AF522350

HISTORY OF THE BRITISH EMPIRE

POLITICAL DIVISIONS OF THE BRITISH EMPIRE.

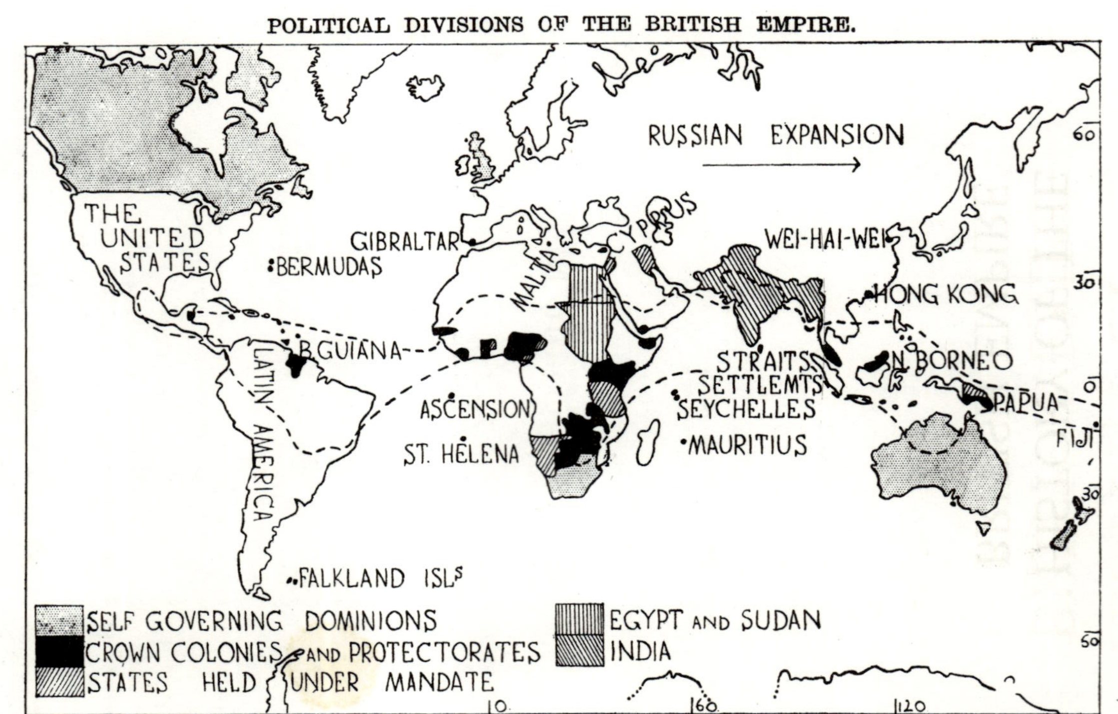

E. H. H. H. del.

The dotted line encloses the area within which the mean annual temperature is 80° Fahr. Notice how almost the whole of the Dependent Empire falls within this zone.

HISTORY OF THE BRITISH EMPIRE

C.S.S. Higham, M.A.

First Published in India 2017

ISBN 978–93–83723–23–2

Published by
LG PUBLISHERS DISTRIBUTORS
49, Street No. 14, Pratap Nagar,
Mayur Vihar Phase I, Delhi 110091
Email: lgpdist@gmail.com

Printed at
Sapra Brothers, Delhi 110 092

PREFACE

In writing this little account of the expansion of British power beyond the seas I have tried to trace the origin and development of some of the many Imperial problems which citizens are called upon to face to-day. For this purpose I have dealt, as far as my space allows, with social and economic movements, as well as with strictly political history, for it is only by appreciating the different sides of the story that we can hope to understand present problems. Any attempt to link history to the events of the present is liable to many dangers; but any value that such a book as this may have lies chiefly in its attempt to tell the story as a whole. The division into books has been adopted in order to mark the main periods in the development of the Empire, and particularly to emphasise the nineteenth century division into Self-governing Dominions and Dependent Empire.

At the end of each chapter I have added a short list of books. They are intended to be interesting books which can be easily obtained by any one who wishes to read further. I have also added references to original authorities which can be consulted in a handy form: big books and monographs I have deliberately omitted. The maps should be supplemented with a good atlas, such as Ramsay Muir's *Student's Atlas*, which has the advantage of showing the physical features of the various countries, and thus explaining many points which the glaring colours of a political map generally hide from the eye.

In writing a book of this sort it is impossible to offer more than a general acknowledgment to the many writers whose books have been consulted. I should say, however, that I have referred to most of the books mentioned in my notes; and I must also acknowledge the help I have received from Professor Egerton's *Short History of British Colonial Policy*, from the volumes of Sir Charles Lucas' *Historical Geography*, and from the Colonial Office List. I am indebted to my friend, Professor Ramsay Muir, for encouragement and advice.

C. S. S. HIGHAM.

MANCHESTER,
January, 1921.

CONTENTS

BOOK IV

THE DEPENDENT EMPIRE, 1815–1920

LIST OF MAPS

ERRATUM

Page 15, line 37, *read* "in the early days of James I."

DIAGRAM OF THE ADMINISTRATIVE RELATIONS OF THE BRITISH EMPIRE

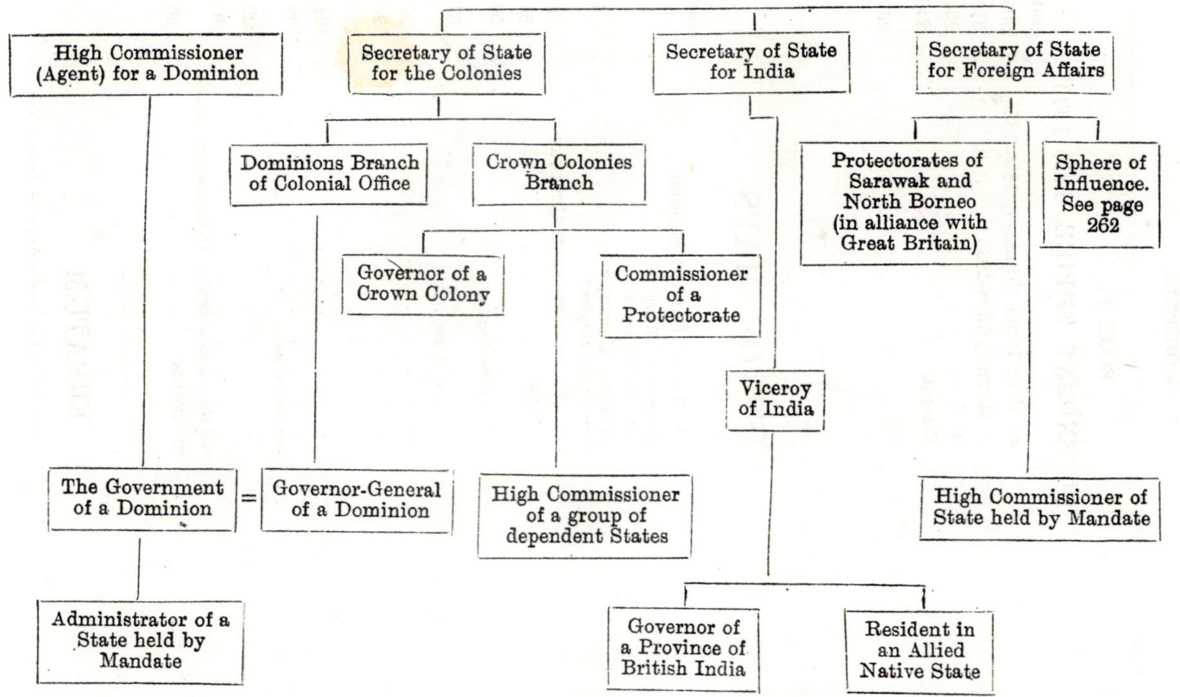

THE OLD TRADE ROUTES TO THE EAST.

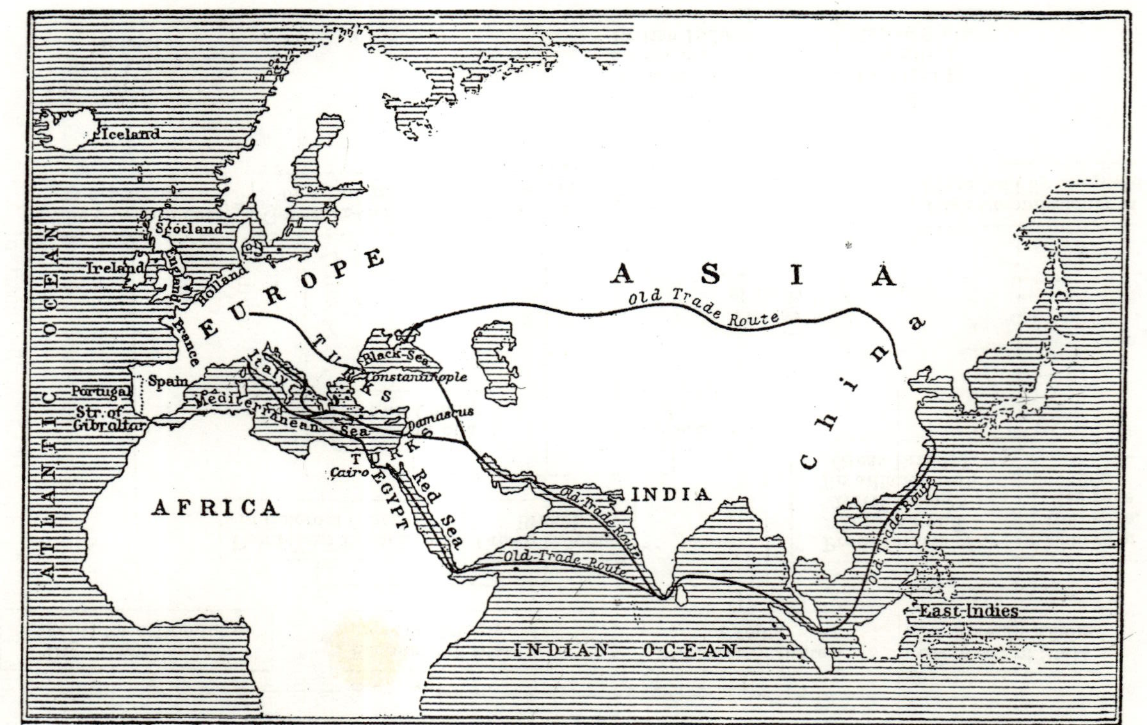

Longmans, Green & Co. London, New York, Bombay, Calcutta & Madras

HISTORY OF THE BRITISH EMPIRE

CHAPTER I

The Beginnings of English Colonisation

Of all those great movements which mark the beginning of what we call Modern Times, such as the Revival of Learning, the Reformation, and the development of strong monarchies ruling over national states, perhaps the most striking is the great series of discoveries which opened the New World and the distant East to the trade and settlement of Western Europe. During the Middle Ages the Mediterranean had been the highway of the world, and the Italian states became immensely wealthy, producing the greatest bankers, traders, and navigators in Europe. The new discoveries soon transferred both wealth and power to those nations which lived on the shores of the Atlantic, and made the Mediterranean little more than an inland lake. The old trade routes from India and the East, by caravan across the desert or by ship up the Red Sea, had been badly interrupted by the Turkish conquests, and merchants began to think of a new route to the East by which they might more safely import the familiar spices used in daily cookery. The revival of learning soon showed that the ancients knew more of geography than mediæval man, and, fired by the re-discovery of old maps, people began once more to speculate on the shape of the world, and the possibility of reaching the Indies by sailing towards the west.

Portuguese discoveries.

The Portuguese, however, determined to try another route, and with the help of Italian seamen, and with Italian instruments and charts, they sought to re-open the way around Africa, which story said had been known in days of old. The coast of Africa itself was forbidding, and at first few dared to sail into the unknown tropics, but in 1419 Prince Henry the Navigator built his palace at Cape St. Vincent, whence he could overlook the sea, and spent his life encouraging his sailors in their task. Cape "No Further" was passed, and year after year ships came sailing back bringing reports of new lands discovered and new wonders seen. Though Prince Henry died long before the discoveries were completed, his energy had shown men the way, and his bold spirit drove them on until in 1487 Bartholomew Diaz rounded the Cape of Storms, and frightened at the terrific gales he met, came back to tell of his success. Realising the importance of his discovery, the King of Portugal renamed the new land the Cape of Good Hope, and in 1495 sent Vasco da Gama, who passed the Cape, touched at Natal on Christmas Day, and reached India in May of the following year. Thus, after eighty years' courageous venture, the Portuguese had at last opened a sea route to India and the East, and for many years they held a monopoly of it.

Spanish discoveries.

While the Portuguese were searching the coast of Africa the Spaniards tried another route. Old legend spoke of an island out in the Atlantic, and men began again to believe the old teaching that the world was round: they thought that by sailing westward they would ultimately reach India. Though not the only holder of these ideas, Christopher Columbus, an Italian, managed to persuade Ferdinand and Isabella to assist him: in 1492 he set sail with the double intention of converting the Grand Khan of China, and opening a western route to the East. Picking up the north-east trade wind, he stood across the Atlantic and reached the West Indies on October 12, 1492. In all his three voyages Columbus never reached the mainland of North America, though he discovered most of the West Indian islands and part of South America. He firmly believed that he had reached the East Indies, and died without knowing that he had really discovered a new continent. Later discoverers, however, crossed the Isthmus of Panama and found the South Sea (the Pacific), and were then reluctantly forced to realise that another great ocean lay between them and their long-sought goal.

Spain was not long in putting her new discoveries to use: she neglected the smaller outlying islands, but quickly settled Cuba and Hispaniola. Thence the Spaniards spread to the mainland, and fascinated by tales of wealth Cortes and a few comrades pressed on to Mexico City, and with the help of some native allies conquered the country, but he utterly destroyed the great city and its wonderful civilisation. Soon other Spaniards settled on the Isthmus, and another great leader, Pizarro, hearing of the riches possessed by the Incas of Peru, led a chosen band of comrades to the conquest of that mountainous country. From Peru Pizarro extended his sway southward to Chile, and later still some Spaniards settled on the eastern coast along the River Plate. Thus by the reign of Elizabeth the Spaniards had occupied the larger islands of the West Indies, Mexico, the Isthmus, the northern shore and the whole of the western coast of South America, though their power hardly stretched beyond the Andes. It was not till 1520 that Magellan discovered the Straits that still bear his name, and later the Spaniards forbade any ships to sail in by this back-door. Thus the usual route to Spanish America was by sea to Porto Bello, thence by land across the Isthmus, on a route nearly the same as that now taken by the Canal, to Panama, and so by sea once more.

Papal Bull dividing the world. 1493.

Portugal and Spain both claimed the lands which they had discovered for themselves, and forbade any other peoples to sail to them at all. These claims were recognised by the Pope in 1493 when he issued a Bull dividing the world by a line running north and south one hundred leagues west of the Azores: thus the two nations started back to back; westward discoveries were to belong to Spain, eastward to Portugal. Next year the line was moved, by agreement, further west, and when in 1500 a Portuguese ship reached Brazil, that country was found to lie on the Portuguese side of the line. Thus Portugal gained a foothold in America. How far the Pope intended to bind other countries is not certain, though Spain and Portugal interpreted the Bull in that light and treated trespassers as mere pirates. But such preposterous claims were all in vain, and the northern nations soon

THE WORLD IN THE SIXTEENTH CENTURY.

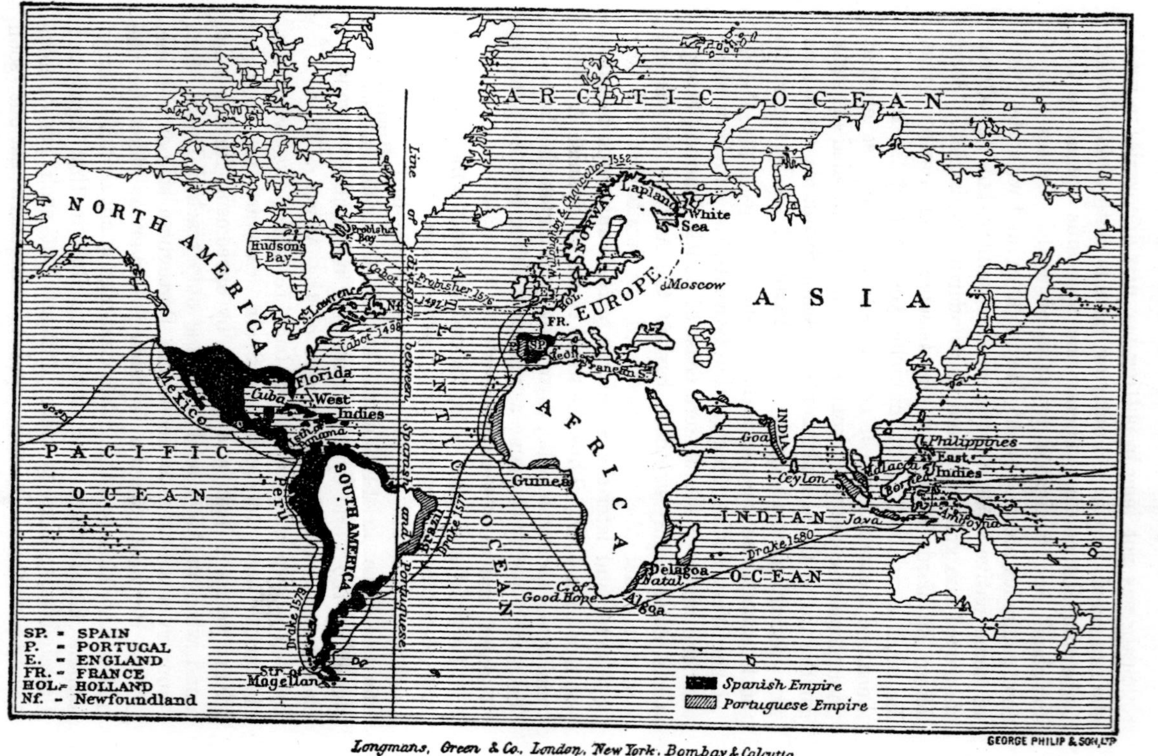

followed the earlier explorers: France, Holland, and England each began to take a share in the new trade and to lay the foundations of an overseas empire.

The Spaniards organised their empire in America with great care. Their main object was to obtain a vast supply of the precious metals, and they adopted a system of compulsory labour in the mines which soon destroyed the wretched Indians whom they forced to work there. The gold of Mexico and the silver from Potosi in Peru poured into the coffers of Spain, and enabled that country for a time to play a great part in the politics of Europe. The attacks of privateers soon forced the Spaniards to protect their shipping, and yearly convoys sailed from Spain—the Flota to Mexico, and the galleons to Carthagena and Porto Bello. Then was held the annual fair at Porto Bello, and the silver from Potosi, which had come on pack-mules across the Isthmus from Panama, was laded on the ships. The two fleets then met at Havana, and standing north picked up the anti-trade wind, sailing home to Spain by way of the Azores. The very regularity of these arrangements, and the clear way in which the prevailing winds marked out the great sea highways, made an attack on the Spanish plate-fleet not a very difficult achievement, and the riches of the New World sometimes found their way into other treasuries than those of the King of Spain.

Organisation of Spanish treasure-fleets.

While these great events were taking place, a change was coming over England which was soon to fit her to take her share in the spoils of the new discoveries. In 1487, when Bartholomew Diaz reached the Cape, England was still a country of little account on the very outskirts of Europe. Her people were bold sailors and skilful fishermen, her richest industry was the woollen trade, but primarily England was an agricultural country, and her general prosperity had suffered much from a long series of civil wars. With the accession of Henry VII in 1485 these struggles came to an end, and under the Tudors England was soon to gain an efficient administrative system, and to learn once more the rule of law. Under the Tudors too there continued to grow that keen feeling of nationality which expressed itself so strongly in the

Elizabethan age. Though at first the Reformation threatened to split England in two, yet the feeling of nationalism triumphed and the Reformation gave a religious excuse to the growing desire for plundering the wealth of Spain. Thus nationalism and the reformed religion joined to urge England into a war with Spain.

The English Navy.

Under the watchful care of the Tudors the foundations of England's naval power were securely laid. In old days the royal ships were the private property of the King, and on Henry V's death were actually sold to pay his personal debts. Under the Tudors, however, the Navy was steadily improved, and though royal ships were still hired out to merchants for trading voyages, the ship of war became a special type of vessel. Henry VII built new ships and tried to buy others from the Spaniards, but it is to his son that the great improvement in the Navy was due. Henry VIII was genuinely interested in his fleet ; he delighted to wear full naval rig with the officer's badge of rank, the golden whistle, and he took personal notice of the design and trials of his new ships. He brought over Italians to improve the building, he increased the size of men-of-war, and arranged for a bounty to encourage the building of merchantmen, then as always the true basis of real sea-power. Armament, too, underwent a change, and Henry favoured fewer and heavier guns instead of the many light and ineffective weapons which ships had carried heretofore. Henry also reorganised the administration of the Navy by creating a Navy Board in 1546, which was responsible for the administrative work under the Lord High Admiral. Though Elizabeth preferred diplomacy to the use of force, she maintained the strength of her fleet, and even arranged a compulsory form of insurance. The pay of the different ratings aboard ship was graduated, and a small proportion was deducted regularly and paid into the Chatham chest. From this fund widows and orphans, and also disabled seamen, could obtain some relief. The ships of this period were clumsy and very unlike a sailing ship of to-day. They had two or three masts, rigged with square sails, and a lateen sail on the aftermast. High fore and aft castles, and fighting tops on the masts, were forts from which the soldiers fired at their enemy, while the heavy guns pounded the side of the enemy ship. In a sea-way the handling of these top-heavy ships was not easy, but the skill and courage of the sailors overcame great difficulties: the ships could not sail close to the wind, and if the winds were contrary often spent many weeks trying to beat against them. The ship was sailed by the master, who was the navigating officer, but she was commanded by the captain, often a soldier, and the fighting of the ship was done by him. By Elizabeth's reign the Navy was a powerful weapon, well gunned and manned, and ready to take its part in the destruction of the Armada and the subsequent fight against Spain.

In another way, too, England was changing: her seamen were beginning to push out on longer voyages, seeking new trade routes, while at home new trading companies were being formed to discover new countries and open trade with them. At first only small attempts were made; the Cabots sailed from Bristol with a patent from Henry VII and discovered land near Cape Breton Island. Thence began those fisheries which were such a nursery for English seamen. From Plymouth, too, sailed William Hawkins on a voyage to Guinea and Brazil. But Englishmen were haunted with the desire to find a route to the Indies for themselves, and so to emulate both Spaniards and Portuguese. They determined to seek for it in another direction, and so in 1553 a company was formed which sought for a North-East passage to India; after incredible hardships Chancellor reached Archangel, travelled by sleigh across the snow to Moscow, and arranged with the Czar to open up direct trade relations with Russia. On his return to England the Russia Company was formed, which for many years traded through Archangel, and later through the Baltic, when the Russian capture of Narva gave them a port on that sea. For a short time the Company even opened up a direct overland trade with the East. Besides its trading business the Russia Company did not forget its original function of discovery, and it encouraged Frobisher's attempt to find a North-West passage and Gilbert's proposed settlement of Newfoundland. Several other companies

New trading companies.

The Russia Company. 1553.

Levant Company. 1581.

soon followed. The Levant Company in 1581 began to trade with Persia through the Mediterranean, while, in attempting to open another route, this Company formed the East India Company, whose fame soon eclipsed that of its parent. These various trading companies each received a charter from the Crown granting them a monopoly of the right to trade within a certain area: often, however, they were troubled by "interlopers" or smugglers, who trafficked within the special zone, although they were not members of the Company.

East India Company. 1600.

Despite this trade activity along eastern routes, English interest was turning to America. The fabulous stories of Spanish wealth made men long to trade with those regions, or at least to plunder the Spanish treasure-ships, while the dreams of a western route to India still haunted men's minds for over a century. Explorers, traders, privateers, and would-be settlers are all found among the early English seamen, but the age of Elizabeth is essentially the age of the privateer. At first the English had been held back from western enterprise by many things: the religious strife at home was at first a hindrance, while the success of the eastward trade was sufficient to keep the merchants well employed. The Papal Bull was not without its influence, and Mary's marriage with Philip of Spain tended to confirm it. But the long line of creaking waggons laden with silver bullion from South America, which Philip sent to the Tower to reform the English coinage, stirred men's imagination, and, when Elizabeth became Queen, interest in American ventures grew quickly. Though she was forced to play a careful game, and at first to look with disfavour on her robber seamen, events pushed the Queen along the road of a breach with Spain. The Huguenots in France, and the Dutch fighting for religious and political independence against Spain, both looked to Elizabeth for help, and, almost in her own despite, she found herself the open champion of the Reformation, face to face with the power of Spain. The great challenge came in 1588, when the Armada sailed up the Channel to transport Spanish troops from the Low Countries for the invasion of England. The English fleet lay waiting in

The Armada. 1588.

Plymouth Sound until the Spaniards had passed by, and then harried the lumbering galleons all up the Channel until they anchored off Calais. There the English attacked the close-anchored lines with fire-ships, and terrified at their danger the Spanish captains cut their cables and stood out into the North Sea in grave disorder. "God blew, and they were scattered," says the Armada medal, and but few of the fleeing ships escaped around the rocky coasts of Scotland and so home to Spain. This great victory was the turning-point in the struggle with Spain: Englishmen now rather despised the power of their enemy, and the piratical raids into the West Indies became lawful expeditions, for open war between England and Spain continued until James I made peace in 1604.

Westward voyages: Martin Frobisher.

The search for a new way to India led Martin Frobisher in 1576 to attempt a north-west route, but though he explored the shores of Labrador his only cheer was a find of spiders, "which, as many affirm, are signs of great store of gold." Two other voyages proved equally disappointing, but explorers did not readily give up the quest. Off Newfoundland the fisheries were growing, and Humphrey Gilbert planned a settlement there which was ultimately to spread southward and turn the Spaniard out of America, but it only ended in failure. Returning homeward in 1583, he stoutly refused to leave his ship, the *Squirrel*, and was lost at sea with all hands. Said Gilbert: "I will not forsake my little company going homeward with whom I have passed so many storms and perils." Of such stuff were the Elizabethan seamen made.

Humphrey Gilbert.

Francis Drake.

The keynote of the Elizabethan age is the heroic struggle with Spain, and of this struggle Francis Drake was the popular hero. A Devon man, around his life and doings there grew a tradition which caused every Spaniard to tremble in his shoes, while in Plymouth men still believe that in time of danger they will hear his drum, and that Drake will come again to save his country. From early days he took part in privateering expeditions to the West Indies, and when in 1573 he caught sight of the Pacific from the heights of Panama he knelt and prayed God "to give him life and leave to sail once in an English ship upon that sea."

The chance came a few years later: setting sail from Plymouth in 1577, he reached the forbidden South Sea through the Straits of Magellan. Driven south and east by storms, he discovered Cape Horn, and then working back into the Pacific he captured the annual treasure-ship off Panama. He then returned to England round the Cape—the first Englishman to circumnavigate the world. Despite the protests of the Spanish Ambassador, the Queen smiled upon his enterprise and knighted him on his return. Drake was now the English champion: in 1587 he sailed boldly into Cadiz harbour and "singed the King of Spain's beard," by burning the store-ships assembled there. Next year he played an important part in the defeat of the Armada, and at last, in 1595, both Drake and his friend Hawkins died during a raid on the West Indies, and were buried at sea in Nombre de Dios Bay.

Courtier and scholar, a man of great ideas and wide sympathies, Sir Walter Raleigh is a different sort of man from Drake, but he is no less a typical Elizabethan. Though anxious to prosecute the war with Spain he realised that more could be done by imitating them in "planting" colonies than by mere buccaneering expeditions. So he obtained from the Queen permission to "discover barbarous countries, not actually possessed by any Christian prince, or inhabited by Christian people, to occupy and enjoy the same for ever." With careful forethought he sent two ships to reconnoitre, and next year (1585) the *Lyon* and the *Tiger* with five other ships took a party of emigrants to Virginia. The attempt, however, proved a failure; the governor spent his time exploring and prospecting for gold, while the "gentlemen" of the emigrants were disagreeably surprised at the nature of the country and the absence of "dainty food, soft beds of down or feathers." The settlers had been ill chosen, and as they got into trouble with the Indians they were only too willing for Drake to take them home next year. Raleigh's attention was soon after turned to South America. The rumour of the golden city of Manoa, and the possibility of founding a colony in the south, took Raleigh in 1594 on his first voyage to the New World. Pushing up the Orinoco river, Raleigh spent two months in exploring the

Walter Raleigh.

tropical forests, and on his return published a wonderful description of all he had seen. Raleigh's influence ended with the Queen's death: James threw him into prison for taking part in an intrigue against Cecil, and he was only released in 1616 in order to seek once more the golden city of Manoa. Returning from Guiana, weak with sickness and unsuccessful in his quest, the great Elizabethan was executed to satisfy the vengeance of the Spanish Ambassador.

New period: colonisation instead of piracy. 1603.

Though there is no break between the reign of Elizabeth and that of James I, yet English enterprise takes on a new character; there were attempts, though unsuccessful, at colonising under Elizabeth, while the game of harrying the Spaniard went on yet for many a year, even after formal peace was made in 1604; but the spacious days of Queen Elizabeth give place to the more prosaic though no less important time of the early Stuarts. This new period is a time of serious colonial settlement and of definite attempts to develop trade as opposed to piracy. The older ideas of discovering a route to the Indies and of finding illimitable store of the precious metals still linger on, but as the colonists took to agriculture and their numbers increased, so the trading interests grew. Again, it was thought that the plantations would afford a refuge for the poor from England, who might win riches in a new land, though at times the steady drain of men from England to America made some thinkers anxious, for there were no accurate statistics in those days and the most alarming guesses were made as to the effect of emigration on the population. Nor must we forget the influence of the missionary ideas of the time, for though they produced little real missionary effort, men always felt that they had a duty to take Christianity to the natives, and this motive for colonisation is repeated in the various charters of the day.

As Drake is the prophet of sea-power, so Raleigh is the apostle of careful and systematic colonisation. Men set themselves to think out the great problems of colonisation, and the influence of their new ideas is seen in a Dedication to Raleigh by Richard Hakluyt, the great chronicler of Elizabethan seamen. Hakluyt explained that his object in translating the French history of Florida was that Raleigh's colonists might be "forewarned and admonished as well to beware of the gross negligence in providing of sufficiency of victuals, the securitie, disorders, and mutinies that fell out among the French, with the great inconveniences that thereupon ensued, that by others' mishaps they might learne to prevent and avoid the like." Bacon too thought carefully about the matter, and in his essay *Of Plantations* lays down the best method of founding colonies. Those who undertake the enterprise must not look for an immediate return on their outlay, for at least twenty years are needed for the colonists to settle down. Emigrants must be chosen with skill. "It is a Shameful and Unblessed Thing, to take the Scumme of the People, and Wicked Condemned Men, to be the People with whom you Plant. . . . For they will ever live like Rogues, and not fall to worke, but be Lazie, and do Mischiefe, and spend Victuals." The basis of successful colonisation, Bacon explains, is the development of agriculture. The government should be in the hands of a strong governor, with but few councillors, while the promoters of the colony in England should be a "temperate Number," and gentlemen rather than merchants, "for they looke ever to the present Gaine."

The plantations that were now sent out were generally organised by companies formed for the purpose, who obtained a grant of land and powers from the Crown. The Company financed the expeditions and in return looked to make profits from rents and other duties, as well as from the trade which they hoped to develop. Thus the growth of plantations is only another aspect of that trade activity which we have seen at work in the Russia or Levant Company. The colonising companies often came to loggerheads with their colonists, who had all the seventeenth-century Englishman's ideas of liberty and self-government, and objected to the autocratic methods of the Company. After a time some companies lost their charters, and thus the plantation became a "royal" colony, under the direct control of the Crown.

Despite his failure in Virginia, Raleigh had never despaired: "I shall yet see it an English nation," he declared. Fired by his ideas there were formed two companies of merchants in

1606: the London or Virginia Company, for settling the southern shores of North America, and the Plymouth Company, whose sphere lay further north. The London Company sent out its first fleet in 1607, and thus was founded Virginia, the first successful English colony in America. Settling on the River James, the colonists soon found themselves in trouble with the Indians, and in want of food. They were saved from utter disaster by Captain John Smith, a versatile soldier of fortune, who had fought and marched over half the continent of Europe, and who had now come to try his hand as a colonist. Enforcing discipline among the dispirited settlers, he made each man dig and plant foodstuffs while his energetic action saved them from destruction by the Indians. Though Smith soon returned to England and did not come back to Virginia again, he had undoubtedly saved the colony, and he continued to interest himself in the work of plantations and in voyages of discovery. By writing books and pamphlets, and by publishing "hints to settlers," he called the attention of Englishmen to the possibilities of colonial settlement, and emphasised the need for practical knowledge and experience in carrying out their schemes.

Virginia Company. 1606.

After Smith's departure the colony was still in a bad way: sickness and wars with the Indians, quarrels between the settlers and their martinet of a governor, and friction between them and the Company, who were not content to wait the twenty years stipulated by Bacon, all hindered development, while the constant intrigues of the Spanish Ambassador added to the troubles of the Company. At last in 1623 an inquiry was held, the Company's charter was cancelled, and thus Virginia became the first royal colony, the "old Dominion."

Virginia Coy. loses its charter. 1623.

Virginia was saved not by the loss of its charter and its transfer to the Crown, but by the cultivation of tobacco as a staple crop, and in a short time its planters became a wealthy aristocracy. At first the introduction of tobacco into England was regarded by most men with horror, and tobacco-smoking was loathed as opium-smoking is to-day. James I published a violent attack on smoking;

Tobacco.

"there cannot be a more base, and yet hurtful corruption in this countrey, than is the vile use or rather abuse of taking Tobacco," wrote the King. Another writer declared: "Men beganne to grow mad and crazed in the brain in that they would adventure to suck the smoke of a weed . . . at all times, feasting and fasting, in health as well as sicknesse, without regard held to persons, ages, sexes, times, temperatures, moist or dry, hot or cold." But men would smoke, despite the thunders of the moralists, and so the King made the best of a bad bargain, and clapped a heavy import duty on tobacco. A much heavier duty was put on foreign-grown tobacco, and its cultivation in England was strictly forbidden: thus colonial tobacco had a monopoly of the ever-growing English market, and the Crown made a very handsome revenue from the tax. The development of this staple crop had a great effect on the social organisation of Virginia: slaves were soon imported to clear the ground and to cultivate the tobacco plant. Huge plantations sprang up where the planter lived in almost mediæval state, surrounded by his slaves, and many miles from his nearest neighbours. Roads were bad, towns were few and straggling, schools there were hardly any: indeed, in 1671 Governor Berkeley wrote, "I thank God there are no free schools nor printing, and I hope we shall not have these hundred years." Political life was backward: under the Company the governor and his council ruled the colony, though in 1619 the governor obeyed instructions and summoned an assembly of elected burgesses. The royal governor, too, used to call assemblies regularly, but despite some quarrels there is no sign of that intense local energy and political independence which was such a marked feature of the New England colonies. Still, in this first colony of Englishmen beyond the seas, a "Parliament" had been called only twelve years after the first settlers had arrived; though its powers were slight and not even defined, its assembly is significant of the outlook of Englishmen in the seventeenth century. It was inconceivable that Englishmen should settle anywhere without having a share in their own government. This feeling has continued, and its development is one of the clues to the story of the British Empire.

Just north of Virginia was planted the colony of Maryland, founded in 1633 by Lord Baltimore by virtue of a charter from Charles I. The proprietor was a Roman Catholic, and though a policy of toleration was adopted, religious quarrels broke out which overthrew Baltimore's authority for a time, until it was restored in 1660. Maryland soon became a prosperous colony, growing tobacco like its southern neighbour.

Plymouth Company. 1606.

The second company founded in 1606, the Plymouth Company, was given the right of settling on the northern shores of America, and it was hoped, as the name well shows, that capital would be subscribed in Plymouth and the other western outports. But money did not come in regularly, and even when the Company was reorganised in 1620 as the Council for New England, it did little more than organise fishing voyages, which proved a very useful speculation. Captain John Smith had popularised the name of New England, and was tireless in singing the praises of the country, but it needed a stronger force to start the colonisation of the New England shore. This was found in the growth of the Puritan movement, which started under Elizabeth as a protest against ceremonies and as an attempt at living a stricter life, but soon became such a revolutionary force that it called down on its head the thunders of Church and State. In the first half of the seventeenth century there began a great emigration of Puritans to America, where the new colonists hoped to develop a religious system after their own tastes, but with the growth of political troubles in England Puritan energy found another outlet, and the civil war ended in a Puritan revolution in England itself. The religious ideas of the Puritan colonists tinged their political outlook; they developed a very democratic system of government, and until Charles II took the matter in hand they were practically independent of the home country.

Puritan movement.

Foundation of New Plymouth. 1620.

The first colony in New England was founded by a body of Independents or Congregationalists, who had fled to Holland in the days of Elizabeth. Much to their distress they found that their children "by these occasions (and ye great licentiousness of youth in yt countrie) and ye manifold Temptations of the place, were drawne away by evill examples into extravagante, dangerous courses, getting ye raines off their neks and departing from their parents. Some became souldgers, others took upon them farr viages by Sea ; and others some worse courses . . . so that they saw their posteritie would be in danger to degenerate and be corrupted." They therefore determined to remove bodily to America, and there to found a little community free from the defiling touch of the outside world. A few friends in England subscribed some money, and in 1620 the *Mayflower* sailed from Plymouth and landed the Pilgrim Fathers at New Plymouth, near Cape Cod. The settlers found that they were within the jurisdiction of the New England Council, and so obtained a grant from them. More friends came to join them, and when a few years later the colonists paid off those English friends who had financed the voyage, there was settled at New Plymouth a small organised state, which owed obedience to no one in England except the general allegiance which they owed to the King as Englishmen. For some time they were left quite alone, and they remained a separate colony until absorbed by Massachusetts in 1691.

An event of more importance was the formation, by a number of Puritans in England, of the Massachusetts Company.

Massachusetts Company. 1629.

These men wished to emigrate, and obtained a grant of land from the New England Council, but they thought it wise also to get a charter from the King, by which they were incorporated into a Company. This Company was not the usual type of trading company, where merchants resident in England subscribed for purposes of trade or exploitation ; most of the members of this Company were men who proposed actually to settle in the new land. As no restriction had been placed on the meetings of the Company, it was decided that the Company should migrate as a whole to Massachusetts, and a few years later the shares of any members who had remained in England were bought up by the colonists. Thus Massachusetts was like Plymouth, an independent settlement owing obedience to the King alone, but Massachusetts was in a very strong position. It possessed a charter which guaranteed its right to self-government, and it quickly developed a democratic constitution. The governor was elected annually, and with him were chosen a number of assistants who acted as his council: the assembly at first consisted of all the inhabitants, but as the settlement developed such a meeting became unwieldy, and representatives were chosen by each township. A stream of newcomers continued to arrive until the beginning of the civil war, and by that time Massachusetts was becoming very strong, and even aggressive towards her smaller neighbours.

In New England the settlers lived in small townships, quite unlike the vast plantations of Virginia, for the northern climate was much like that of Old England, and unsuited to the growth of tropical plants. The newcomers had to hew their way through the great forests, and in the clearing around the settlement they grew much the same crops as they had grown at home. Each township was built of log-houses, and surrounded by a palisade for protection against the Indians: within was built the church and the village school. Thus New England was far ahead of Virginia in education, and within six years the colonists had founded Harvard College. Though the Puritans of Massachusetts had emigrated for religious freedom, such freedom was only meant for those who saw eye to eye with them in religious matters. Toleration was thought mere weakness, and the right of citizenship was soon restricted to those who were Church members. Any who disagreed with their religious ideas were quickly bundled out of the colony, and went off to found new settlements of their own: the Quakers especially received most ferocious treatment, being whipped and tortured for their religious beliefs. Massachusetts was thus an austere place, where people took life very seriously; men were fined if absent from church, while to import playing-cards was a serious offence. Work and worship were the two ends of life, and the country soon became a prosperous agricultural community. At first there was little commerce, for the colony had little to export, but Boston soon developed into a port, shipping wood and barrel-staves to Virginia and the West Indies, and it quickly became one of the most important towns in America. New England produced very little that was needed by the Old Country except masts for shipbuilding, and thus there was never that economic bond which held Virginia and the West Indies so closely to the English markets.

Besides Massachusetts there were a number of little settlements in New England, some of which were absorbed by their stronger neighbours, while others managed to retain their independence, and finally became separate members of the United States. Connecticut was founded partly by sectaries flying from the persecution of Massachusetts, and partly by fresh settlers from the Puritan families of England. One of its townships, Saybrook, was to contain "such houses as may receive men of quality," and the story runs that the great Puritan leaders, Pym and Hampden, were planning to emigrate to America, but that the quarrel over the payment of ship-money turned their thoughts to other things. Connecticut produced a written constitution in which it adopted the institutions of Massachusetts, modified by the rule that a citizen need not be a Church member. This colony was important as an outpost against the Dutch settlement on the River Hudson. In 1662 it absorbed the small settlement of Newhaven. Providence and Rhode Island lay between Connecticut and New Plymouth, and were founded by religious outcasts from Massachusetts. They obtained a charter of incorporation in 1647, and maintained their policy of toleration, much to the chagrin of Massachusetts, who desired to enforce a general policy of rigid uniformity throughout New England. North of Massachusetts lay New Hampshire, a number of small settlements made at different times by merchants and promoters, but the colonists were so weak that, between 1642 and 1643, they were absorbed by the energetic government of Massachusetts. After the Restoration the King forced the larger colony to disgorge New Hampshire, which remained a separate colony thenceforth. Still further north was the last of the English

Other New England Colonies: (1) Connecticut. 1631.

(2) Providence and Rhode Island. 1635.

(3) New Hampshire. 1635.

(4) Maine. 1623.

coast-line colonies, Maine, founded by Sir Ferdinando Gorges in 1623; Gorges relied on a grant from the King, but other would-be proprietors disputed his title, claiming grants from the New England Council. Here, too, the weaker colony was practically absorbed by Massachusetts, and in 1668 it was definitely annexed by the larger colony. Thus the whole of the coast-line under the control of the New England Council was divided up into little settlements, or large areas awaiting effective colonisation: the Council had done but little to bring this about, and it was dissolved in 1635.

New England Federation. 1643.

The New England settlements were at first weak and isolated; the thin fringe of townships along the coast or on the river banks were always exposed to sudden Indian raids, or to attacks from the French in Canada, or the Dutch at New Amsterdam. Some form of common effort was a necessity, but it was fear of interference from home that led to the first attempt at union in America. The growth of Archbishop Laud's power, and his known hostility to Puritans, were a source of constant alarm. In 1634 he had been appointed a commissioner for supervising the colonies, and next year an attempt was made to cancel Massachusetts' charter. The colonists grew even more fearful lest the political quarrel in England should spread to America. So in 1643 there was founded the United Colonies of New England, which consisted of Massachusetts, Connecticut, Newhaven, and New Plymouth. A written agreement was drawn up, and the Federation adopted a very independent attitude towards England. There were, however, local quarrels: Massachusetts in particular objected to paying so large a share of expenses, and yet having no larger vote. Though the commissioners continued to meet for some time, the real power of the Federation died out after the Restoration.

West Indies: (1) Somers Island.

Meanwhile Englishmen were planting colonies in that centre of the Spanish preserve, the West Indies. The old game of harrying the Spaniard began to give place to a new policy of settlement on the smaller islands, which the Spaniards had neglected in their haste for gold. An offshoot of the Virginia Company had been formed in 1615, to colonise the Somers

Islands (Bermudas), which had been re-discovered by Sir George Somers, who was blown off his course when sailing to Virginia in 1609. The company forced their colonists to trade direct with them, and this caused much discontent; but the islands soon became a market-garden and exported honey, "cabidghoes," and other vegetables to the West Indies or America. The Providence Company, an offshoot of the Somers Company, was formed of Puritan gentlemen with Pym at their head, who tried to build up a colony on the island of Old Providence. The plantation, however, soon got into difficulties, and it was attacked by the Spaniards, who succeeded in capturing the island in 1641. The story of the Providence Company is really part of the great story of the Puritan migration; but a Puritan colony in the West Indies is almost an absurdity, for it could not there develop its typical form of township and local government.

(2) Old Providence.

The real interest of the West Indian colonisation belongs to the doings of independent traders and a royalist noble, Lord Carlisle. In 1623 some settlers led by Thomas Warner, a Suffolk gentleman, landed on St. Christopher and agreed to divide the island with some Frenchmen who arrived soon after. From St. Christopher the English spread to Antigua and Nevis, while Montserrat was settled with Irishmen, and the negroes there speak with an Irish accent to this day. These four islands were called the Leeward Islands. In thus settling on the very outskirts of the Spanish preserves, the French and English felt themselves allied in a great adventure. They drew up a treaty for mutual help against the Spaniard, and agreed not to fight among themselves even if war broke out in Europe. With the Dutch, who were founding trading depots on the neighbouring islands and carrying on a flourishing trade with the Spanish Main, despite the Spaniards' vigilance, both French and English kept on excellent terms. At first almost all their trade was carried in Dutch ships, and Dutchmen began to import negro slaves to the islands. Indigo and tobacco were the first crops grown; and when there was the threat of a glut of tobacco the French and English

(3) Leeward Islands.

governors arranged to restrict their output. In 1617 the newly settled islands were granted by the King to Lord Carlisle, and to him also fell the island of Barbados, which had been already settled by Englishmen. Thus the West Indies became a proprietary colony, but owned by an individual instead of a company. Their wealth and importance were soon increased by the introduction of sugar from Brazil. The great storm which was brewing at home led men of every shade of opinion to emigrate to Barbados, and the island soon had plenty of labour. The local assembly passed a law forbidding the use of provoking terms such as Cavalier or Roundhead, and fining the offender a turkey, which had to be provided for a mutual feast of reconciliation. But the turkey did not succeed in keeping the peace, for after the King's execution Barbados proclaimed King Charles II, and published a Declaration of Independence. This bold defiance could not be overlooked by Parliament, which despatched an expedition under Ayscue to recall the island to obedience (1651). After some time an agreement was reached, and the fleet sailed on to force the Leeward Islands and then Virginia to recognise the Commonwealth. Barbados under a new governor had an uneventful time of great progress, while the labour-market was constantly improved, by Cromwell's policy of sending out captured royalists to work on the sugar plantations, and by the negro slaves brought by the Dutch traders. The success of Ayscue's expedition was followed very soon by a war with the Dutch. Holland was England's trade rival in both the East and West Indies, and Parliament was now itching to use the magnificent fleet which had been built up to defeat Rupert and to reconquer Barbados. A deliberate attack had already been made on the Dutch carrying trade by two Acts of Parliament. That of 1650, passed in connection with the rebellious attitude of Barbados and Virginia, had forbidden any foreign ship to trade with the American colonies. Next year the great Navigation Act was passed. The terms of this Act are most important. (1) Goods from Asia, Africa, or America must be imported into England in ships owned and manned by Englishmen. (2) Goods from

(4) Barbados.

Navigation Act. 1651.

Europe must be imported in English ships, or ships owned by the country in which the goods were made. (3) Foreign goods must be shipped to England direct from the country in which they were manufactured. (4) The English coasting trade was reserved for English shipping. This great law was a shrewd blow at the Dutch, for though they were not great manufacturers, they were the carriers of the world, and as far as England was concerned, this carrying trade was prohibited by the new Act. The Dutch protested in vain, and war broke out in 1652. The war was disastrous to both sides, despite the brilliant victories of Blake, the great soldier-sailor, and of the Dutchman Van Tromp. But the Dutch suffered worse, for England was able to strangle their trade by the hold she kept on the Channel. When peace was made in 1654 it was really a truce, for the great question of sea-power was still unsettled.

Dutch War. 1652-1654.

Though Cromwell's policy of maintaining a strong fleet, and keeping a squadron stationed in the Mediterranean, laid the firm foundations of Britain's sea-power, yet his policy in the West Indies was like a return to the Elizabethan system of buccaneering expeditions. Possessing a strong fleet, he could not bear to see it idle, and he dreamt of employing it on some great design against Spain in the West Indies. That England was at peace with Spain did not matter, the capture of Old Providence in 1641 was a sufficient excuse, and so in 1654 an expedition was secretly prepared and sent off on a "Westward design," under the command of General Venables and Admiral Penn, the father of the great Quaker. The scheme was ill-managed from the start; the soldiers were badly chosen, many of them being raw recruits, and when the expedition landed on Hispaniola it was soon routed by a handful of Spaniards. In despair the expedition fell on the small island of Jamaica, and as there were but few Spaniards in the place it was easily captured. Thus Cromwell's grandiose scheme gave the English another island in the Caribbean Sea, which for some time was a very doubtful gain, and it also led to a lengthy war with Spain. Once again English commerce lay open to the attacks of an enemy, and heavy taxation

Cromwell's Policy.

Capture of Jamaica. 1655.

in England meant grumbling and discontent. At sea the English fleets were gaining further successes, and the Navy was becoming a separate profession. The long period of active service under Cromwell shaped the traditions of that Navy which was to play an ever-increasing part in the development of the empire.

One other important development took place during the Protectorate, and that was the great increase in the power of the merchants. Their influence is seen in the framing of the Navigation Acts, and they were freely employed in the committees appointed at this period, for dealing with the affairs of America. Their papers and letters which still survive show the interest they took in colonial administration and the part they played in influencing appointments and general policy. These merchants admired the organisation and energy of the Dutch, and they were anxious to reorganise the governmental control of colonies and trade on Dutch lines. Their proposals gained the day after the Restoration.

Books.—Hakluyt's account of the great voyages can be obtained in the Everyman Series. There is an edition of selected voyages, edited by Payne and Beesley. Bacon's essay *Of Plantations* should be read by every one. C. P. Lucas, *The Beginnings of English Overseas Enterprise*, tells the story of the early trading companies. R. W. Jeffery, *The Thirteen Colonies of North America*, is a concise and readable account of the early colonies with illustrations. There are biographies of Drake, Raleigh, and Captain John Smith in the English Men of Action Series.

1492. Columbus first reaches America.
1495. Vasco da Gama reaches India by the Cape.
1577. Drake sails round the world.
1606. Virginia Company. [Loses Charter, 1623.]
1620. Pilgrim Fathers found New Plymouth.
1623. Leeward Islands settled by Warner.
1629. Massachusetts Company.
1655. Cromwell's capture of Jamaica.

CHAPTER II

The Organisation of the Old Empire, 1660–1688

Development of the Empire. 1660–1688.

THE reign of Charles II is crowded with picturesque events and fascinating mysteries, but amongst the intrigues of the secret Treaty of Dover, and the still unsolved riddles of the Popish Plot, we are apt to overlook the story of the colonies. The truth is that the Restoration period is one of the most important in the development of the Empire; in the twenty-eight years between the landing of Charles at Dover and the flight of his brother James, not only was the Empire enlarged beyond all knowledge, but the whole framework of the old Imperial system was deliberately built up. This organisation took three lines: a code of trade laws was devised to guide trade into those channels which seemed best to the thinkers of that day; secondly, the general control of the colonies was centralised in an efficient committee which established a careful office system; and, thirdly, a regular supply of labour was guaranteed to the colonies by means of a monopolist slave-trading company. This great outburst of colonial activity is due to several causes. During the troublesome days that were past there had been a constant stream of refugees to the West Indies: Barbados, that "little England," had been peopled by Roundhead and Royalist, and then by forced emigrants. This ready supply of labour came at a time when an improved method of sugar manufacture was introduced, and the Barbadian planter became fabulously wealthy. This increased the power of the merchants in England, so that they practically directed the economic and colonial policy of the Protector. Under the Restoration they retained this influence, and even increased it by persuading the King to follow the Dutch example and appoint prominent merchants to a Council of Trade. Though many of the Restoration statesmen were interested in the colonies, two gave special attention to colonial business

THE OCEAN HIGHWAYS IN THE SEVENTEENTH CENTURY.

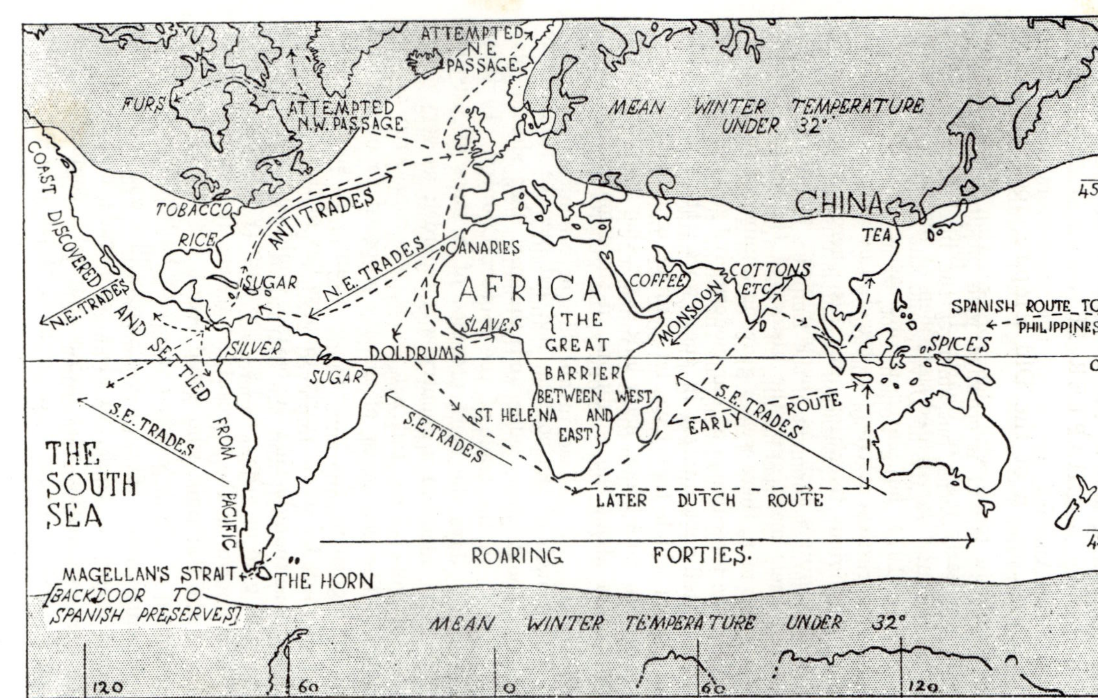

E. H. H. H. del.

Arrows show prevalent winds: dotted lines usual trade routes. The dark portion shows the cold area over which the average winter temperature is below freezing point.

Even while in exile Lord Clarendon had kept in touch with plantation affairs, and at the Restoration he found time to act as leading member of a special committee of the Privy Council for America: as one of the proprietors of the new colony of Carolina, and as the King's chief minister, Clarendon was closely in touch with the reorganisation of the Empire during the early years of Charles II. Lord Shaftesbury was one of the most far-sighted statesmen of his time, and until his fall in 1674 he played an increasing part in colonial affairs; his restless activity, his broad-minded ideas about the value of religious toleration, and his energy in organising colonial ventures such as the plantation of the Carolinas, have left their mark upon the history of the time. Besides these great men, there were a growing number of subordinate officials, the forerunners of our modern civil service, who took a most intelligent interest in their work; their memoranda and papers which they have left behind, and their carefully kept private note-books, show how eager they were to obtain information about the conditions in the colonies from every source.

Economic ideas of the period.

The growth of the colonies had led men to think more carefully about their value and the part they should play in the trade of the Mother Country. In those days the mere presence of a mass of precious metal in a country was regarded as very desirable, for gold alone, and not goods, was considered as true wealth. The economist of the day proposed to obtain this end by regulating the trade of the country in such a way as to "sell more to others yearly than we buy of them in value." Thus it was thought that the balance would be made up by the import of gold or silver, and so the country would grow rich. This is known as the Mercantilist system, in contrast to the idea of the Bullionist who would obtain his end by the direct regulation of the import and export of bullion, instead of by regulating trade. Though the mercantilist was feeling after a true theory of trade, his ideas were crude, and he missed the true explanation that metals too are a commodity, and that a constant inflow of the precious metals into one country would infallibly send up the price of all other commodities.

The desire to rival the Spaniard and discover rich mines had been an important cause of early colonisation; in Virginia it had been a case of "no talk, no hope, no work, but dig gold, work gold, refine gold, and load gold." But the failure to find the precious metals forced the colonies to adopt the sounder plan of agriculture, and the mercantilists began to apply their idea of the balance of trade to the colonies. Colonies, they thought, were of no value if foreigners were allowed to trade with them; this would mean loss of wealth to England and decay of shipping. Nor were colonies useful if they produced the same things as the Mother Country, for then they would not form a market for English goods, and might even compete with England itself. Those colonies were best which grew things not obtainable in England; thus the tropical colonies were the most favoured—the West Indies for their sugar, and Virginia for its tobacco. The New England colonies were regarded as rivals, while the East India trade was looked upon with suspicion as it brought in "luxuries," and tended to drain out gold instead of goods in exchange. On the basis of these theories were built up the Navigation Laws; and under this system the colonies were controlled until the early nineteenth century, when men's ideas of the laws of wealth had undergone a complete change and the whole system was swept away.

The organisation of the Empire. A. The Navigation Code.

Cromwell had attempted to exclude the Dutch from the carrying trade, but now a regular code of trade laws was drawn up. The ideal was a self-supporting Empire, the colonies producing the raw materials, and England manufacturing all necessary goods, supplying the colonies and exporting the surplus to Europe. The Act of 1651 was reinforced by the great Navigation Act of 1660, and the new Enumeration clause named a number of commodities, such as sugar, indigo, tobacco, and later rice, which could only be shipped direct to England. These enumerated commodities were just those tropical products which England needed either for her own consumption or for re-export to the Continent at a large profit. Thus England became the mart for colonial produce, and in 1663, by the Staple Act, she was made the depôt from which all goods were shipped to the colonies, for, with few exceptions, nothing might be sent thither which was not laded in an English port. Finally, in 1673, the plantation duties were imposed, by which goods shipped from one colony to another paid on export the same duty which they would have paid if imported into England. This Act was designed to prevent the smuggling of enumerated goods to foreign markets. In addition to these laws all colonial goods paid an import duty in England, but were protected against foreign competition by high tariffs.

Under the navigation system both Scotland and, to a large extent, Ireland, were excluded from the benefits of plantation trade, and the Scotch Parliament soon took action by way of reprisals. It passed a Navigation Act excluding Englishmen from the Scottish coasting trade, and in 1695 tried to form a colony of its own at Darien, on the Isthmus of Panama. The Scots hoped to gain a large share in the trade with India, by way of the Pacific, but the Company was ill-managed, the settlers were thinned by disease and by attacks of the Spaniards, and in 1700 the Company collapsed. Stung by this failure, and by their exclusion from English colonial trade, the Scotch Parliament passed the Act of Security in 1703, refusing to recognise George I as Anne's successor unless they were granted the same rights of trade as Englishmen. A scare ensued, the frontier fortresses were garrisoned, and it looked as if the quarrel might come to blows, but after some negotiation the Act of Union (1707) was adopted. Thus two separate kingdoms, united only by the chance that they had the same king, became the United Kingdom with a common flag, a common Parliament, and common rights of trade.

The plantations, however, were treated differently, for "English" was specially defined as including colonial, and under the protection of the Navigation Laws colonial, and especially New England, shipping developed very fast. At first the Act of 1660 was strongly criticised. Lord Willoughby, Governor of Barbados, complained that the ports of the Leeward Islands, hitherto dependent upon the Dutch, were destitute of shipping, while the Barbados Assembly protested against the plantation duties, explaining "how impracticable it was for them (Parliament) to lay a tax on those that had no members in their House." Though frigates were stationed at American ports, and an elaborate customs system organised, there was always smuggling, but it must be remembered that the navigation system had two sides. It has been denounced as a tyrannical system which hampered colonial trade in the interests of England, but in its original form it actually encouraged colonial trade, though along certain routes. The inclusion of colonial shipping, the virtual monopoly of the home market, and the protection given to the colonies by the English fleet, must be weighed against the disadvantages of trading in special ships and to English ports. For England the system meant the partial exclusion of the Dutch from the colonial carrying-trade, and a great increase in shipping, But security as well as profit was in men's minds, and the Navigation Laws were designed to give England a strong fleet, and so to secure to her the mastery of the seas. In this they were successful. The system was the expression of the economic theories of the day, and as such it was accepted, with some grumbling, by the colonists. In the next century fresh restrictions were imposed which limited colonial manufactures, but this was no part of the original scheme.

B. Administrative organisation.

The development of a special administrative department for the control of plantation business again reflects the intimate relation between trade and colonisation. The merchants persuaded Clarendon to establish two councils, one for trade and one for plantations, but although these councils comprised merchants and sea-captains, as well as the great noblemen of the day, they soon proved unwieldy. After some further experiments, there came, in 1670, Shaftesbury's Council of ten paid members, of whom Evelyn was one, and Locke the secretary. Maps, charts, globes, a small library of books, a number of carefully kept official registers, and frequent reports from the colonial governors, all mark the activity of this Council and the energy of Shaftesbury, and its efficiency is proved by the fact that the old Council of Trade was soon amalgamated with it. In 1674, after four years of hard work, the Council was dissolved on

Shaftesbury's fall, and by its dissolution the needy King saved £8000 a year in salaries and expenses. The control of the plantations now fell into the hands of a committee of the Privy Council, the "Lords of Trade," who had all along kept a general eye on colonial affairs; their labours were great, but their efficiency was largely hampered by the King's chronic lack of money, and by his secret machinations with France. Finally, in 1696, colonial matters were given to a "Board of Trade and Plantations." These different bodies maintained an increasing hold over the royal governors, drafting their instructions, receiving their reports, and ordering their behaviour on all occasions. Attempts were made to gain independent information by demanding regular despatches from the local assemblies, but these bodies objected to letter-writing. Colonial business was pushed in committee by merchants who were interested in trade, or by planters sent home on special missions, and the custom gradually arose of appointing a paid agent to conduct the business of a colony. The Board of Trade encouraged this policy, but the various colonies were always chary of putting their hands in their pockets, and they sometimes combined to appoint a joint representative or even refused to employ a regular agent at all. The increase of imperial control is seen in attempts at influencing colonial legislation; the Lords of Trade examined the Acts of the colonial assemblies and recommended the King to pass or annul the different laws. The interests of the merchants in England were often opposed to those of the planters, and the views of men in London had great weight with the Lords of Trade. An attempt, however, to dictate legislation from England, and to force a code of ready-made laws on Jamaica was vigorously resisted and failed, and the custom remained that governors gave their assent to a colonial law, but that the King had still a right of veto, and this right was frequently exercised.

The Lords of Trade and Plantations. 1675-1696.

One of the great problems of early colonisation is the question of labour, and Virginia and the West Indies soon felt the need of a regular supply of labourers who were capable of working in the hot climate. This demand was supplied by the organisation of the slave trade

C. The Slave Trade.

Before 1660 the few slaves imported were usually brought by the Dutch, but the economic ideas of the day could not see the Dutchman gaining wealth from selling slaves to the colonies, and shipping in return sugar and tobacco to Europe. The merchants determined to form companies of their own, and after the failure of a couple of ventures, in one of which the King himself lost money, there was floated in 1671 the Royal African Company, which successfully established a regular slave trade between the West Coast of Africa and the West Indies. Its great vellum-bound books, stamped with the crest of the golden elephant, contain a story of misery and cruelty which we to-day can scarcely realise, but the men of the seventeenth century saw nothing wrong in the trade—negroes were looked upon as beasts of burden, and though there are isolated protests against ill-treatment in the plantations, those who had money readily subscribed, and the King, as well as the Duke of York and Prince Rupert, was among the shareholders. The mercantilists' ideal circle of exchange is seen in the slave trade. The outward ship carried a special cargo of manufactured goods likely to appeal to the native—beads, ironwork, and such like. Working down the coast of Africa, the skipper called at one of the Company's forts, and bought his slaves from the Arab traders; then standing north, he picked up the north-east trade wind, and so across to the West Indies—the notorious "middle passage," during which the human cargo was usually kept stifling below, shackled to iron bars, so that the average loss in some years was about 30 per cent. of the slaves. In the West Indies the slaves were traded for sugar, which was brought back to England to be refined and sold, or the balance re-exported at a good profit to the Continent. The Company was given a monopoly of this lucrative human traffic, but there was continual trouble with the interlopers, who were able to undersell the Company, since they had no standing charge to pay for forts and guard-boats. At the time men were careless enough of the evil which they did, but all unconsciously the Royal African Company was sowing the seeds of a crop of troubles in the West Indies, and in the future Southern States, that are by no means over even in the present day.

This was a time of colonial development for other countries, as well as for England. The Dutch had trading posts in both Indies; the Spice Islands were claimed by them as a monopoly, while their few islands in the West Indies were but depôts from which they absorbed most of the trade from the English and French settlements there: at first they had almost a monopoly of the slave trade, while their colony of New Amsterdam on the Hudson was a shop from which they traded with the English colonies on either hand, and with the French in Canada. But the Dutch were traders rather than planters: they sought "to secure the sole commerce of the Places, and with the people, which they conquer, not by clearing, breaking up of the grounds, and planting, as the English have done. . . ." The commercial jealousy between Dutch and English had not been appeased by Cromwell's war, and the navigation system was aimed directly at the Dutch carrying-trade, while the rival slave traders on the African coast soon fell out and came to blows. Thus war broke out in 1665 and the Dutch lost New Amsterdam, but French help saved them, while the plague and fire combined to fight against the English. At last, in 1667, De Ruyter managed to raid the fleet lying up in the Medway, while peace negotiations were actually on foot. The Treaty of Breda arranged for a mutual restoration of conquests, but left England with New Amsterdam. A few years later, in 1672, the secret negotiations between Charles and Louis led to a joint attack on the Dutch, but Parliament, suspicious of the alliance with the great Roman Catholic power, forced Charles to withdraw from the struggle, thus leaving France and Holland to fight the matter out. As English trade and shipping increased, so her old rivalry with Holland was giving place to a new fear of France.

Other colonial powers: Holland.

The end of the civil wars in France had given unity at home, while in Colbert the young King Louis XIV had a great minister who fully realised the importance of colonies, and determined to develop all their resources. He hedged French commerce round with a series of restrictive laws, much like the English navigation system, and set himself to win the carrying trade of French colonies

France.

for French shipping. He promoted great trading companies, giving them the monopoly of trade in different areas, often finding capital for them from the coffers of the State. He encouraged shipbuilding by every means in his power. Thus the French East India Company entered into competition with the English Company, and began to build up such a strong position that it soon became a question which should control the Eastern trade. In America the French had two groups of colonies. The West Indian islands of Guadeloupe and Martinique had fallen into the hands of individual proprietors, but Colbert floated a West India Company, which encouraged sugar-growing and succeeded in transferring the trade from Dutch to French shipping. In the north the French had early explored and settled in Acadie and along the shores of the St. Lawrence. Quebec was founded in 1608, and fired by the wish to find a way along the river and thus to China, Champlain had pushed westward and thus discovered the Great Lakes, leaving a memory of his hopes in the name of La Chine Rapids. In 1664 Colbert founded the great "Company of the West," which was given a monopoly of trading privileges on the whole of the mainland of America, but the high officials of Canada were still nominated by the King, who also appointed a General-in-Chief for all the French possessions in the New World. A great outburst of activity and exploration now took place: under Governor Frontenac, a brave Jesuit named Marquette found his way to the Mississippi, and, hoping it would lead him to the South Sea, began to sail down the river. When, however, his compass told him that he would arrive at the Gulf of Mexico, he turned back, fearing to fall into Spanish hands. A few years later, La Salle with a small party succeeded in reaching the mouth of the river, and, realising the great possibilities of his discovery, hastened home to France to get permission to found a colony. Louis, who was at enmity with Spain, was pleased with the idea, and so in 1684 Louisiana was founded at the mouth of the great river. The colony, however, was ill-fated, and what with disease and Indian murders, this first attempt at a colony proved a failure.

West Indian Colonies.

Canada.

Louisiana. 1684.

The French system in Canada was that of extreme centralisation: officials appointed from home ruled the people according to directions received from the royal ministers, and there was nothing to correspond to the local government of the English colonies, or to their very independent attitude towards the home authorities. As trappers and woodmen the French colonists had a hard life, earning their living as fur-traders, and frequently intermarrying with their friends the Indians, so that there soon grew up a race of French-Canadian half-breeds. The Jesuits came early to Canada, and as missionaries, teachers, explorers, and map-makers played a very important part in its development.

The growth of this French Empire in America, and the grandiose schemes of Louis XIV in Europe, altered the balance of power and made Englishmen think of France as the great rival. Spain, England's old bugbear, was falling into the background; Holland, her recent rival, was being outstripped; and in England there grew up a new policy of seeking alliance with either of these powers against the ambitions of France. At first this policy had but few supporters, and during the Stuart reigns it was nullified by the royal friendship with Louis; but when William of Orange became King of England the old hostility between Dutch and English was merged in a common hostility to the increasing power of France.

The friction between England and France in America during Charles' reign was greatest in the West Indies, but as Canada grew more important so the quarrel developed on the mainland too. The change in the balance of power in the West Indies was early realised by an English governor there, who wrote in 1664, "The question is whether His Majesty or the King of France will be the King of the West Indies, for the King of Spain cannot hold them long." Things had greatly changed since the days of the treaty for the mutual defence of St. Christopher against the Spaniard, and all that the local governors could do was to promise each other that if news of the outbreak of war arrived from Europe, they would not commence hostilities without due notice. When in 1666 the French came to the aid of the Dutch, they captured the

War with France: Peace of Breda. 1667.

English part of St. Christopher, and their delay in handing it back, as promised by the Treaty of Breda, only increased the mutual ill-feeling.

The sugar-planters of the Leeward Islands suspected that their rivals, the planters of Barbados, were not too friendly towards them, and so in 1671 the four northern islands were cut off from Barbados and formed into the separate government of the Leeward Islands. Their new governor, a witty

THE WEST INDIES ABOUT 1660.

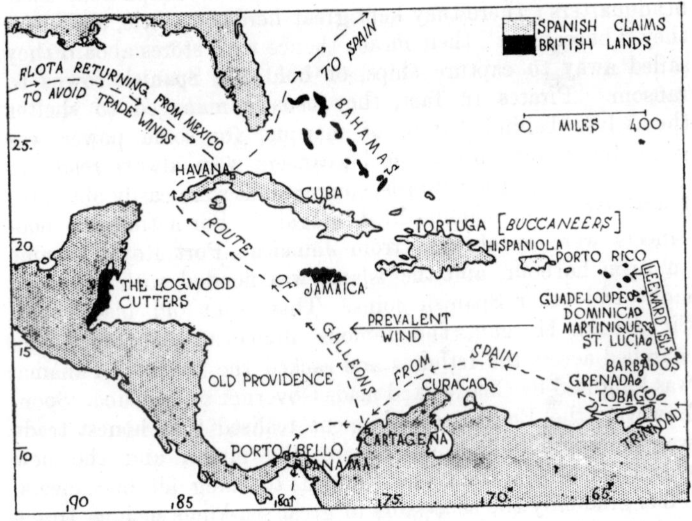

E. H. H. del.

The Logwood cutters were at this time only squatters on Spanish territory.

Irishman, Sir William Stapleton, ruled them for many years, and protected them alike from Dutch ships and from the raids of Carib Indians. He was devoutly thankful when England withdrew from helping the French in the second Dutch war; he hated even to hear of a French victory, for "it gave them but fresh occasion for vapouring." Meanwhile, Cromwell's favourite colony of Jamaica had received a royal governor, and, strengthened with settlers from Barbados, was rapidly becoming an important place. On the coast of Honduras, English squatters were busily engaged in cutting logwood with the help of friendly Indians, and the export of these woods for making dyes grew steadily, despite the Spanish opposition. These squatters were not a formal colony with a governor, and never became so until the nineteenth century. More troublesome to the Spaniards, and indeed to traders in general, were the buccaneers. These picturesque ruffians were dare-devil sailors of all nations, but chiefly French and English, who made Tortuga and the north-west of Hispaniola their headquarters; there they kept great herds of cattle, and there they "buccanned" their meat; thence with stores aboard they sailed away to capture ships, or hold the Spanish towns to ransom. Pirates in fact, they usually managed to shelter themselves behind letters of marque, for some power was generally at war, and as the buccaneers were always ready to sell their swords, commissions were easily obtained, but seldom called in again. For a time the buccaneers were encouraged from Jamaica: Port Royal became an open harbour, and the island was flooded with pieces of eight and other Spanish coins. That stout old blackguard, Sir Henry Morgan, the famous Jamaican buccaneer who marched across the Isthmus and sacked the town of Panama, was knighted by Charles and made Governor of Jamaica. Soon, however, the English Government realised that honest trade was more profitable than playing the pirate, and the new Governor of Jamaica was ordered to hang all buccaneers. Thus gradually the successors of great sea-kings such as Drake and Hawkins sank lower still and became mere pirates, and for many years the seas of the West Indies were haunted by these pests. Cruel and callous as were most of the buccaneers, yet they had a bravery all their own; in quite small ships they made amazing voyages, and in battle feared no odds. They even pushed into the sacred preserve of the Pacific, and made the Indian seas a useful hunting ground.

The Buccaneers.

Barbados was at this time the richest of all the West Indian colonies: at the Restoration it had, together with the Leeward Islands, voted a perpetual export duty of 4½ per cent. in return for the cancelling of the proprietor's rights. Thus the islands became a royal colony, and, despite the duty, their trade flourished greatly. The Sugar Islands, as the West Indies were called, were very popular in England, and offered a continual market to the slave traders, though the planter was always more ready to buy on credit than to pay over his casks of sugar. Soon, too, a system of indentured labour sprang up: English men and women sold their services for a number of years in return for their passage and a gratuity after four years' service. This system had the advantage that it helped poor people to emigrate, but it was abused by masters who overworked and defrauded their servants, and in England by crimps or "spirits," who seized upon unsuspecting people in the street or on the seashore, and sold them forcibly into slavery beyond the seas. Strong steps were taken to put down this villainy, and Virginia and the Sugar Islands complained loud and long of the difficulty of obtaining labour. Still another form of labour was employed. The agent of St. Christopher suggested that it would be better to send criminals to work in the plantations than to let them rot in English gaols. After lengthy negotiations, and much money spent in "presents," a number of prisoners were sent out to work as indentured servants, with a promise of freedom after eight years, provided they never returned to England. Such transportation had already played its part in colonising Ireland and Virginia.

The planters crushed and boiled their canes, and the coarse brown Muscovado sugar which they made was then shipped home to England to be refined. The molasses, like thick treacle, was also shipped to Bristol or New England to be made into rum. The English sugar-refiners continually opposed the attempts of the planters to refine their own sugar, and were generally successful. The sugar industry was very wealthy, since the English merchant sold his sugar on the Continent cheaper than could the Portuguese, and this trade created a powerful sugar interest in England, but the growing competition of the French islands was soon to make the English merchants very uneasy.

The Sugar Islands grew wealthy during Charles' reign, but on the mainland even larger changes took place. Here the colonising activity of the time found its vent in the settling of several new plantations. For some time Englishmen had looked with desire on the land south of Virginia which was vaguely called Florida. During Cromwell's time some merchants who had a scheme for colonisation succeeded in persuading a native to come home to England, where he was dignified with the title of Ambassador, but the plan fell through. Now, in 1663, Charles granted the land to a number of proprietors, of whom Clarendon and Ashley (Lord Shaftesbury) were the chief. The proprietors were entitled to grant religious liberty "because it may happen that some of the people cannot in their private opinions conform to the public exercise according to the Church of England." In this justification of toleration we may perhaps see the influence of Shaftesbury, who always stood for religious freedom, though the normal instructions to royal governors at this time order freedom of worship for private individuals. It seems that several settlements were intended, but two only were planted, those of North and South Carolina. The former, which was settled first, drew its men largely from Barbados, despite the protest of the Governor, who declared it was but taking money out of one pocket and putting it into the other. On the whole the settlers were a poor lot, and the colony, shut in by swamp and forest from its neighbours, long remained in a backward state. The southern colony was more of a success, but, despite better selected emigrants and good governors, the country still grew slowly, for the hot climate made the breaking up of the land a slow and arduous task. It was not until the introduction of slave labour and the concentration on rice as a staple crop that Carolina really prospered. Then it became the typical aristocratic slave-owning state; rice was enumerated, and from the port of Charlestown a steady supply was shipped to England. If the Carolinas were not immediately a great success, this was not due to any lack of thought or interest on the part of the proprietors. The philosopher Locke had drawn up a careful, if somewhat fantastic constitution, in which queer names like "cacique" and "landgrave" appear; but this constitution was found impracticable, and the Carolinas developed the

New Plantations: Carolina.

normal colonial institutions. Shaftesbury himself paid great attention to his colony, and his papers, which are still preserved, show his interest in every detail of its administration.

Further north, the capture of New Amsterdam from the Dutch gave England the land between Maryland and the New England colonies, and from this territory the "middle" colonies were created. The conquest meant the removal of a constant threat to the peace and security of New England, and enabled the navigation system to be better enforced, but though England secured a continuous line of coastal colonies from Maine to South Carolina, this did not really improve communications between the various colonies, for roads were very bad, and for many years the easiest way to get from colony to colony was still by ship. The Dutch with their usual aptitude for seizing upon strategic positions had settled on the Hudson, and now that great river highway to Canada was in English hands, for trade or war as the case might be. By the capture of this Dutch plantation the English were faced for the first time with the problem of ruling another European people, a problem which was often to occur again in the development of the Empire.[1] The King granted the land to his brother the Duke of York as proprietor, and his governor did not call an assembly till 1683. When James succeeded to the throne New York became a royal colony, and naturally remained so after 1688. The population of New York was very mixed, for the religious freedom permitted by the Dutch, and their permission for residents to trade, had drawn men of all nations, and it was said that eighteen tongues could be heard at New Amsterdam. This mixture of nationalities meant that the new settlement must be wide and comprehensive. The Dutch were left in possession of their lands, and only called upon to pay a small fee; religious liberty was likewise granted, each township was to have a church, and the choice of denomination was left to the inhabitants. Under this generous system the Dutch quickly settled down, and despite trouble with the Indians, who were egged on by the French, New York soon became a flourishing colony and what Governor Nicholls hoped it would be, "a

The Middle Colonies: (1) New York. 1664.

[1] The number of Spaniards in Jamaica had been but small.

School of better religion and obedience to God and the King than was to be found in New England."

The southern lands of the Dutch colony as far as the Delaware were granted by the Duke of York to his friends Carteret and Berkeley, and called New Jersey in memory of the Duke's stay in the Channel Isles during his exile. Several experiments in colonising were made, and a number of Quakers bought a share in the proprietary rights and settled fellow Quakers there, where they might be free from the persecution they had suffered in Massachusetts, or from the disabilities they were under at home. But this experiment was not enough for William Penn, son of the admiral who had taken Jamaica, a famous Quaker and a man of the highest ideals, though limited sometimes in his practical outlook. In 1681 he received from the King a grant of land on the Delaware river on which to found a colony. The King's advisers had learnt wisdom from past troubles, and determined to keep a tight hold upon this new proprietary colony, especially in matters of trade. The royal charter provided that the King's customs officials should be present in the colony, and that the proprietor should always keep a responsible agent in London ready to answer for the colony. In founding this new colony Penn did not wish to make a settlement for Quakers alone, but a place where his ideal of colonisation should be carried out, where all men who acknowledged a God might come and live free from forms and interference, and where the relations between the colonists and the Indians should be on an honest footing. Penn drew up a constitution for his colony, with a large council and still larger assembly, both to be elected by the colonists, and with some modifications this became the constitution under which the colony was governed. In his laws Penn insisted on honest treatment for the natives ; crimes against them were to be tried by a mixed jury of natives and colonists, while elaborate precautions were taken to prevent their being cheated in trade. Penn saw in the Indian not a bloodthirsty savage to be destroyed, or at best to be regarded with mistrust, but a brother man who also knew of God, though he worshipped Him under different forms. On his first visit Penn founded the city of Philadelphia

(2) The Jerseys.

(3) Pennsylvania. 1681.

(or Brotherly Love), and so apt was the choice of a site that by 1681 he was able to grant his city a charter of incorporation. "Of all the many places I have seen in the world," wrote Penn, in 1683, "I remember not one better seated ; so that it seems to have been appointed for a Town." Penn's colony did not start with quite a clean slate, for there had been earlier settlers, Swedes, and then their conquerors the Dutch; these people lived chiefly in the land south of the Delaware, which had been granted to Penn by the Duke of York. These "territories" caused Penn much trouble, for the inhabitants quarrelled frequently with the men of Pennsylvania, and finally demanded a separate assembly: this Penn granted to them, and later they broke away entirely, so becoming the separate colony of Delaware.

(4) Delaware.

Pennsylvania flourished quickly, and so many settlers came that Penn soon found it difficult to keep to his ideal of a colony ; his rules for dealings with the Indians were often ignored, while quarrels soon arose with Penn himself. Men began to forget what he had done for the colony, to dispute over the question of the payment of quit rents, to quarrel with his governor and the other officials. Thus Penn's latter years were years of trouble and contention, and the high ideals with which he had set out were found most difficult of achievement. In 1689 Penn lost his rights owing to his friendship with James, and for a short time Pennsylvania was joined to New York, but Penn was soon back in favour, and the old system was restored.

Still further north two settlements were organised which were to play an important part in the relations of French and English in America. The French claimed all the coastline north of Maine, but their settlement of Acadie had been captured in the war of 1666 ; though it was returned by the Treaty of Breda, England retained a right to Nova Scotia. A clearer knowledge of geography soon showed that Nova Scotia was really a part of Acadie, and so the English claim was valueless except as a pawn in the diplomatic game. Newfoundland with its fogs and fisheries was more important, for along its shore had gradually grown up a small settlement of Englishmen, who traded with the fishing-fleets that came there every summer, and even began to

Newfoundland.

fish on their own account. It was proposed to send out a governor to organise a regular plantation, but this suggestion was vigorously opposed by Sir Josiah Child, a famous mercantilist writer. He argued that a governor would mean more expenses, taxes, and so an increase in the cost of fish, while such a colony would compete in the fishery, trade exclusively with New England, and thus not benefit England at all. But facts were harder than theories, the men were there and would not leave, and so a governor was sent out. The French, however, retained the right to fish and had vague claims on the island, which resulted in frequent disputes and a spirit of misunderstanding which has only been cleared away by the Entente Agreement of 1904.

Hudson's Bay Company. 1670.

The French made much of their fur trade in Canada, and the English wished to gain a footing there, so in 1670 the King granted to Prince Rupert and a number of other adventurers a monopoly of trade with the northernmost parts of America. Thus was founded the Hudson's Bay Company, who traded by summer through Hudson's Strait with Rupertsland. Here they established a few trading-forts, and hardy trappers set out to pit their skill against their quarry. At the outset vast tracts of virgin forest shut them off from the French, but the claims of both nations were very vague, and their trappers and explorers were soon to meet and to come into bitter conflict.

The relations between the restored monarchy and the southern colonies were good, for Virginia and Maryland were largely royalist in sympathy, but the New England Federation had treated Cromwell's government in a very independent manner, and were loth to come to heel. They had even set up a mint and coined money of their own. These "Boston shillings" with their device of an oak tree and "God my Help" as their legend, were badly needed for purposes of exchange, for in the whole of America there was so little coin that goods were bought and sold by barter, and in the South sugar and tobacco were used as the normal measures of value; thus the new coins quickly spread to the other colonies, and to the West Indies. This assumption of the royal prerogative was very objectionable to the King, but despite protests the mint went on. In other matters, too, New England was unaccommodating, the omission of the royal name in legal processes, and the extensive evasion of the Navigation Laws all caused complaint. So in 1664 Clarendon sent out commissioners to try to remedy matters, but they were treated in a most discourteous manner, and it was only the outbreak of the Dutch war, and an opportune present of masts and tar for the Royal Navy that averted the King's wrath for the moment. After the war things went from bad to worse; Massachusetts deliberately annexed Maine, although it was known that the King was inquiring into various claims to that colony, and for several years the Lords of Trade tried to arrange for greater control over the executive of this practically independent colony. Finally, in despair, legal proceedings were begun, and in 1683 Massachusetts forfeited its charter. The New England Confederation itself had been gradually weakened, and it finally broke up in the following year.

Massachusetts loses its Charter. 1683.

The Council of Plantations had early recommended that all proprietary rights be acquired by the Crown, and that no further proprietary colonies be created. This far-seeing recommendation was not carried out, but it was not merely favouritism which led the King to create new proprietary governments. It was a method of securing private energy and capital for colonising ventures which the Crown was unable or indisposed to undertake directly; but the evils of proprietary governments, whether the proprietors were companies or individuals, became more and more evident; Massachusetts is an extreme case, but the reservations in the grant of Pennsylvania show which way the wind was blowing. During the reign of James II there grew up a policy of centralising control in America and of attempting to secure co-operation between the colonies, both in matters of customs and of joint defence against the Indians. This policy is no mere expression of arbitrary instincts on the part of the King, but a practical attempt to solve a practical problem. The Lords of Trade had come to the conclusion that it would be best to unite all colonies north of Maryland under a common governor. In 1686, Edmund Andros, who had already been Governor of

Attempt to unite colonies under Andros.

New York, was sent out as Governor of Maine, New Hampshire, and Massachusetts; by 1688, all colonies north of Pennsylvania were under his control, and plans were in hand for cancelling the other proprietary charters. The Revolution of 1688 drove James from his throne, and Andros, a still more hated man, from his control of America: thus the scheme fell through, and things reverted to the old condition of separate colonies with separate interests and governments.

The fall of Governor Andros is of great importance for the future development of America. Two schemes of union had now been tried and had failed. The New England Federation represents voluntary union from below, and it failed partly because of mutual jealousies, and partly because of the hostility of the home government to its independent attitude. Andros' governorship represents union from above, forced on the colonies by the King, and its failure was due partly to colonial feelings of liberty and sectional independence, but largely to the fall of James in England. The great problem was now shelved indefinitely until Grenville took the matter up in a new form, and only succeeded in precipitating the War of Independence. Had the Andros policy been successful, the future development of America must have been very different.

If we review the British Empire at the Revolution we are able to appreciate the importance of the reign of Charles II in colonial history. We see a well-organised central administration in constant touch and control of the colonies, a carefully devised system of trade legislation expressing the economic ideas of the day, and attempting to build up the wealth of the country by regulating the trade of the world, a wealthy company bringing a continual supply of slave labour to the colonies, and exploiting the riches of tropical soil by their means. This is the framework of empire. In America we find a continuous line of colonies along the Atlantic sea-board, from Maine in the North to Carolina in the South, with outposts at Newfoundland and Rupertsland. In the West Indies there are three groups: Jamaica, the Leeward Islands, and Barbados, all flourishing on a monopoly of slave-grown sugar; the Bahamas and the Bermudas are still of small account. In the East, the great East India Company is firmly established with its factories at the three Presidency towns of Bombay, Madras, and Calcutta, while the tea supply of England depends on the Company's annual voyages to China. So rich is the Company that a violent attack on its monopoly is already preparing among the jealous merchants who are not in the privileged clique. Thus the reign of Charles II saw the empire extended, consolidated, and organised ready for the struggles of the eighteenth century.

BOOKS.—See note to Chapter I. John Masefield, *On the Spanish Main*, is a picturesque account of the buccaneering days.

1660. **The Navigation Act. [1663. Staple Act. 1673. Plantation Duties Act.]**
1663. **Carolina founded.**
1664. **New Amsterdam captured: it becomes New York.**
1670. **Hudson's Bay Company founded.**
1671. **Royal African Company founded.**
1681. **William Penn founds Pennsylvania.**

CHAPTER III

The Development of America and the Struggle with France [1688–1763]

THE most picturesque aspect of English history in the eighteenth century is the long struggle with France, which was fought out in India, on the rivers and backwoods of America, and on all the seas of the world. The story of the struggle is told in vivid fashion by Seeley in his famous book *The Expansion of England*, but there is another side of colonial history which must not be forgotten, or else the War of Independence comes as a sudden shock which seems quite unconnected with all that went before. In fact, the long period of apparent quiet before the passing of the Stamp Act was filled with a continuous series of small quarrels between the colonies and the Mother Country which are the true preface to that great struggle. Though these two points of view are separated in the telling, it must always be remembered that they were closely interwoven ; thus it was the fear of the French power in America which prevented the colonial quarrels from coming to an open rupture until after 1763, while a few years later the French made use of a domestic quarrel between England and her colonies to interfere and win back some of the prestige which they had lost in the Seven Years' War. Then was formed that long friendship between France and the United States which has so influenced the development of both countries, and which has been cemented yet more firmly by joint sacrifices in the European War.

Eighteenth-century characteristics.

During the greater part of the eighteenth century colonial affairs were in the hands of the Board of Trade, which was created in 1696 and took over plantation business from the Lords of Trade. Although William III had been greatly affronted at Parliament's attempt to nominate the members of the Board, yet throughout the century Parliament was constantly enlarging its control over colonial affairs : in the seventeenth century a member who raised the question of America had been told that he was out of order, but things soon became very different. In 1763 the terms of the Peace of Paris were hotly debated in the Commons, while a few years later the whole question of American taxation was thrashed out in the House. The Board of Trade was a consultative body, and had little executive authority of its own. The chief power lay in the hands of the Secretary of State for the Southern Department, who was responsible for colonial matters, and if he was not interested the Board of Trade would report in vain. The lengthy period of Walpole's ascendancy, when Newcastle was Secretary of State from 1724 to 1748, was a time when colonial problems were ignored ; Walpole prided himself on leaving things alone, while Newcastle's ignorance of colonial matters became a byeword. This vicious system of letting matters slide only heaped up trouble for the future : the Board of Trade pursued a consistent and, on the whole, a statesmanlike policy, but its frequent reports were simply laid aside, and its advice neglected.

Board of Trade. 1696.

Thus, although the first half of the century might seem a time of peace when the old disputes between England and the colonies had disappeared, there was all the time going on beneath the surface that fermentation which was to break out in the War of Independence. Thus Walpole rather than Grenville should be held responsible for that disaster.

The early colonists took with them from England the idea of self-government, and, unlike the colonies of other nations, quickly developed a system of popular government by means of a governor, council, and elected assembly. The theories of political freedom, which had bulked so large in Englishmen's minds during the stirring days of the seventeenth century, had apparently triumphed with the successful Revolution of 1688. The colonists were English too, and it was only natural that they should have similar feelings, and the struggles between governor and local assembly in the colonies are a reflection of similar struggles between King and Parliament in England. The colonists were rather suspicious of control by England, and of their governor as an English agent. Thus one of the hardest fought disputes was over the question of the governor's salary : in most of the colonies there was a permanent fund for this payment, and the Board of Trade tried to force New York and Massachusetts to make similar arrangements. These two colonies, however, paid their governor every year, and valued this custom as they were enabled to control him by threatening to cut off his salary. This struggle ended in success for the colonists, for though the Board directed the governor to refuse all "presents," as they were pleased to call the annual payments of salary, the assembly remained firm and would not be frightened by talk of a Stamp Act, or threats of Imperial legislation. So the governors went unpaid, and the Board had to give way. Another cause of friction was connected with the appointment of judges. These officers were appointed and paid locally, but the Board wished to alter the wording of their commissions to prevent the local assemblies from influencing the course of justice. The assemblies threatened to refuse payment if this was done, and it

Disputes between colonies and Board of Trade.

(1) Governor's salary.

(2) Judiciary.

was not till the death of George II in 1760 made all the old commissions void that the Board was able to gain its point. This honest attempt by the Board to secure clean justice for America was afterwards cited in the Declaration of Independence as an instance of cruel oppression and arbitrary interference with local rights. Yet another cause of irritation was the King's power to veto colonial legislation. Although this power had been exercised from early days, and was recognised as part of the royal prerogative, yet in many cases it caused discontent, and the colonists attempted to defeat it by means of "tacking" and such parliamentary tricks. Defence was always an important problem for people who had treacherous Indians as near neighbours, but the local jealousies of the colonies prevented common action. In time of peace no regular troops were stationed in America, each colony had to rely upon its militia, and the Assembly was quick to resent English attempts to control this local citizen force. The practice of giving a governor a commission to command the militia of several adjoining colonies was usually met with protests and opposition, while the joint campaigns of Imperial and colonial troops were often the cause of further ill-feeling. The open scorn of colonial officers for regular generals, who were unused to the tactics of backwoods fighting, was repaid by a contempt for colonial dress and colonial soldiers which deeply offended the military pride of the colonists. Though competent officers such as Howe and Wolfe admired the skill of the militia and even made their troops adopt the local dress and tactics, these joint expeditions usually ended in mutual misunderstanding.

(3) Veto on legislation.

(4) Control of militia.

Still another cause of friction is to be found in the navigation system, though the ill-feeling which it caused must not be over-emphasised. The system of Charles II had been accepted with but little grumbling, and though there was always some smuggling it does not appear to have been very great. In two directions, however, the original system was altered. As the New England colonies grew they soon began to develop small industries of their own, first to supply local demands, and then with a view to export. Thus, beaver hats were made, wool was grown and manufactured locally, and a little iron was mined and smelted. This development was watched with anxiety by English manufacturers, who foresaw not only the loss of colonial markets, but also actual competition in other countries. A series of restrictive Acts were passed, which practically prohibited these manufactures, but, though these measures doubtless caused some inconvenience and loss of money to a few, they were not a general cause of ill-feeling. In another way, too, the navigation system was extended: a large trade in molasses had sprung up between the French West Indies and the northern colonies, especially New York. The molasses were distilled in the colonies and re-exported as rum. This trade was regarded with suspicion by the English planters, who declared that it was ruining the West Indies, and, after much agitation, they procured the passing of the Molasses Act (1733), which forbade this trade. Had this Act been enforced it would have caused very great discontent, for molasses from the English islands cost more, and, indeed, all the English islands, so it was alleged, were unable to produce sufficient molasses to meet the demand of the northern colonies. For practical purposes the Act was a dead letter: a vast amount of smuggling went on and was openly winked at.

(5) Navigation system extended.

Despite all these disputes between the colonies and the home country, it would be wrong to think that the different colonies co-operated in their protests, or that colonists felt any community of interest with the men of the next colony. This was far from the case; indeed, antagonism between the various colonies was often much sharper than feeling against the governor or Board of Trade. A fruitful cause of trouble was the frequent boundary disputes between adjacent colonies: the original grants had often been very vague, and, as the colonies grew, the question of accurate frontiers became important. It was often a problem how far westward a colony extended, and this was no empty question, for westward lay the Indians, and the hardy pioneers who pushed into the woods for Indian trade were often anxious to escape authority and to deny the jurisdiction of the colony. But the local

Inter-colonial disputes.

(1) Boundary disputes.

government had to keep a watchful eye on such men, lest a private quarrel with the Indians should lead to sudden war and rapine all along the frontier. Boundary disputes were often bitter, and the settlers of Maryland and Pennsylvania actually came to blows. Trouble, too, occurred between Virginia and North Carolina, for the Virginian assembly refused to allow tobacco to be imported from their southern neighbour, on the grounds that it was inferior stuff and would ruin the reputation of Virginian tobacco. They policed their frontier, but the home government forced them to give way.

(2) Defence against Indians.

These local quarrels were most fatal in the case of Indian affairs, for the follies of one colony might ruin the good understanding between another colony and its savage neighbours. Indeed, the Indians could hardly understand how the different colonies all belonged to the same nation, and compared them very unfavourably with Canada and its centralised government. The Quakers of Pennsylvania would not fight, and many later settlers sheltered themselves under the plea of conscience: the Dutch of New York were suspected of trading with the enemy, while Washington complained most bitterly of the supineness of his Virginian fellow-colonists after Braddock's defeat in 1755.

Causes of disputes.

This lack of co-operation was due to several causes. The colonies had been founded at different times by different types of people: the Puritan of New England felt little in common with the planter of Virginia. Various other nationalities, too, were incorporated in the English colonies—Dutch at New York, Swedes in Delaware, Moravians, Huguenots, Highlanders—and this prevented a ready amalgamation. Even the economic interests of the colonies were very different. The more southerly the colony, the more it depended upon England: while, from the very first, Massachusetts could almost do without England at all, and for periods was practically independent: South Carolina, on the other hand, with its staple crop of rice, was, for practical purposes, nearer to England than to New York. Above all, the lack of easy communications, good roads and bridges, prevented the colonies from drawing together; men went from colony to colony by sea, and although some sort of post was established, it might take as much as seven weeks for a letter to get from Boston to Virginia.[1]

This keen local jealousy is typical of the colonies in the eighteenth century, and nothing was more distasteful to them than attempts to unite them under a common authority. The Board of Trade, however, realised that the crux of the problem of defence was this local disunion, and that the proprietary and charter colonies were the centres of discontent and opposition to the home government. Its general policy was, therefore, to do away with these anomalies, and to force all the colonies into the common mould of the royal colony—as a step to something further. "The independency they thirst after is now so notorious," wrote the Board in 1700, "that it has been thought fit that those considerations, together with other objections against those colonies, should be laid before Parliament, and a Bill has been brought into the House of Lords for resuming the right of government in those colonies to the Crown." Nothing, however, came of the matter, and despite the frequent recommendations of the Board the question was always shelved. In 1721, however, the Board produced a definite scheme for union: they proposed the appointment of a Lord-Lieutenant for America, who was to have in constant attendance two councillors from each colony. This scheme also came to nothing, and it was only the fear of a French war in 1754 that led to the famous Albany Conference. Deputies from the different colonies had met at Albany, a frontier town in New York, on several previous occasions, to deal jointly with Indian business, but the Conference of 1754 is of great importance because it also discussed the problem of union. The Conference voted that a union was absolutely necessary for security and defence, and drew up a plan for a "President-General" appointed by the Crown, and an annual council elected by the local assemblies, to sit at

Policy of Board of Trade.

Abolition of proprietary colonies.

Union.

Albany Conference, 1754.

[1] See the vivid description in Doyle: *The Colonies under the House of Hanover*, Chap. I.

Philadelphia. This council was to have power over new settlements, military, naval, and Indian affairs, and the right of levying taxes. Though accepted by the Conference, the colonial assemblies would have nothing to do with the plan. Connecticut declared that it was "a very extraordinary thing, and against the rights and privileges of Englishmen," while Governor Shirley of Virginia thought "their different constitutions, situations, circumstances, and tempers . . . an invincible obstacle to their agreement upon any one plan in every article, or, if they should ever happen to agree upon one, to their duly carrying it into execution." Only twenty-two years after this conference these same colonies signed the Declaration of Independence. If we ask what had brought about so great a change in so short a time we can see two causes. First, the Seven Years' War, which had removed the continual menace of the French, had taught the colonial militia its powers, and had left an undeserved slur on British arms; and next, the attempt to solve these very problems which Walpole had burked.

The West Indies: Economic changes.

In the West Indies too there were constitutional struggles between the assemblies and their governors, but a gradual change was taking place in the population of the islands, which made them so dependent upon England that any chance of a violent quarrel was out of the question. The regular importation of slaves soon had an effect which those who first organised the trade never foresaw; the number of blacks in the islands grew apace while the whites increased but slowly, and after a time actually diminished. Thus in Jamaica, the most important island during the eighteenth century, the negroes in 1739 outnumbered the whites by nearly ten to one, and this danger quickly alarmed the planters. They saw the possibility of a slave-revolt, and they feared the attack of French or Spaniards, for the slaves could not serve in the local militia, and might even help the enemy. In an attempt to remedy matters laws were passed requiring each planter to keep one white servant to every so many slaves, but it was cheaper to pay the fine imposed than to comply with the law, and these Acts quickly became nothing more than a

Slaves outnumber whites.

normal method of local taxation. Other economic causes were also at work. In the first rush to secure sugar fortunes some land had been cultivated that was scarcely worth the expense; it was quickly exhausted and either abandoned or sold to larger planters. It was cheaper to work huge plantations with large gangs of slaves, and so the small planter who worked with two or three slaves and a few indentured servants soon disappeared. The inflow of white men practically stopped, as it was increasingly difficult to get indentured servants. Thus, by the middle of the century, the Sugar Islands consisted of large plantations owned by a few wealthy planters, who were often absentees living in London or Bristol, and working their plantations by means of local managers and overseers. The whites who still lived in the islands formed a little society with their parish churches, their local assemblies, and in Barbados with a weekly newspaper composed of essays, letters, gazettes from England, and local news. This white society was fashionable and hospitable. A writer of 1740 praises the planters of St. Christopher: "I can't enough commend their generosity; they used us well; and when we were about to depart, expressed the same concern, as if we had been their long and intimate Acquaintance." Below were the slaves, vastly outnumbering their masters and often treated very harshly, for they were regarded as scarcely human, and certainly not as fit objects for Christianity. It was not until the arrival of the Moravians and the Wesleyans about the middle of the century that anything was done for the negro slaves. A few, however, gained their freedom, through the gift of kindly masters, and there grew up a class of half-castes whose position in the economy of the islands was not always pleasant. At times the slaves escaped; those from the Leeward Islands generally fled to the Caribs at Dominica, whence by inter-marriage there sprang up a fierce and implacable race of savages; in Jamaica the escaped maroons took to the mountains, and long and bloodthirsty wars had to be waged against them. Despite these changes in the West Indies, the merchants and planters who lived in England remained a powerful factor in political circles. This sugar interest secured the passing of the Molasses Act to check French competition,

Absentee proprietors.

and when in 1763 the terms of the Peace of Paris were being discussed, it was seriously proposed to accept Guadeloupe, one of the French Sugar Islands, instead of Canada. This suggestion shows how valuable the Sugar Islands were considered, but it fell through because the sugar interest feared competition from the plantations of Guadeloupe, if annexation brought that island within the sacred circle of the navigation system.

The French exploited their islands with great energy: their plantations on St. Domingo, where previously the buccaneers had kept their herds of cattle, were very successful, and owing to the fertility of their islands and the good treatment of their slaves, the French were able to undersell the English, and to take from them much of the continental sugar trade. This competition was always a great annoyance to England, and in every European war an English fleet was despatched to the West Indies to seize or destroy the French plantations.

French competition.

The great struggle between England and France which runs all through the eighteenth century began definitely with the accession of William of Orange to the English throne in 1688. At first the European wars have merely an echo in America; colonists fought because the home countries were at war, but as the plantations grew there soon arose disputes between the two nations in America, and then there was often fighting in the colonies long before war had broken out in Europe. Thus both in America and India hostilities had begun between the French and English some time before the outbreak of the Seven Years' War. On the mainland of America the French held besides Acadie, Canada, which comprised their settlements along the St. Lawrence from Quebec to the Lakes, with hunting posts further inland, and their new colony of Louisiana with vague claims to the Mississippi valley. The New England colonies were much exposed to the danger of raids by Indians encouraged by Jesuit missionaries, but New York was really the key to the situation.

The struggle with France.

Routes to Canada.

The River Hudson formed then, as it does to-day, the great highway to Canada. From the frontier town of Albany the trader or general could chose between two routes: he could go west along the Mohawk and so to Lake

Ontario, or north by Lake Champlain and the Richelieu river to Montreal. There was a third route to Canada, by sea up the St. Lawrence, but that was a difficult voyage, hampered by fogs and the shallows of the river, and quite impossible in winter because of the ice. Further south, Pennsylvania, Maryland, and Virginia backed on the Alleghany mountains, and had untrustworthy Indians for their neighbours; when the French began to spread to the Ohio valley, another route lay open to attack, and armies pushed westward across the Alleghanies. The strategy of the American wars depends on these four highways.

The two wars against Louis XIV saw fighting in America as well as Europe: "King William's war" was largely a tale of Indian raids and massacres, marked by the successful capture of Acadie from the French, and by the mismanagement and failure of an attempt on Quebec. The Peace of Ryswick (1697) was a restoration of the *status quo*, but the war is important as it saw the first conference at Albany to arrange for common action in defence. The War of the Spanish Succession, or "Queen Anne's war" as it was called in the colonies, is very important for colonial development. Though most of the fighting took place in Europe, the great victories of Marlborough were really the guarantee that France should not control Spain, and absorb her whole colonial empire. The home government was too busy with the war in Europe to pay much attention to America, though Vetch, the Massachusetts agent, already dreamt of ousting the French from America, so that "Her Majesty shall be sole Empress of the vast North American continent." In 1710 British and colonial troops took Port Royal in Acadie, and in the following year the Tories, who were now in power, hoping to eclipse the victories of Marlborough, sent five thousand troops to America. The story of their doings is not a happy one; quarrels arose with the colonies about the question of billeting, while a joint expedition on land by Lake Champlain, and on sea up the St. Lawrence, ended in disaster and the wreck of the fleet. In 1713, however, the Peace of Utrecht proved of great advantage to the

Queen Anne's war. 1702–1713.

Peace of Utrecht. 1713.

AMERICA IN 1713.

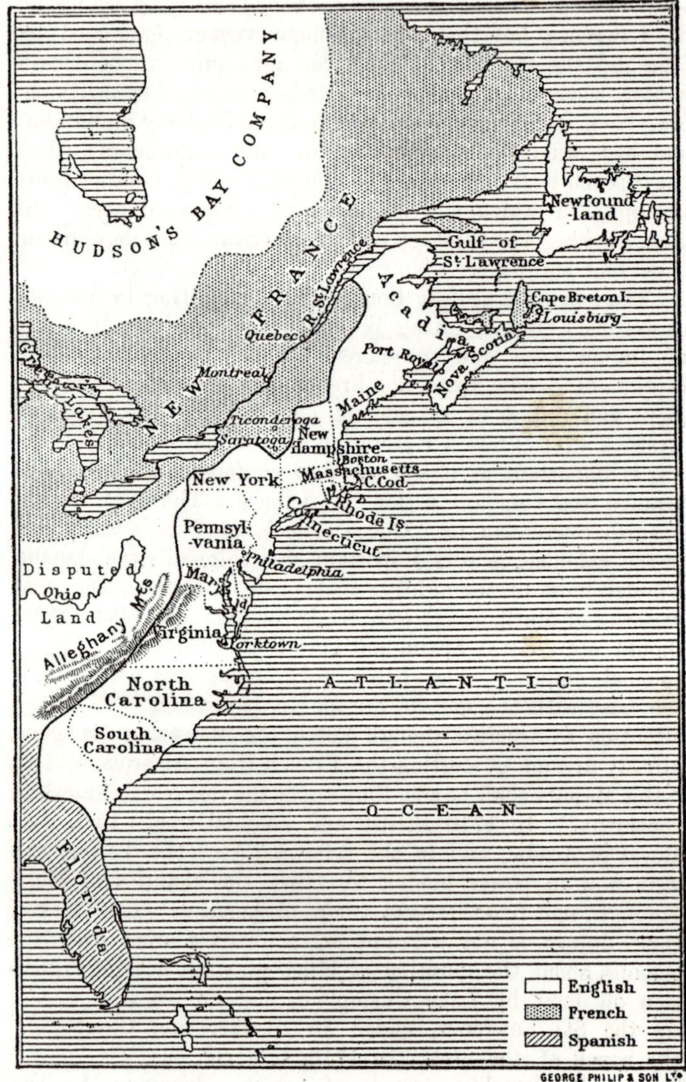

colonies and to English merchants. In the West Indies, where the French portion of St. Christopher had twice been captured by the English, the whole of the island was now resigned to England. Acadie too became English, though the French retained Cape Breton Island and certain fishing rights off Newfoundland—a fruitful scource of future trouble and dispute. Lastly, England gained the right to send one ship-load of goods each year to Spanish America, while the Asiento permitted her to supply the Spaniards with slaves; but this successful breach in the ring of Spanish trade monopoly was quickly widened by smugglers, and soon led to yet another war.

The Peace of Utrecht was rather a starting-point for further quarrels than a settlement of past disputes. It did not decide the essential question who was to be the dominant power in America; it did not even settle the problems with which it was supposed to deal. "The ancient bounds" of Acadie were hotly disputed, and the very name of the country meant different things to French and English. The feeling of antagonism is shown by the outburst of fort-building on both sides. The French, deprived of Acadie, built the strong harbour and fort of Louisbourg on Cape Breton Island, which served alike as a threat to New England and as a protection to "the river that leads to New France." As long as Louisbourg remained hidden away amongst its fogs in the north, the English colonists could never feel secure, and their first thought in any war was to seize that place. On the mainland too the French began that system of regular fortification which in time threatened to hem in the English completely. In 1720 they built Fort Niagara. Burnet, the energetic governor of New York, replied by building Fort Oswego on Lake Ontario at the end of the Mohawk route from Albany, and when his assembly refused to vote the money he paid for it himself. "I have this spring," he wrote in 1727, "sent up workmen to build a stone house of strength at a place called Oswego, at the mouth of the Onnondaga river, where our principal trade with the far nations is carried on. I have obtained the consent of the Six Nations to build it." The French determined to control the

Fresh rivalries. Fort-building: (1) Louisbourg.

(2) Niagara, 1720. Oswego, 1727. Crown Point, 1731.

other route at least, and owing to disputes between the English colonies, were able in 1731 to seize and fortify Crown Point on Lake Champlain, and so to bar that highway to Canada.

At the other end of the colonies, too, the English secured their power. Here the last colony of South

(3) Georgia. 1732.

Carolina lay open to attack by the Spaniards in Florida, and since Spain had been co-operating with France, and quarrels were arising from the Asiento, the danger of war was no idle dream. Hence the proposals for a new colony were readily received, and in 1732 Georgia was founded by General Oglethorpe. The charter granted the right of government to the proprietors for twenty-one years, after which time it was to revert to the Crown, and this actually occurred in 1753. Oglethorpe's scheme in founding Georgia was twofold: he intended to erect a series of fortified posts at good defensible points within his territory, and so secure himself from Spanish attack. He also planned to people his colony with debtors and others whom he took from the prisons in England, and to whom he gave an opportunity of starting life anew in Georgia. For this philanthropic work Parliament voted a small grant, and thus Georgia was the only American colony to be founded with the aid of public funds. To ensure that his "assisted emigrants" actually worked and so redeemed their character, Oglethorpe provided that no slaves should be imported: estates were to descend from father to son, and plans were made for small compact settlements, easy to defend. As time went on, the proprietors, anxious to strengthen their colony, admitted bodies of Highlanders and German Moravians, who were planted in small villages. Thus the ideal of a pauper reformatory was gradually lost to sight, and the settlers soon began to grumble because they had no slaves. The proprietors declared that negroes were "a baneful commodity, which, it is well known by sad experience, has brought our neighbour Colonies to the Brink of Ruin, by driving out their White Inhabitants, who were their Glory and Strength, to make room for Black, who are now become the Terror of their unadvised Masters." After a time the rule of exclusion could be maintained no longer, and Georgia became a slave-owning colony. Quarrels too arose with Carolina over the question of traders' rights and the treatment of Indians. In one way, however, the colony was a success: it had been founded as an outpost against the Spaniards, and when war came Oglethorpe was able to give a very good account of himself indeed. His victory at Frederica in 1742 saved the colony from the Spaniards.

Thus the years following the Peace of Utrecht were a time when French and English watched each other anxiously, waiting for the next struggle: this was soon to come. The treaty by which the English were allowed to ship one cargo of goods annually to Spanish America soon became a mere cloak for wholesale smuggling: the Spanish coastguards and patrol-ships did their best to stop this illegal trade, and in many a rough-and-tumble skirmish blood was shed. At home there was an increasing cry for war, which Walpole steadily refused, until in 1739 he had to give way. The "War of Jenkin's Ear" is well named if we recognise that ear in its bottle of spirits as a symbol of trade and sea-power for which the war was really fought. At home the struggle was soon merged in the War of the Austrian Succession, and once again England and France had come to blows. In the West Indies Admiral Vernon sacked Porto Bello in 1739, but failed two years later to capture Carthagena, while Anson in the *Centurion*, sent into the Pacific to plunder the Spaniard, found himself forced, like Drake of old, to return home by sailing round the world. Though most of his men were enfeebled with sickness, he captured the Manilla treasure-galleon, and reached England with his prize in tow, after nearly four years' absence (1741–1744). Soon after France had joined in the struggle, the English scored a great success in America, In 1745 Shirley, the energetic governor of Massachusetts, persuaded his assembly to make an attempt on Louisbourg. Pepperell, a local merchant, was made general, and with a small force composed only of colonial militia, but supported by a British fleet, he made a dash on what the French considered an impregnable fortress. Dragging his heavy guns on rough sleighs across the mud of the foreshore, he set up his batteries, and soon succeeded in forcing the astonished and unprepared garrison to surrender. This striking victory greatly

War of Jenkin's Ear. 1739–1748.

elated the colonists and gave them much self-confidence in their arms, and their chagrin can well be imagined when in 1748, at the Peace of Aix-la-Chapelle, Louisbourg was restored to the French in exchange for Madras. It is true that Parliament voted a large sum to the colony as compensation for its expenses, but the blow to their military pride was not to be healed by a mere gift of money.

Peace of Aix-la-Chapelle. 1748.

As far as America and India are concerned, the Peace of Aix-la-Chapelle was hardly even a truce: there was almost continuous fighting until 1763, and some of the greatest battles were fought overseas when England and France were nominally at peace in Europe. In America the trouble centred in two places, Acadie and the Ohio Valley. The boundaries of Acadie had never been satisfactorily defined: commissioners were appointed under the Peace of 1748 to settle this question, but they only succeeded in disagreeing; the forts of Beauséjour and St. Lawrence glowered at each other across the narrow neck which joined Acadie to the mainland, while the old French inhabitants proved a doubtful factor in the situation. Immediately after the Peace, the English Government had built Halifax (1749) on the south-eastern side of Acadie, as a port and fortress to act as a check on Louisbourg. The French inhabitants, who still dwelt among their pleasant orchards on the western coast, had persistently refused to take the oath of allegiance and had posed as "neutrals" during the recent war. They were constantly set against their English masters by French agents, and some even joined in bands to murder the soldiers of the garrison. At last in 1755, with the certainty of another war with France before his eyes, the English governor decided that something must be done: the Acadians were ordered to take the oath within a certain time, and as they did not comply, they were secretly surrounded by night and deported from the colony, being allowed to settle wherever they willed. This action, however necessary it may have seemed at the time, has left a blot on the story of the English in Nova Scotia.

Acadie (Nova Scotia).

The real clash, however, came in the Ohio Valley. The French had claimed this country because of La Salle's discovery of the Mississippi long ago in 1682, and now, just as Virginian traders were forming the Ohio Company to push across the Alleghanies and exploit the territories of the Ohio, the French governor of Canada determined to reinforce his claims. At times the Mississippi still washes up the leaden plates buried by his prospecting party. "Year 1749 in the reign of Louis XV, King of France," ran the inscription, "we have buried this plate . . . as a mark of the renewal of possession which we had formerly taken of the aforesaid river Ohio, and all its feeders, and all territory upon both sides of the aforesaid streams as former Kings of France have enjoyed, or ought to have enjoyed, and which they have maintained by force of arms and by treaties, especially those of Ryswick, Utrecht, and Aix-la-Chapelle." These sweeping claims were but empty words unless some definite steps were taken to hold the land so claimed, and so in 1752 Duquesne, the new governor, built the fort of Lebœuf, and two years later caught the English napping by building Fort Duquesne on the Ohio forks, the very spot already chosen by Washington for an English fort. This action was a challenge which could not be overlooked. The question was whether the English colonies were to be hemmed in between the Alleghanies and the sea and remain a mere strip of coastwise settlement, while the French established their hold on the Ohio and the Mississippi, thus linking Canada to Louisiana, or whether they were to expel the French from the Ohio and secure freedom to expand westward as they developed. Governor Dinwiddie of Virginia saw the situation and promptly sent George Washington, a promising young colonel of militia, to protest: a mistake was made, blood was shed, and nothing could now expel the French but force. Though both countries were at peace, each sent reinforcements, and General Braddock, with three regular regiments and four hundred militia, slowly cut a road through the backwoods of Virginia to attack Fort Duquesne. Crossing the river in the summer sunlight, with drums rolling and colours flying, he was suddenly attacked by the French backwoodsmen and their Indian allies. His troops, though crack regiments, were not used to wood fighting, their serried ranks of scarlet uniforms offered a target which none

The Ohio Valley.

could miss, and they were shot down in confusion. Braddock fell and was buried in the forest, his troops retired on Philadelphia, and Washington, with a handful of militia, was left to protect the frontiers of Virginia and Pennsylvania, ablaze with the fires of Indian massacres.

Seven Years' War. 1756-1763.

Meanwhile, in Europe war was openly declared, and England ranged herself on the side of Prussia against the joint attacks of France and Russia. This outbreak of the Seven Years' War did not at once improve affairs in America, for the English generals sent there were by no means skilful in their art. The French, however, gave the command of Canada to Montcalm, a brave and capable soldier who found himself sadly handicapped by the red tape of his government and the dishonesty of the Intendant Bigot. The weakness of the French at sea also proved a great drawback, as reinforcements and supplies were hard to send, and when most needed seldom came.

In 1756 the English lost Oswego on Lake Ontario, while in the following year the arrival of Lord Loudon with eight thousand men from Ireland did not have the desired result. He concentrated all his forces in an ill-planned attack on Louisbourg, which ended in disaster, and while he was employing the colonial militia there the French captured Fort William Henry at the southern end of Lake Champlain. Montcalm was greatly to blame for not keeping his Indian allies in hand, and their massacre of the English prisoners made the catchword, "Remember Fort William Henry," a bloody war-cry for the rest of the campaign.

Pitt's policy. June, 1757-Sept., 1761.

In England, the accession of Pitt to power in June, 1757, changed the whole conduct of affairs: his choice of young and brilliant generals infused new life into the colonial campaigns, while his European policy was no less successful. By means of a rigid blockade he prevented the French from sending their ships across the seas, and he eventually brought their fleets to action. His policy of conquering America on the fields of Germany was accomplished both by giving heavy subsidies to Frederick of Prussia and by supporting him with English troops. This policy, and his frequent raids upon the coast of France, kept a large number of French troops at home in Europe which might have been employed across the seas. During Pitt's short years of office he raised England to such a pitch of glory and success as never has been known before or since: as Horace Walpole said, it was necessary to inquire each morning what fresh success had been achieved, for fear of missing the news of some great victory.

In America the change was quickly felt. In July of 1758 Louisbourg fell to a joint attack led by General Amherst and by Admiral Boscawen; while Forbes, despite his fatal sickness, pushed over the Alleghanies to Fort Duquesne only to find it abandoned, as Montcalm had been forced to concentrate his men for the defence of Canada. The abandoned post was re-named Fort Pitt in honour of the national hero, and the name of Pittsburg still recalls the days when the smoky city was only a fort wrapped in the silent forest. Pitt's men had been successful: there was only one failure, for Abercromby had not been recalled. Pushing up the Hudson with fifteen thousand troops to attack the French fort of Ticonderoga on Lake Champlain, he caught Montcalm and three thousand men sheltering in a temporary stockade. Abercromby flung his men to certain death in a frontal attack, and suffered a cruel defeat, leaving Montcalm wondering at the madness of a soldier who neglected his artillery in such a case.

Amherst captures Louisbourg. 1758.

Next year a triple attack was planned on Canada itself. Amherst was to take Ticonderoga and push on up the Richelieu river, Prideaux was to re-build Oswego and capture Niagara, while Wolfe was to sail up the St. Lawrence and besiege Quebec, where the other generals were to join him. The operations were successful, though Amherst's deliberate movements made him too late to join Wolfe as planned, and so the whole success of the attack on Quebec depended upon Wolfe's courage and ingenuity. While sick in bed, with winter coming on, and after he had failed in an attack on the impregnable Beauport lines, Wolfe held a council of war and adopted a plan which only genius would dare to undertake. He sailed on up the river, and, dropping down in boats by night, succeeded in

Wolfe captures Quebec. 1759.

scaling the cliffs above the city. Next morning Montcalm saw an army drawn up above the city, and was forced to leave his trenches and give battle in the open. The victory cost both generals their lives, but ended in the surrender of the city. Matters were still precarious, for a small British force was left to winter in Quebec while the fleet went home. Everything now depended on which side first received reinforcements in the New Year. The English command of the sea really settled the question, and with the arrival of a fleet and the junction of Amherst's troops, the army was able to march on Montreal and to receive the surrender of the whole of Canada.

Fall of Montreal. End of campaign. 1760.

England owed her great victories in the Seven Years' War, and, indeed, all her successes in the wars of the eighteenth century, to her command of the sea. This sea-power was no sudden growth, but was due to the long training of the Navy, the improvement of administration, and the development of sound theories of strategy in the grouping of fleets and of the fighting tactics of ships in action. The union of the two sea-powers of England and Holland in 1688 led to victories from which the English gained much more than their allies, while by the Peace of Utrecht in 1713 England's sea-power was still further strengthened. Gibraltar and Minorca gave her firm bases for her Mediterranean fleet, while the Asiento was an important trading concession. "Before that war England was one of the Sea-Powers; after it she became the Sea-Power without any exception." The long peace under Walpole was only possible because of the supremacy of English fleets at sea, but this same time saw a decline in the efficiency of the Navy. A bad type of ship was built, old officers retained command, and there developed a cautious type of tactics that made the early years of the War of Jenkin's Ear anything but famous in the annals of the Navy. That war, however, brought better men to the front: Anson was an inspiring commander, daring in action, and sound in theory. Soon after his famous voyage round the world, which he accomplished despite incredible hardships, he was appointed to the Admiralty, and he soon put matters in a better state.

Sea-power.

In war, the first duty of the English fleet was to retain command of the narrow seas and to prevent invasion, or landings in Scotland or Ireland. To do this a system of blockade was gradually developed, both to prevent French fleets slipping from their ports, and to force them to action; for, while there was still "a fleet in being," it was capable of doing infinite damage. The two great harbours of Brest and Toulon were usually blockaded, the former by fleets based on the Western Channel ports, the latter from Minorca or Gibraltar; but westerly gales might blow off the blockading squadrons, who had to run for shelter, and when the wind changed it was a race, the French fleet trying to get away to sea before the English appeared. Lastly, the English Navy had to send fleets to India and America, not merely for protection, but to join with local militia and regular troops against the French colonies. Anson's reforms at the Admiralty included a new build of ship, new uniforms for the officers, the choice of young and energetic admirals, and the issue of a new set of fighting instructions, which made it a capital offence to neglect to help a comrade's ship in action.

Anson's work bore fruit in the Seven Years' War. The decisive year was 1759, when French fleets lay blockaded at Brest and Toulon, waiting the opportunity to join for an invasion of Ireland. From Toulon the French escaped, but were brought to action by Boscawen, who sailed from Gibraltar and defeated them off Lagos in Portugal. Meanwhile, Hawke had been blown off Brest by an autumn gale from the west, and, when he managed to beat back, found the French had sailed south to Quiberon Bay. With a winter night fast closing in, and a rising gale blowing him on to a lee shore, he boldly followed them in between the rocks and shallows of that dangerous anchorage. There he gained a famous victory, breaking the naval power of France for the rest of the war, and thus securing English conquests in India and America. The lessons of sea-power were well learnt in the Seven Years' War, and though political jobbery and discontent again impaired the efficiency of the Navy, they were never wholly forgotten. Through the evil time of the War of American Independence,

Battle of Quiberon Bay. 1759.

it was still the Navy that saved England from ruin, and she has never since lost that command of the sea which she gained so securely in the glorious days of the eighteenth century.

Peace of Paris. 1763.

The Peace of Paris in 1763 expelled the French entirely from the mainland of America, thus confirming the great victories in Canada. Spain, who had, to her own misfortune, entered the war in 1761, surrendered Florida to England, and received in return the vague French claims beyond the Mississippi. In the West Indies, where English fleets had captured most of the French colonies, the larger islands were restored, but Grenada, St. Vincent, Dominica, and Tobago, which had long been a source of dispute, were kept by England, and she also had confirmed her right to cut log-wood in Honduras. In the East, where Clive had captured the French settlements, these places were returned, but a limit was placed on the number of troops which the French might keep in Pondicherry. Thus it was hoped to limit their ambitious plans in India.

The effects of this great settlement were far-reaching. For France they meant the complete ruin of her vast schemes in the West, and her monarchy received a blow from which it never properly recovered, while she conceived a hatred of England which was long in dying out. In America, the removal of the French menace meant the removal of the firmest guarantee of colonial loyalty. "The death of Wolfe upon the plains of Abraham meant not only the conquest of Canada, but the birth of the United States of America." For Canada, too, the Peace of Paris was the opening of a new era: England found herself faced by the problem of governing a conquered body of Europeans, but by sympathetic statesmanship she was able to deal with problems at least as difficult as those she failed to solve in her own colonies. For England, the Peace marked the zenith of her power, which was soon so rudely to be shaken.

Books.—J. R. Seeley, *The Expansion of England*, should be read by every one. C. M. Andrews, *The Old Colonial Period*, is a brilliant little book, describing the internal condition of the colonies. The first chapter of J. A. Doyle: *The Colonies under the House of Hanover* ives a good picture of colonies at this period. A. G. Bradley, *The*

AMERICA IN 1763.

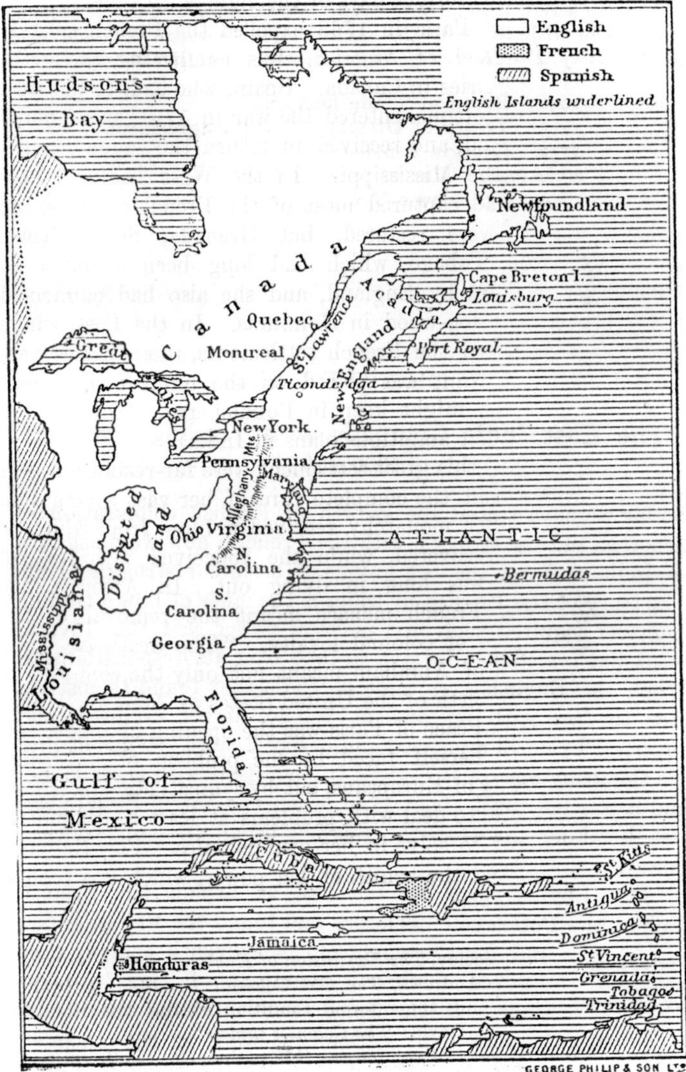

Longmans, Green & Co., London, New York, Bombay & Calcutta.

Fight with France for North America, is a picturesque account of the great struggle. *Anson's Voyage round the World* is published in the Everyman series, with an interesting introduction by John Masefield. Those who wish to study the subject more thoroughly should read W. H. Lecky, *The History of England in the XVIIIth Century*.

1696. Board of Trade founded.
1713. Treaty of Utrecht. Asiento agreement.
1732. Georgia founded.
1739-1748. War of Jenkin's Ear.
1756-1763. Seven Years' War.

CHAPTER IV

The East India Company as a Trading Venture [1600-1763]

So far we have traced the growth of English colonisation in America, and the struggle with the French ; now we must turn to India and see the beginnings of a similar struggle there. The story of the English in India is the story of how a trading company acquired such vast political power, that the Government was forced step by step to take over its responsibilities. When the English first came to India they found themselves face to face with an ancient people, highly civilised, and governed by an ill-organised and despotic state. Thus at first the Company was quite content to busy itself with trade alone, and it was not until about 1760, when the Mogul Empire was fast breaking up, that the English began to gain political power.

Portuguese monopoly. XVI Century.

The English were not the first to exploit the Eastern traffic : the Portuguese explorers had found the way to India, and for the whole of the sixteenth century they enjoyed a virtual monopoly of this lucrative trade. In the Spice Islands, beyond the Straits of Malacca, they had their settlements, while on the coasts of India their chief factory was at Goa, a place which they still hold : the present Portuguese colonies on the coast of Africa are a reminder of their greatness in days long past. But the Portuguese were vigorous crusaders rather than cunning traders, and their cruel treatment of the natives and piratical plundering of merchant ships often hindered their trade. They freely intermarried with the Indians, and lost some of their former vigour. The Portuguese had other interests besides India, and the attempt to develop the sugar industry in their new found colony of Brazil absorbed much of their energy, and thus their settlements in the East could offer little resistance to the increasing number of foreign traders.

English and Dutch as rivals. XVII Century.

The Portuguese monopoly ended with the sixteenth century, when the Dutch and English appeared together as keen rivals for the Eastern trade. In 1600, after much discussion, the East India Company was formed in London and granted a charter by Elizabeth. The attempt of English merchants to open a trade with the East had led to the formation of several companies ; the Russia Company, then the Levant Company, and now this new venture which was to make the voyage round the Cape, thus showing in a practical way the scorn of Protestant England for Papal authority. The royal charter gave the Company a monopoly of the Eastern trade for fifteen years, and allowed them to export a certain amount of coin every voyage. This unusual privilege of exporting coin was looked upon with grave suspicion, and formed a convenient method of attack for the Company's enemies. The first fleet sailed in 1601, with a cargo consisting chiefly of coin, glass, cutlery, and so on, and after trading successfully with the Spice Islands, returned in 1603 laden with a valuable cargo, and paid a dividend of about 95 per cent. Two further voyages were made to the Spice Islands, and it was not till 1608 that, during the third voyage, India proper was visited.

East India Company. 1600.

The revolt of the United Provinces from Spain had been helped, to a certain extent, by Elizabeth ; but now the English recognised in them a formidable rival to their trade and growing sea-power. Dutch traders had visited India a few years before the English ; their great East India Company was founded in 1602 and backed with all the influence of the State. The Portuguese Crown had been joined to Spain in 1580, and the Dutch seized the opportunity of attacking the Portuguese in India with the greatest energy, driving them out of the Spice Islands and capturing their trade. But the Hollanders were determined to keep the Spice Islands for themselves, and they opposed the English traders by every means in their power. In 1619 an arrangement was made between England and Holland, by which James agreed that his subjects should only retain one fortified post in the Spice Islands, but though they were nominally allowed to trade in other places, the Dutch still put every obstacle in their way. A few years later, in 1623, the judicial murder of the English Company's servants at Amboyna, by the Dutch, led to a great outcry in England: the matter was referred to arbitration and dragged on for many years until in 1653 a small sum was awarded to the English as compensation. Amboyna, however, settled one thing; the Spice Islands became a Dutch preserve, and the spice trade a Dutch monopoly, and the Dutch wars of Cromwell and Charles II failed to alter this decision. Thus the East India Company, which had already begun to traffic with India, was forced to rely on that trade more than ever.

Dutch and English struggle for Spice Islands.

India itself is a huge triangle, shut in on the north by the Himalayas, and surrounded on east and west by the sea. Though in modern times the Europeans reached India by sea, from the earliest days invasion after invasion poured through the passes of the North-West frontier, for the great mountain ranges were a much less formidable barrier than they seemed. Thus when the English reached the East they found the whole of Northern India ruled by the Grand Mogul, with his capital at Delhi, while in the south were other Mohammedan states. This Mohammedan Empire was a military despotism of Afghan rulers, which had been founded by Baber in 1526, and extended and organised by his successors. It was but the last of a series of empires established by invaders from the north. The majority of the Indians were Hindus by religion and they were then, as now, rigidly divided by the system of caste, connected with the trade or

Mogul Empire. 1526.

employment of the individual, and upheld by the strictest religious rules. The sacred caste of Brahmins were the interpreters of the religious laws, and it was to their advantage to emphasise the caste system and their own superiority. Intermarriage was strictly forbidden, no man could rise from one caste to another, and so the civilisation of India became fixed, and altered little for many hundreds of years. Great towns there were but few, though manufactures such as the making of silks, cotton fabrics, and jewellery were carried on by village craftsmen. Most of the Indians were peasants, dwelling in their village communities and waging a constant warfare against famine on the one hand, and the jungle on the other: it was of but little importance to them that empires rose and fell above their heads.

Such was India when the English first came to it, and it was early decided to send a man "of pregnant understanding, well-spoken, learned, industrious, and of a comelie personage," as envoy to the Mogul. Sir Thomas Roe was chosen for this important mission, and lived at the Mogul's court for three years (1615-1618), and obtained permission for the establishment of factories. Roe strongly advised the Company to avoid interference in local politics, a game at which both Dutch and Portuguese were only too ready to play. "It is the beggaring of the Portugal, notwithstanding his many rich residences and territories, that he keeps soldiers that spend it, yet his garrisons are mean. He never profited by the Indies, since he defended them. Observe this well. It hath been also the error of the Dutch, who seek plantation here by the sword. They turn a wonderful stock, they prowl in all places, they possess some of the best; yet their dead payes consume all their gain. Let this be received as a rule that if you will profit, seek it at sea, and in quiet trade; for without controversey it is an error to affect garrisons and land wars in India." Similar objections to the waste of money on forts were often repeated: a pamphleteer of 1698 declares rather glibly, "Nothing can be more ridiculous than to have Forts there to secure the Trade of the Coasts of 10,000 Miles; as if we should have a Fort at Archangel to secure the Trade to Turky." With one disastrous exception, the Company

Sir T. Roe's dispatch.

followed Roe's advice for nearly one hundred and fifty years, and during that time it became by far the richest and most influential trading company in England, if not in the world.

English Settlements: Surat. 1613.

Fort St. George (Madras). 1640.

Fort William (Calcutta). 1690.

Bombay. 1662.

The first English settlement on the mainland was at Surat, which was founded in 1613, and for a time became the chief English settlement in the East; by 1640 Fort St. George had been founded on the south-east or Coromandel coast, and under its protection grew up the town of Madras with its separate quarters for natives and Europeans. Further north in 1651 the English had settled on the wealthy delta of the Ganges at Hughli, near-by to rival settlements of the Dutch and Portuguese, and it was not until 1690, after an unsuccessful war with the Mogul, that Calcutta was founded. On the western coast, Bombay, the dowry given by Portugal to Charles II with his wife Catherine of Braganza, was handed over to the Company, and soon took the place of Surat as the chief western town. Thus by the end of the century we find the three "Presidency" towns, Bombay, Fort St. George (Madras), and Fort William (Calcutta), firmly established with their governors and councils, controlling the trade and organisation of the other English settlements within their area. Though the Company was becoming more and more interested in trade with India, it had other stations and other trade as well. The earliest factory at Bantam in Sumatra was long an important post, and controlled Madras until 1653, while a factory was established in Persia and coffee was imported from Mocha and other Arabian ports, despite the Arab pirates. Further eastward, stations were established in Cochin China and Tonquin, and though these were later abandoned, trade was carried on with China for its tea, and with Japan.

Financial development.

The trading companies of mediæval England, such as the Staplers and the Merchant Adventurers, had been "regulated" companies, in which each member traded individually provided he kept the rules of his company. But the trading companies of Elizabeth, faced by the new problems of distant voyages and by the need of obtaining capital from outside the narrow ring of merchants, began to trade upon a joint-stock basis. At first subscriptions were raised from members for each particular voyage, and when the fleet returned the capital was repaid and the profits divided. The East India Company soon found that this system also had its disadvantages, and it became customary to carry over capital from voyage to voyage, and thus permanent clerks and traders could be retained in the East. After being much troubled by "interlopers" and a rival firm, which had circulated base coin in India, the Company received a new charter from Cromwell in 1657, and was reorganised as a joint-stock company of the modern sort: its shares were sold at the Exchange, and dividends declared from time to time.

Factory organisation.

The affairs of the Company were ably managed by a governor and committee-men annually elected by the shareholders and these officials endeavoured, though not always with success, to keep a tight hold over their employees in the East. The "factories" were much like colleges, with common chapel and dining-hall, and the governor had large disciplinary powers over the junior members. As time went on the factories grew, hospitals, warehouses, and other buildings sprang up, and the whole were amply fortified. The Company's servants were but poorly paid, and generally made up for this by private trade, a practice the Company often tried in vain to suppress. From the letter-books of the Company we can gain amusing side-lights on the life of the English in the East. At times they tried to make up for their weary exile from home by various amusements, which brought down sharp reproofs upon their heads from the vigilant directors. Madras was reproved in 1721 for its gambling mania. "It is with great concern we hear the Itch of gaming hath spread itself over Madras, that even the gentlewomen play for great sums, and that Captain Seaton makes a trade of it to the stripping of several of the young men there." The factory of Bencoolen received a severe reprimand for the immoderate drinking of its staff. "It is a wonder to us," wrote the directors, "that any of you live six months to an end, or that there are not more quarrellings and duellings among you, if half the liquors he charged were guzzled down." The latter then recounts "the monstrous expense of July . . . seventy-four dozen and a half of wine, of which 8 dozen and 5 were double bottles, and 50 dozen and 5 single bottles of French claret, 24½ dozen of Burton ale and Pale Beer, two pipes and 42 gallons of Madeira wine, six flasks of Shyrash, 274 bottles of Toddy, three leagers (casks) and ¾ of Batavia Arrack, and 164 gallons of Goa."[1] As this is alleged to have been drunk by nineteen people, it seems, perhaps, fairer to believe that the steward was forging his accounts.

The Company's ships sailed together in fleets from the Thames, well armed and equipped to meet an enemy if necessary. Calling at St. Helena, that sea-tavern of the Company which played for them the same part as the Cape did for the Dutch, they stood away for the south, and usually took six months to reach the Indies. A writer of 1750 estimated that three-quarters of the outward cargoes consisted of precious metal, and the rest of lead, iron, guns, powder, clothes, and such like. In return they brought two classes of goods: pepper, tea, coffee, and some spices, which could not be grown in England, and silks and cotton goods, which the mercantilist statesman regarded with great distrust.

The trading fleets.

Soon after the accession of William III, the East India Company fell on evil days. Between 1686 and 1690, a deliberate attempt to gain political power in India had failed disastrously, and peace had only been obtained by promising an indemnity to Aurungzeb, the Mogul Emperor. Now in England, the vast wealth of the Company stirred the jealousy of those merchants who were not members to oppose the renewal of the charter. It was only by spending fabulous sums in bribery that Sir Josiah Child, the energetic governor of the Company, succeeded in obtaining a new charter in 1693, but the victory was short-lived. The opponents joined with the Whigs, who were now in power, and succeeded in their plans. The attack on the

Attack on Company in England.

[1] Quoted in Roberts: *India*.

Company was made along three lines. The economist of the day objected to the export of silver, and also to many of the goods imported by the Company. "The consumption among ourselves of the wrought silks, Bengals, and printed Callicoes of India," he declared, "is prejudicial to this Nation, and not only carries out our Mony, but hinders our silk and woollen Manufacturers at home." The only part of the trade he approved was the import of such tropical goods as could not be grown in England, and he wished that the Dutch monopoly of the spice trade could be broken down. The Company was stoutly defended by Sir Josiah Child, in his *Discourse of Trade*. "It will not be denied by the honourable East India Company, but they import more goods into England than they export, and that to purchase the same, they carry out quantities of gold and silver annually ; yet no man that understands anything of the Trade of the World will affirm that England loses by that Trade." The balance of trade, he explains, must be looked at from a wider point of view, for besides the strong fleet the Company maintains, and the annual import of saltpetre (necessary for gunpowder), a large amount of the objectionable imports are re-exported to the Continent and sold at a huge profit. At the moment this defence did not carry much weight, and the Company's trade was long regarded with suspicion, but Child's opinion gradually gained ground, and in 1750 a merchant, writing of the East Indian Trade, declares "notwithstanding the many specious arguments that have been used to the contrary, I must consider it a general benefit to the nation." Another line of attack was on the narrow monopoly of the Company : it was proposed to meet this by issuing new shares, and so allowing the discontented outsiders to obtain a share of the trade, but this was vigorously opposed by Child. Others again wished to reorganise the Company on a "regulated" basis, so that each member could trade for himself.

Reply in Child's "Discourse of Trade."

In 1698, when the Government was hard put to it to raise money, a charter was granted to a New Company in return for a loan of £2,000,000 : the charter of the Old Company was not immediately revoked, and thus for several years there were two companies trading to India. Such a state of affairs could not last long; in the East there was constant quarrelling between the companies' servants, while the competition led to a serious rise in prices of Indian goods, a development that neither company could regard with satisfaction. In England the strife between the two companies was so keen that it overshadowed the division into political parties and split the country into two camps: William was most anxious to heal this dispute and at last in 1702 the two companies were amalgamated. The failure of the New Company is easy to understand. It was burdened with a vast loan it had been forced to find for the Government, it had little or no experience in Eastern trading, and it had no old-established factories or well-trained body of merchants and servants in the East. The very merchants it employed were discharged servants of the Old Company, and proved dishonest or incapable, and their bungling diplomacy failed to get the hoped-for privileges from the Mogul. The United Company became stronger than ever; its new charter granted it very large powers, while at home it was backed by the Government and the whole of the City.

The New Company. 1698.

Union. 1702.

For nearly forty years after the union of the two companies, there is little exciting to tell of the East India Company, but though this was a period of quiet growth and development for the Company, it saw the break-up of the Mogul Empire, and the need for a new policy on the part of the Europeans. After the death of the great Emperor Aurungzeb in 1707, the Mogul power soon became little more than a name: emperor succeeded emperor at the will of a general or powerful minister, but the actual control over his vast dominions was very small. In an attempt to assert his authority in Southern India, Aurungzeb had destroyed two powerful Mohammedan states, and so the Deccan became the hunting-ground for adventurers. The decay of the Mogul Empire was hastened by the growth of the power of the Mahrattas, a confederacy of Hindu princes of Central India, who rose in revolt against the Mohammedan

Break-up of Old System. 1700–1744.

(1) Decay of Mogul Empire.

(2) Rise of Mahrattas.

power at Delhi. Led by Shivaji (1627–1680), a great soldier prince, the "mountain rats of the Deccan" ate the heart out of the Mogul Empire. Ranging far and wide, they levied blackmail or destroyed all settled government, and soon the Mahratta states formed a great wedge across Central India, cutting off the northern parts of the Mogul Empire from the Deccan. After Shivaji's death the power passed to the Brahmin minister, the Peshwa, and under the rule of the Peshwas the Mahratta power still grew, until it was finally checked by the victories of Wellesley and Hastings early in the nineteenth century. As the Mogul's power declined, so his deputies, the nawabs, became more powerful. In South India the Nizam of Hyderabad was actually an independent sovereign, though he owed nominal allegiance to the Mogul, the Carnatic under its nawab was officially subordinate to the Nizam, while in the north-east the Nawab of Bengal was almost independent also.

(3) Growth of independent kingdoms.

This change in the balance of power affected the position of the English factories; although their trade increased steadily so that an annual dividend of 10 per cent. was usually declared, it seemed that they might soon have to fight to retain their position. While all these troubles were going on in India, the sea-coast settlements strengthened themselves by building more fortifications and by obtaining new grants of recognition and privileges from the successive Moguls, or from the local nawabs. The Company had an armed force consisting chiefly of Sepoys, which was steadily growing, while at Bombay the governor was forced to maintain a large force and a navy to protect himself and his trade against the constant peril from the pirates.

(4) Growth of English power.

It was, however, the spread of the French quarrel to India that put an end to this period of peaceful trade development. At first French and English had lived peaceably together in India: there was trade enough for both, and the wars in Europe did not spread to India, though on the seas men regarded each other as enemies. Indeed, the early French attempts in India were not very successful, and

(5) The French.

caused but little anxiety to the English. The French companies were largely State-controlled concerns, and they lacked the healthy activity of private enterprise, which had been the basis of the English Company. Even the East India Company started by Colbert was not a great success; it was practically ruined by the European policy of Louis XIV, for his continual wars with the Dutch (1672–1713) made peaceful trade impossible. The fortunes of the Company fell so low that from 1708 to 1720 it was forced to let all its privileges to some other merchants. After 1720 it was reorganised, and, owing to a policy of peace in Europe, its trade increased very rapidly. When the War of the Austrian Succession was threatening in Europe, the French Company tried to negotiate for neutrality in India, but the scheme broke down, and so, in 1744, the struggle between French and English spread also to the East.

French power in India. 1744.

The French power in India might at the moment appear very strong, but it was not as firmly founded as the English. The French had suffered a number of serious checks, and even now their great prosperity was but of recent date. Their Company was practically a department of State: its officials and directors were appointed by the King: its shareholders took no part in the control of the Company, but received dividends at a fixed rate guaranteed them by the State. In India its chief settlement, Pondicherry, was as fine a town as its neighbour, Madras, but the other settlements were not nearly so important as the English factories, while the islands of Bourbon and Mauritius (Isle de France), though a useful sea-base for attacking India, were sometimes used as a convenient refuge for French fleets, which should have remained off the Indian coast.

The War of the Austrian Succession. 1744–1748.

La Bourdonnais, the French governor of Mauritius, had planned to attack the English settlements as soon as war broke out, but he got tired of waiting and sent his fleet home. Thus, it was not till 1746 that he arrived off Pondicherry, and concerted plans with its governor, Dupleix, to seize Madras. The English fleet left Madras to defend itself, and it was soon surrendered to La Bourdonnais, who astounded Dupleix by restoring it to the English in return for a heavy indemnity. Dupleix was furious, and, after a gale had driven La Bourdonnais to Mauritius, he denounced the treaty, marched upon Madras, and seized it once again. Soon after, a strong English fleet arrived and besieged Pondicherry in vain, and the Peace of Aix-la-Chapelle restored Madras to the English in exchange for Louisbourg: the wealthy factory seemed of much greater value to the English merchants than the fog-bound harbour on Cape Breton Island.

Peace of Aix-la-Chapelle. 1748.

Dupleix was a man of wide ideas and a vivid imagination, and, despite this temporary check, he schemed to extend the power of France until she was supreme in the whole of India. His plan was to interfere in the quarrels and disputes of the local nawabs, and thus gain influence by supporting a successful candidate: the very policy against which Sir Thomas Roe had warned the English Company at the beginning of its career. Dupleix's policy soon forced the English of Madras to play a similar game, and thus, though France and England were nominally at peace, they soon found themselves face to face on Indian battlefields, much to the displeasure of the directors of both companies at home, who saw trade profits being rapidly eaten up by useless and expensive wars.

Dupleix's schemes.

Dupleix soon found an opportunity to put his plans into practice. He championed the claims of Chunda Sahib to the Carnatic and Muzzuffir Jung to the Deccan, and soon succeeded, despite English opposition, in conquering the Carnatic for his nominee; by 1750 he was hailed as Suzerain of Southern India, and began to build a city to commemorate his victories. Meanwhile Dupleix proclaimed Muzzuffir Jung Subadar (or Viceroy) of the Deccan, and sent him off with the French soldier, Bussy, to seize his capital of Hyderabad. Here Bussy stayed for several years organising and drilling a native army, and bolstering up the authority of a new Subadar, whom he had created on Muzuffir Jung's death. Thus by 1751 it seemed that Dupleix's schemes were all successful, and that the French power had far surpassed the English in Southern

India. It was soon seen, however, on how unstable a basis that power really stood. While Dupleix was besieging Trichinopoly in 1751, Robert Clive, then a captain in the Company's army, setting out from Madras with one hundred men, seized Arcot, the capital of the Carnatic. This forced Dupleix to send some of his troops northward to try to regain this important fortress, but Clive with his scanty garrison succeeded in defeating them. After this reverse fortune never smiled on him again, and, in 1754, he was recalled by the French Company, who had become thoroughly alarmed at his policy and the emptiness of their treasury. Meanwhile, the two rival companies came to an agreement, by which they both undertook to renounce a policy of conquest, but the terms of this treaty were never really carried out, and it was but an unmeaning truce for a few years until the outbreak of war in 1756. The romantic story of Dupleix, his recall by the Company, and his death in poverty and neglect, have coloured the whole of this period of Indian history. But a careful examination of the facts shows that the French success was more apparent than real: the Company's treasury was exhausted, Dupleix was a man who never knew when to stop, and the French influence at the native courts might easily have been overturned by a domestic revolution.

Clive captures Arcot. 1751.

Dupleix recalled.

The Seven Years' War was a time of victory for the English in India as well as in America, but in India, too, it started with successes for the enemy. When the French commander Lally, the son of an Irish Jacobite, landed at Pondicherry early in 1758, he found the English at a disadvantage, for the capture of Calcutta by Siraj-ud-Daula, and the massacre of the "Black Hole" (1756), had forced the governor of Madras to send Clive and his best troops to Bengal. Thus Lally quickly captured Fort St. David, but after some indecisive actions with the British fleet, the French admiral retired to Mauritius, and Lally was left unsupported at sea. His attempt to besiege Madras was a failure, for he could only blockade it by land, but it was not till 1760 that the tide definitely turned in favour of the English. In the Indian campaign, no less than

Seven Years' War.

the Canadian, sea-power was a decisive factor, and Hawke's victory at Quiberon (Nov. 1759) cut off the last hope of French help from home. Despite his protests, Bussy had been ordered to throw up his work at Hyderabad and join Lally with what troops he could, and, in January, 1760, their united forces were defeated by Sir Eyre Coote at Wandewash, just north of Pondicherry. The fall of that fortress was now only a matter of time; it was surrendered just a year later, and with its surrender fell French power in India.

Wandewash. 1760.

The Peace of Paris in 1763 gave the English the Northern Circars, a strip of land on the east coast: Pondicherry went back to the French, but the number of troops they might keep there was strictly limited, and in future disputes Pondicherry was always an easy prey to an English force. Though the Peace still left the French some factories in India, and did not expel them as completely from the East as from America, yet it marks decisively the failure of Dupleix's great dream. On several later occasions the French were still to find means of stirring up trouble for the English in India, but it was generally by means of alliance with native rulers, and the loan of French officers to train and organise their armies, rather than by great expeditions of French troops. The English command of the sea made it increasingly difficult for the French to send fleets to the East in time of war.

Peace of Paris. 1763.

BOOKS.—P. E. Roberts, *India: History to the end of the East India Company* [Vol. VII. of Lucas' "Historical Geography"] is a readable text-book which deals with social and economic as well as political matters. Ramsay Muir, *The Making of British India*, 1756–1858, is a series of interesting documents with a valuable explanatory introduction. More advanced reading will be found in W. W. Hunter, *History of British India*.

1495. The Portuguese in India: Goa becomes their port.
1600. E. I. C. formed (first voyage, 1601–1603).
1623. Massacre of Amboyna: English practically excluded from Spice Islands.

1701–1708. United Company formed by amalgamation.
1744–1748. War of Austrian Succession spreads to India. 1746. French capture Madras.
1756–1763. Seven Years' War.

CHAPTER V

The Independence of America, 1763–1783

THE War of American Independence is a great turning-point in the history of the Empire, for then the earliest English colonies broke away in anger from the Mother Country and set up an independent state, which for many years remained a hostile and suspicious critic of Britain and all her doings. For a long time this feeling coloured all the writings about the origin of the United States. In America, political orators and "patriot" historians magnified the doings of the Fathers of the Revolution, and painted Britain as a brutal tyrant, while in England Whig writers threw all the blame on North, and refused to see that their party had any share in the responsibility for the disaster. Now, however, such feelings are dying away, and we can examine the story with less prejudice and a clearer understanding.

"As to the English colonies, one essential point should be known; it is that they are never taxed. . . . She should have taxed them from the foundation; I have certain advice that all the colonies would take fire at being taxed now." This shrewd remark was made by Montcalm in 1757, and its truth was proved immediately after the Seven Years' War. Pitt, the Great Commoner, had organised victory all over the world, until the jealousy of the new King, George III, thrust him from office in 1761: Bute, the King's friend, forced through the unpopular Peace of Paris and then resigned. To George Grenville, the new Prime Minister, was left the thankless task of reconstructing the Empire and reorganising the finances.

An expert financier, an honest and indefatigable worker, Grenville was hampered by a legal type of mind which sometimes prevented him from taking a really broad view of affairs. He lectured the King upon his duty, and George, who objected to these discourses and disliked Grenville personally, got rid of him as soon as he could find a substitute. But before he went, Grenville had done irreparable harm.

In every part of the Empire Grenville was faced with difficult problems. In India the conquests of Clive were followed by gross scandals in the government of Bengal, and in 1765 Clive was sent out again to put an end to the evil state of affairs. The government of the conquered province of Canada had to be organised by a royal proclamation, though this settlement was only a temporary expedient. But the most important problem was that of the American colonies, who were engaged immediately after the war in a bloody struggle with the Indians, led by their chief Pontiac, who rightly foresaw that the expulsion of the French meant that the Redskins could no longer hold the balance of power between the Europeans, and would soon be squeezed out by the white man.

George Grenville and Imperial problems.

Of the three great problems which had led to so much friction between the colonies and the Mother Country—the organisation of the administrative system, the control of trade, and the defence of America—Grenville tackled the two last, but in his mind they were closely connected. He saw that the Navigation Laws were but little observed; the cost of collection was far greater than the value of the customs revenue, and smuggling was rife. Grenville determined to alter this, for to his orderly mind it was absurd to retain laws on the statute-book unless they were enforced, and so with infinite care he studied the problem in all its bearings, and worked through the numerous Acts of Parliament. He began to tighten up the whole system, sending absentee officials back to their posts, and in 1764 passed the Sugar Act, lowering the duty on molasses, so that smuggling should be unprofitable. Grenville's policy was very unpopular

Sugar Act, 1764.

in America, and it was shrewdly observed that it was "this new invention of collecting taxes which makes them burdensome"; but Parliament had always regulated the trade of the plantations, and the Americans grumbled and paid. It needed something further to give a handle to their discontent.

The defence of the Empire by sea was secured by the Navy, to whose upkeep the colonies paid nothing, but by land the colonial militia was the only force in time of peace, and the Indian war had shown how exposed the colonies were to attack. Grenville thought that a standing army should be maintained in America for defence against the Indians, or against French attempts at revenge. Only a small part of the cost of this army could be met from the customs revenue, and Grenville proposed that England should pay a third of the balance, and that the rest should be raised in America. He suggested that this should be done by means of a stamp duty, but left the colonies a year in which they might propose an alternative. As this was not done, the Stamp Act was passed in 1765. By this measure government stamps had to be bought and placed on all newspapers, documents, and many other things, much as an excise stamp is placed on patent medicines to-day. This Act raised a storm of objection in America, and all the discontent at the reinforcement of the trade regulations vented itself in an outcry against the stamps. A congress of representatives from the various colonies was held at New York, and the Act was denounced, while riots were organised, offices burnt, and the hated stamps destroyed. This opposition found its echo in England, where Pitt, who had been ill when the Act was passed, came down to the House and denounced the policy. "If I could have endured to be carried in my bed," he declared, "so great was the agitation of my mind for the consequences, I would have solicited some kind hand to have laid me down on this floor, to have borne my testimony against it."

Stamp Act, 1765.

Meanwhile, Grenville had left office, and largely owing to Pitt's efforts the Stamp Act was repealed by the new ministry, but in its place was passed the Declaratory Act, which stated that Parliament had the right to tax America. For the moment, the clamour died down; few saw the danger of the Declaratory Act, while the citizens of Charlestown in South Carolina erected a statue, which still stands, to Pitt, "who gloriously exerted himself in defending the freedom of Americans, the true sons of England." Grenville's policy then had failed, and a serious crisis had only been averted by the Repeal. A wit declared that Grenville lost America because, unlike his predecessors, he read the American despatches, but the Whig neglect of colonial problems during the first half of the century was partly responsible for the catastrophe that was yet to come.

Stamp Act repealed. Declaratory Act, 1766.

Legally Parliament was quite within its rights in taxing the colonies, despite Pitt's unhistorical argument that it possessed the legislative, but not the taxative powers, and despite the other contention which admitted the right of taxation for the control of trade, but not for raising a revenue. Though claims to "rights" and "liberty" were bandied to and fro, the real question was one of expediency and of constitutional development. Just as in the seventeenth century Parliament fought against the King, so now the Americans were striving against Parliament for rights which were really usurpations, and in each case the side of liberty won the day. The Americans flung in the teeth of Parliament those very phrases which Parliament itself had used as a rallying-cry against the King. Thus we should think of the Americans rather as champions of a more liberal form of government than as "rebels." Our chief regret must be that the contest could not be settled without the bloodshed of civil war, and the hatred which it left behind.

It is one of the ironies of history that the Act which finally led the Americans to fight was actually passed under the shadow of Pitt's authority. Called on to form a ministry on the basis of reconciliation, Pitt had no sooner accomplished his task than he retired to the House of Lords as Earl of Chatham. This action of the Great Commoner seemed to throw a blight over affairs: he himself fell sick of a mysterious disease, and was quite unable to attend to business, while his patchwork ministry, deprived of his supervision and lacking the influence of his great name, soon broke up. But before the ministry fell, Charles Townshend, a brilliant but unreliable opportunist, had passed his fatal Act. As Chancellor of the Exchequer he boasted coolly that he would raise a revenue from America, and in 1767 laid an import duty on various goods arriving at American ports—a duty so ill-devised that it was actually found to operate largely to the disadvantage of English goods. The discontent aroused by the Stamp Act was small compared with the opposition to these fresh duties imposed for the avowed purpose of raising a revenue, but the trouble had to be faced by a new ministry.

Charles Townshend's Act, 1767.

The accession of Lord North to power in 1770 marked the triumph of the King's attempt to break the grip of the Whig oligarchy, and to set up instead his own personal rule; thus during North's government the Crown possessed a direct power and influence which it had never enjoyed since the Revolution of 1688. Though the American disaster has thrown a cloud over North's ministry, yet his government was responsible for several great constructional reforms. Besides attempting to check the worst abuses in Parliamentary elections, it was responsible for passing the great charter of the French-Canadian liberties (Quebec Act, 1774), while it sought to solve the Indian problem by the Regulating Act, but in dealing with America North found himself in an impossible position. To repeal all the duties would have been the heroic measure, and some there were who pleaded for this course, but this would acknowledge the weakness of Parliament before violence and mob rule; on the other hand, to retain the duties meant yet further trouble in America. North desired a policy of compromise, but he was met by the obstinacy of the King, and, as time went on, by the anger of the country against the Americans and their deeds of violence.

North's ministry. 1770-1782.

North attempted to solve the difficulty by repealing all the duties except that on tea, which was retained on principle, but as usual half-measures pleased neither party. Though the tea duty was modified so that the Americans could buy their tea much cheaper than people in England, they would have none of it,

Duties repealed. Tea duty modified. 1770.

and organised opposition continued until, in 1773, a party of New Englanders, disguised as Redskins, boarded an East Indiaman in Boston harbour, and tumbled all the tea-chests overboard. In England feeling flamed up: the East India Company demanded compensation for their property, and North took the fatal step of attempting compulsion, in the hope of coercing Massachusetts by economic pressure. The Port of Boston was closed, the Massachusetts charter was suspended, while a law was passed removing certain trials from the courts of the colony. At the same time, though not connected with these penal measures, was passed the Quebec Act.[1] This last Act was very unpopular among the Americans, for they saw in it an attempt to rob them of those lands between the Ohio and the Mississippi which had been won from the French in the Seven Years' War, and they feared to see the establishment of the Roman Catholic Church in Canada.

Boston tea-party. 1773.

Acts of repression. 1774.

The Americans were not slow to act in reply: so far opposition had been chiefly local, now it was reorganised and became national. Corresponding societies had been set up in the different colonies, and now a congress was summoned to Philadelphia, which was attended by delegates from all the colonies except Georgia. Here was drawn up a formal Declaration of Rights, which stated that Englishmen did not lose their "natural rights" by going overseas, and enumerated the various Acts to which objection was taken. But the Congress went further than mere platitudes; a Non-Importation agreement was made, by which each colony undertook not to trade with Britain in any way, and arrangements were completed to boycott any trader who tried to make an exorbitant profit out of the resultant shortage of British goods. Thus the Americans had now a central Parliament which had organised an executive to carry out its decisions: this American Parliament had proclaimed economic war on Britain, and the Parliament at Westminster quickly replied to the measures of the upstart by extending the Boston Port Act to other colonies also.

Philadelphia Congress. 1774.

The step from economic war to actual fighting was a

[1] See later, p. 94.

short one. In America radical orators had been inflaming the people by fiery speeches; the Massachusetts militia had been embodied in October, 1774, and Boston was flooded with royal troops. The first blood was shed early next year, when General Gage sent a small force from Boston to destroy some colonial stores at Concord. In a skirmish there, and at Lexington on the road, the colonial militia bore themselves well, and the fight at Bunker's Hill in June, when Howe drove the militia from some fortifications they had seized, cost the royal troops very dear, and showed that the Americans were a formidable foe. Gage was recalled, and Howe found himself practically besieged in Boston. In March next year he withdrew to Halifax, and the capital of New England was in the hands of the Revolutionary government. Meanwhile, Congress had met in May, and had sent Richard Penn with the Olive Branch Petition to the King, but no answer was received. More practical steps were taken when they voted a united or continental army, and chose the experienced George Washington as its commander. In one venture the Americans were less successful, for an autumn raid on Canada was foiled by the loyalty of the French inhabitants and the skill of Governor Carleton, who successfully defended Quebec. Matters quickly drifted towards a crisis: there was actual war, though no formal revolution, and the moderate party in America were continually protesting their desire for a settlement by compromise, though their terms were constantly advancing. A pamphlet by Tom Paine, entitled "Common-Sense," which pointed out to the colonies that the logical result of their actions was to declare that they were separate states, had a great effect on American opinion, and Howe's evacuation of Boston in March, 1776, showed the weakness and vacillation of the British. At last, in July, the extreme party won the day, and Congress issued the "Declaration of Independence," while the moderates, who were ready enough to clamour against taxation, swung round at this fateful step, and enrolled in battalions to fight for union. The issue was now clear-cut, and the war began in earnest.

Bunker's Hill. June, 1775.

Declaration of Independence. July, 1776.

Through all this difficult time, and even after the Declaration of Independence, there were not wanting men in England to protest against the fatal policy of taxation, and the still more fatal policy of war. Burke turned pen and tongue to the service of reconciliation, pouring scorn on the Declaratory Act, and urging the uselessness and folly of provoking civil war for the sake of the unremunerative tea duties. Chatham, too, strove in vain for a more far-sighted policy. "My Lords," he had warned the House, "you cannot conquer America." Yet Chatham protested against independence, and when France came into the war his old fervour awoke once more, and he made a final appeal for unity. Decrepit and old before his time, swathed in flannel and leaning on his crutches, he made his last speech. He mumbled and stuttered, a piteous sight to all, but now and again he burst forth in all the energy of conviction. "I am old and infirm, have one foot, more than one foot, in the grave. I have risen from my bed to stand up in the cause of my country, perhaps never again to speak in this House"; thus with grim foresight he began, and then went on to urge his country never to give way before France. "Let us at least make one effort, and if we must fall, let us fall like men." A little later, springing up to reply, he fell forward in a fit, and with Chatham's death there disappeared the last faint chance of reconciliation with America.

Chatham's last speech. 7th April, 1778.

The evacuation of Boston left New England to the Americans, and after the failure of the raid on Canada New York became the centre of colonial resistance. It was, therefore, determined to attack this city; thither Howe sailed with his troops from Halifax, and there he was reinforced by soldiers from Carolina, and by an English fleet under the command of his brother which had sailed from home. In September, Washington was driven from New York and forced to retire southward, but Howe's neglect to follow up his victory gave Washington time to re-make his army. For next year's operations an elaborate plan was drawn up by Lord George Germaine, the Secretary of State for America. He determined to cut off New England from the southern colonies by a great

The War.

New York captured by Howe. 1776.

campaign along the Hudson Valley. Howe was to move north from New York, while two armies from Canada were to join him, one marching south up the Richelieu river to Lake Champlain, the other by the Mohawk route from Lake Ontario. These careful plans went all awry, and it is said that by some careless oversight Howe never received the necessary orders. In any case, Howe went off on a campaign of his own in the middle colonies, succeeded in capturing Philadelphia, from which Congress had fled in fear the previous year, and then so flagrantly neglected to push on and crush Washington that men suspected his loyalty and good faith. Meanwhile, Burgoyne came down from Canada, took the forts of Ticonderoga and Crown Point upon Lake Champlain, but looked in vain for the armies which were to meet him. The western force had already been defeated, while Clinton at New York had so few men that he could barely secure his own safety. Burgoyne found himself attacked on all sides, and was surrounded at Saratoga and forced to capitulate.

Howe captures Philadelphia. Sept. 1777.

Burgoyne surrenders at Saratoga. 1777.

This great victory of the Americans was really the turning-point of the war. France had already helped them secretly, now she openly recognised their independence and declared war on England. The entry of France into the war changed the whole balance of power. Britain was now forced to look to her control of the sea, and when Spain (1779), and then Holland (1780), joined the enemy, she found herself fighting for very existence. There was even a threat of further trouble, for the armed neutrality of Russia, Sweden, Denmark, and later Prussia and Austria, stood for resistance to the British claims at sea. French fleets and troops came to the help of the Americans, French power interfered in India and stirred up the independent rulers against the Company. In America, Britain found herself able to do much less on the mainland, for all her communications there depended on the sea, and she was forced instead to secure the safety of the West Indies. In 1780, however, orders were received in New York for a big expedition to be sent to the southern colonies. Lord Cornwallis landed with five thousand

France joins the war. Feb. 1778.

troops, as well as loyalists, and recaptured Charlestown from the Americans. He determined to march northward into Virginia, and thus to attack Washington from the south. But he received no help from Clinton at New York, and was forced to take shelter at Yorktown. Here he was blockaded by Washington and anxiously scanned the horizon for Clinton's sails, but the ships which actually arrived were the forerunners of a French fleet under de Grasse. There was nothing left for Cornwallis to do but surrender.

Cornwallis surrenders at Yorktown, Oct. 1781.

The capitulation of Yorktown marks the end of the land campaign, but fifteen months were yet to elapse before peace was signed. During this time the courage and hard work of the British fleets, keeping the seas under the most difficult conditions, maintained the traditions of the Navy, and formed a pleasing contrast to the ill-fortune of the land campaigns. Despite some French successes in the West Indies, Rodney's great victory over the French fleet at The Saints, off Martinique, gave him once more control of the sea, and he was able to retake most of the French conquests. In Europe, the gallant defence of Gibraltar against the joint attack of France and Spain held that post secure, though Minorca was lost. The British naval successes really prevented the Peace Treaty from being more humiliating than it actually was.

Rodney's victory off The Saints. April, 1782.

Thus Britain's failure was chiefly due to her temporary loss of the command of the seas. Faced by a league of the chief sea-powers of Europe, her Navy was yet able to re-establish its superiority, but the damage had already been done, and the American colonies had won their independence. On land Britain's defeat was due to bad generals, and to the bad strategy which was adopted. Instead of concentrating and striking the enemy at his most vulnerable point, the British attempted to hold a long line of towns, between which the only effective communications were by sea. In her choice of generals Britain was equally unfortunate. Lord Howe was especially to blame for not following up his successes and destroying Washington's army at New York in 1776, and again in Pennsylvania in the

Reasons for British failure.

following year. There was lack of co-operation, too, between Howe and Burgoyne at Saratoga, and again between Clinton and Cornwallis in 1781, which ended in Yorktown. The truth seems to be that most of the generals were thoroughly disgusted with their task, and that to natural incapacity was added the lack of a desire to crush the enemy. But when all this is admitted, tribute must be paid to the genius of Washington. His name and his deeds have become a legend, but his true greatness lay in his power to hold together an ill-disciplined body of militia during times of disaster, and to mould such troops into a formidable army. But though it is true that good generalship on the British side might have made a very different story, yet the result of the war can hardly be regretted. Had the Americans been held against their will, they could have been nothing but an evil to the Empire. The war itself was a disaster, but not its result.

The Peace of Versailles, which ended the war, altered somewhat the terms of the Treaty of Paris. (1) The independence of the United States was recognised, and their territory extended to the Mississippi, while beyond that the land was claimed by Spain. (2) Spain received back Florida from England. (3) Canada was restricted to the north of a line drawn from the Great Lakes to the eastern coast, though future disputes arose as to the exact trace of this line: thus the Ohio lands fell to the States.

Peace of Versailles. 1783.

The Peace of Versailles is the low-water mark of British power and prestige in the eighteenth century; though her Navy had saved her from utter disaster, and she was soon to re-establish her sea-power yet more firmly, Britain came out of the war disillusioned. The new office of Secretary for American Affairs, created in 1768, was abolished in 1782, and colonies gradually went out of fashion. Those that still remained were bandied from office to office until, in 1801, the newly created Secretary for War became responsible for the colonies also; but this increase of centralisation and unsympathetic control soon led to further quarrels, though the new problems were to be solved without another civil war.

The War of Independence was the forerunner of great

revolutionary movements in Europe, and it was the beginning of a series of revolts among the colonies of the other European powers: during the Revolutionary and Napoleonic wars the French island of Hayti and the American colonies of Spain revolted and finally secured their independence. Thus Turgot's saying, that colonies were like fruit and would drop off when ripe, seemed amply justified. France got but little from the war except a barren revenge, and a bankruptcy which accelerated the forces of the Revolution, while American phrases and American examples had great influence on the early days of the French Revolution.

If we would appreciate the effects of the war on Canada, we must see what had been happening there since the Peace of 1763, for events in Canada played an important part in the development of the quarrel between Britain and America. After the capture of Quebec, Canada was governed by military rule, but it was obvious that some arrangements would have to be made for its future. There were three great questions to be decided. The Canadians were Roman Catholics, living under the laws of France, and they had long claimed, and but recently fought for, the Indian territories of the Ohio Valley. Now Canada had been conquered, what was to be the official religion of the country, what law was to be administered in Canada, and to whom were the disputed Ohio lands to belong? In 1764, the year after the Peace, a proclamation came into force establishing a government for Canada. The province of Quebec was formed, excluding the Ohio territories, and the governor was given power to call an assembly, but as Roman Catholics were excluded from this assembly it would have been composed of a few hangers-on of the British rule, and the Governor very wisely refrained from summoning such a body. At the same time elaborate and expensive arrangements were made for administering the Ohio territories, and a set of rules was laid down for the honest treatment of the Indians. These arrangements greatly annoyed the colonists of Virginia, who had fought in the Seven Years' War for the right of exploiting the Ohio lands, but they were still more angry at the next step.

Canada. Proclamation of 1764.

Governor Carleton realised that there could be no security

in Canada until the great outstanding questions had been faced, and so he worked for a definite settlement. Thanks to his efforts the Quebec Act was passed in 1774, and became the basis of the reconciliation between the French of Canada and their British conquerors. (1) The province of Quebec was extended, and was now to include the Ohio Valley. (2) The Roman Catholic Church, which had been promised protection by the terms of the surrender of Canada, was now finally guaranteed. (3) The French civil law was confirmed as the law of the land. (4) The English criminal law, which had been administered since the conquest of Canada, was continued because, harsh as were its punishments, they were more certain and more moderate than those of the French law. Though there was no arrangement for calling an assembly this is not surprising: in England at this time Roman Catholics had neither the right to vote, nor to sit in Parliament, and any assembly in Canada which excluded Roman Catholics would be but a farce. The French in Canada accepted the Quebec Act as a veritable charter of liberties, for under its working they were better off than under the old French regime, and their loyalty stood the test both of the American invasion of 1775, and of those difficult years when French fleets were off the coasts of America, and French troops fighting British on the mainland itself. To the American colonists, however, the Act was a hateful measure. They feared the establishment of the Roman Catholic religion, and they were furious at the Ohio arrangement. Thus the Quebec Act became one of the counts against Britain in the Declaration of Independence, and the British Government was accused of "establishing an arbitrary government in Canada," for the Sons of Liberty could understand no liberty but their own.

Quebec Act, 1774.

French-Canadian loyalty.

As we have seen, the Treaty of Versailles gave the Ohio lands to the States, and with them the infinite possibilities of westward expansion. The policy of limiting Canada to the parallel of the Great Lakes has gone on steadily ever since, until the boundary between Canada and the United States is now a straight line stretching from the Lakes to the Pacific. On the other hand, the "arbitrary government" remained for many years, and its essential points, the establishment of the Roman Catholic religion, and the French civil law, are still in force in the province of Quebec. But the war did more for Canada. A great body of loyalist refugees left their homes in the old colonies and settled in Canada, thus adding an English element to balance the French in Quebec. These Americans had fought in Loyalist battalions for the cause of union, and when that cause was lost it was provided in the Treaty that there should be no further confiscations, and that the Loyalists should have a year in which to make their arrangements to

THE BOUNDARIES OF CANADA.

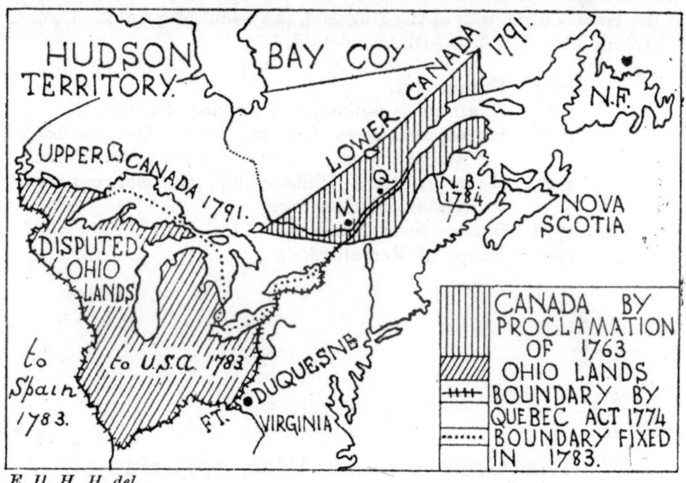

E. H. H. H. del.

emigrate. These terms were not kept, and a veritable persecution of these luckless men broke out, the hatred and ill-feeling of civil war venting itself on the first victims. Thus it was with bitter feelings that the United Empire Loyalists left the States: the majority, about 25,000, went by sea and settled in Nova Scotia and along the shores of the mainland. Others, some 10,000 in all, went by a much more difficult way through the backwoods and up the rivers, and settled in the land between Lakes Huron and Ontario. Here they founded Kingston, in

The British Empire Loyalists.

memory of their loyalty, and soon after English or Upper Canada was made a separate province from French or Lower Canada (Quebec). Thus the migration of the United Empire Loyalists became the nucleus of another set of English colonies on the mainland, but it did still more. It sowed the seeds of hatred and mistrust between Canada and the United States, which were a fruitful cause of friction for many years to come. Men do not quickly forget their wrongs.

BOOKS.—There is as yet no handy account of this period. Burke's *Letters and Speeches on American Affairs*, should be read, and also the Declaration of Independence (printed in W. Macdonald, *Documentary Source Book of American History*). *The Life of George Washington*, by J. H. Harrison [Heroes of the Nations], is a useful biography. Lecky's Chapters XI to XV deal with this period.

1765. **Stamp Act.**
1767. **Chatham's ministry. Townshend's duties.**
1776. **Howe evacuates Boston. July: Declaration of Independence. Howe captures New York.**
1777. **Howe captures Philadelphia, but Burgoyne surrenders at Saratoga.**
1778. **France joins America.**
1783. **Peace of Versailles.**

CHAPTER VI

The Great French War, 1793–1815

AFTER ten years of peace Britain found herself in 1793 face to face with her old enemy once more, and the last act in the great eighteenth-century rivalry between Britain and France began. For some twenty years there was almost continuous war between the two countries, and during that time Britain established such a control over the seas of the world as had never been seen before, and the power she then gained has been maintained ever since.

Thus, as a result of the war, Britain's Navy became the police force of the world. It was the Navy which attacked and destroyed the power of the piratical Dey of Algiers, and freed his Christian slaves in 1816. It was the all-compelling threat of British sea-power which gave force to the Monroe doctrine, and prevented the reactionary powers of Europe from re-establishing the authority of Spain over her revolted colonies (1823). Thus the republics of South America owe their freedom to the British Navy. Again, it was the Navy that suppressed the slave trade, that hunted out the last remnant of the pirates in the East Indies, that examined, sounded, and charted the seas of the world, and thus made the ocean highways safe and easy for the traffic of every nation, securing, in the truest sense of the phrase, the freedom of the seas.

The great war with France decided finally that Britain was to be the predominant power beyond the seas, for French ambitions on the continent hindered her then, as they have before and since, in developing a great colonial empire. The control of the seas gave Britain almost every French possession, and though most of them were returned at the final settlement, some were retained by the conquerors. Thus the British Empire was enlarged during the war by conquests from France, from Spain, and from Holland, though the value of some of these new acquisitions was hardly realised at the time, for few could guess that the little trading-station at the Cape would grow into the Union of South Africa. In India, Britain gained her largest territories during the war, for when French schemes stirred up native rulers against the British power, the energetic and far-seeing Wellesley carried out a policy of annexation and alliance.

At first the French Revolution was welcomed by Englishmen. The Whigs saw in the movement an attempt to imitate their Glorious Revolution of 1688, and various clubs were formed in England to teach the principles of freedom. But feeling quickly began to change, the execution of the King caused a thrill of horror through the country, while the French invasion of Belgium and the opening of the River Scheldt to free navigation alarmed the jealous British merchants, who feared that the great waterway would absorb their trade. Thus the two countries soon found themselves at war, and Britain began that struggle against revolutionary France which was soon to become a great crusade against the military ambitions of Napoleon. Pitt was a peace minister who found himself with a war on his hands, and he fought it on land by building up alliances among the European nations against the common enemy, and by using the Navy to its full extent at sea.

When the war began the British Navy was in good condition: it had done well in the American War despite great odds, and the lessons then learnt had not been forgotten. The ships were well built, and the new practice of sheathing the hull with copper had improved their speed. Anson had developed the 74 as the typical man-of-war, but an increasing number of three-deckers were now built. The fast-sailing frigates were the scouts of the fleet, and it was their duty to form a screen and to gain information about the enemy. Some of the senior officers were old and over-cautious, but there was a group of brilliant commanders, some such as Nelson still only captains, whose names were soon to become world-famous. The crews were not so satisfactory, for voluntary enlistment was supplemented by the press-gang, and even by the shipping of criminals, and this, combined with a harsh system of discipline, actually led to mutiny in 1797. But at heart the men were sound, and it was only the bravery and self-sacrifice of the crews that made the great victories possible. On the other hand, the French navy had suffered seriously from the Revolution; the dockyards were inefficient, discipline was bad, and many of the officers had been guillotined. Thus at first the French were heavily handicapped, though the energy of patriotism reorganised their navy, and the struggle was soon an even one.

State of the Navy.

At the beginning of the war, fleets were sent to the West Indies, to the Mediterranean, and to watch the coasts of France. No very close blockade was kept, but Howe caught a large French fleet returning from the West Indies with a convoy of grain ships. Meeting them on the "Glorious First of June," he attacked them vigorously and won the first great sea victory of the war. Hoping to avoid the fleet, the French made several schemes for the invasion of Ireland, but they were

Howe's victory. 1st June, 1794.

frustrated by the constant pressure of the Navy. In the Mediterranean the indecision of the British commander, and the entrance of Spain into the war on the side of France, had forced the fleet to withdraw (1796), but next year two great victories were won. These victories were badly needed, for 1797 was the critical year for Britain. Austria, her only ally, had signed the Peace of Campo Formio; discontent and the threat of bankruptcy in England, rebellion in Ireland, and mutiny in the fleet at the Nore, all combined to make a very black outlook. But in February, Sir John Jervis, aided by the brilliant disobedience of Nelson, had inflicted a crushing defeat on the Spanish fleet off St. Vincent. At the Nore the mutiny died out, and the fleet sailed to reinfore the blockading squadron off the Texel, and to defeat the Dutch at Camperdown.

A critical year. 1797.

Meanwhile the Mediterranean was left open to the French, and Napoleon's teeming mind dreamt of an Eastern Empire built up with Egypt as its base. A vast armament was prepared at Toulon, and when Nelson's small blockading squadron was blown off, Napoleon slipped out and made for Egypt. Nelson was reinforced and hunted his quarry up and down the Mediterranean, at last bringing them to bay at Aboukir. "We have just been witnesses, my dear Friends, of a Naval combat, the most bloody and unfortunate that for many ages has taken place. As yet we know not all the circumstances; but those we are already acquainted with are frightful in the extreme." Thus wrote a French officer describing the Battle of the Nile in a private letter which was captured at sea by the *Bellerophon*, and he was right in his judgment, for Nelson's destruction of the French fleet cut off Napoleon from his base, forcing him to return to France as best he could, and to leave his army in Egypt to its fate. After this disaster France was almost impotent at sea, but on land she was still terrible, and on reaching France, Napoleon soon broke up Pitt's second coalition by his victories at Marengo and Hohenlinden. The result was the Peace of Amiens, by the terms of which Britain surrendered all her overseas gains except Trinidad and Ceylon (1801).

Battle of the Nile. 1st August, 1798.

The Peace, however, was only a truce: it really settled

nothing, and it still left Napoleon free to mature his great plans and to work out his "destiny." Thus by 1803 war had broken out again, and Britain began by a strict blockade of all the enemy's ports. Napoleon, who had crowned himself Emperor at Paris in 1804, determined to strike at his persistent foe by invasion. On the cliffs at Boulogne, near where the huts of a British rest-camp were to stand during the Great War of 1914, sprang up the tents and bivouacs of the Army of England which Napoleon had destined for the capture of London. The flotilla of flat-bottomed boats could not cross the Channel until he obtained the command of the sea, and so Napoleon planned for his admirals to break out of their ports, meet in the West Indies, and then make for the Channel. But plans on paper often fail in practice, and though Villeneuve escaped from Toulon in March, he found no colleagues at Martinique, and was forced to return homeward. Meanwhile, Nelson had hunted him across the Atlantic, and was hard on his heels again. Villeneuve made for the mouth of the Channel, but there he was headed off by an inconclusive action with Calder, and turned southward. On 21st October Nelson found him in Trafalgar Bay, and after a great struggle captured eighteen of his thirty-three ships. Still others were taken a day or two later.

Trafalgar. 18th October, 1805.

The victory of Trafalgar frustrated Napoleon's invasion schemes, and gave to Britain an almost undisputed command of the sea. For the rest of the war British fleets could sail where they willed, while the fact that the Peninsular War could be carried on is the measure of British sea-power. Privateers might prey upon her shipping, and Napoleon's Continental System might attempt to starve out her goods, but her trade by sea more than doubled. At a distance British fleets acted with equal security, and soon almost every colony belonging to her enemies was in her hands. It was a fitting end to the war that Napoleon should surrender himself to the captain of the *Bellerophon*. In the final settlement which was made at Vienna, when the diplomats of the conquering nations met to rearrange the map of Europe, Britain retained as her share of the spoils some of the colonies she had seized. Thus St. Lucia, Tobago, and Guiana in the West

Indies fell to her, with Malta, the Cape, and Mauritius, all three important as ports on the route to India.

The old Empire had broken up with the American War of Independence, but in the years between the Peace of Versailles in 1783 and the Treaty of Vienna in 1815 there were laid the foundations of a new Empire from which the dominions of to-day were destined to arise. These beginnings were not very promising, and no one could foresee what great developments the future had in store. In Canada the British were represented by refugees, who fled from the anger of their fellow-colonists, now stout republicans of the United States: New South Wales was but a convict-station, while the Cape was merely a "sea-tavern" on the route to India, which the British captured from the Dutch. It was the day of small things.

The founding of the New Empire.

Canada

The influx of British Empire Loyalists from the United States led to new problems in Canada, for the new-comers soon began to agitate for a change in the system of government which had been established by the Quebec Act in 1774. They asked for exemption from the French system of land tenure, and they naturally wished for a government by council and assembly, such as they had been accustomed to live under in the old colonies. In 1791 William Pitt the younger passed his Canada Act, by which the province of Quebec was divided into two, Upper Canada consisting of the land where the loyalists had settled near the Niagara river, and Lower Canada comprising Quebec and Montreal, where the population was chiefly French. In each province there was to be an elected assembly, and Pitt hoped "the division would remove the differences of opinion which had arisen between the old and new inhabitants, since each province would have the right of enacting laws desired in its own house of assembly." In the maritime provinces a similar division had already taken place, and the loyalists or "blue-noses" on the mainland were separated from the old province of Nova Scotia, and formed into the province of New Brunswick (1784).

Pitt's Canada Act, 1791.

The new colonists had hardly time to settle down, to fell their trees and build their farmsteads in Upper Canada, and to plough their lands or start their fisheries in the maritime provinces, before a new trouble was upon them. The interference of both France and Great Britain with the trade of the United States, during the long struggle of the Napoleonic wars, had caused endless recrimination, but finally the crisis was reached: Britain was supreme at sea, and against her the States declared war. For Canada this war was an incalculable disaster, and the evil done was not limited to the burning of towns, or the destruction of villages by frontier raids, for the war left behind it a bitter feeling of hatred between the Canadians and the Americans which hampered their good relations long into the century. The loyalists had already fought for the Empire and lost their farms and homes; once again as old men they turned out to fight the same enemy, and to save their new won homes from his grasp. Such men, when they saw their farms go up in flames, and their families turned out into the cold of a bitter winter, could not soon forget what they had suffered. The maritime provinces were never attacked, and indeed flourished by supplying the needs of British ships, while even Lower Canada felt the war but slightly, since the routes by which it could be reached were few and difficult. The brunt of the war fell upon Upper Canada, whose open frontier could easily be crossed: here for three years small forces of Americans campaigned against Canadians, villages were sacked, forts taken and recaptured, but the invaders found it an impossible task to compel the surrender of the province. Finally, in 1814 peace was made, and the colonists turned to repair the ravages of the war and to face those internal problems of government which were soon to bring the troubles of Canada into prominence once more.

War with United States. 1812-1814.

Australia

The first colonisation of Australia was directly due to the War of Independence. The American colonies had, from time to time, received batches of convicts who had been pardoned on condition that they were transported for life. Although these men hardly made the most desirable colonists, yet in a new country where labour was scarce and an absolute necessity for development, they were tolerated, if not always welcomed. Bound as indentured labourers to work for a term of years, they were able in due course to work out their time, and so receive their freedom. After the Declaration of Independence it was impossible to send any more to America, so in 1787 the first ship-load of convicts sailed to the newly-discovered eastern coast of Australia, and landing at Botany Bay soon moved their little settlement to Sydney Cove. Here, however, conditions were very different from those in America; there were no colonists in Australia ready to receive the convicts, and so a government penal station had to be founded. When the men had served out their time, they were allowed their liberty on condition that they settled near at hand, and so from this unpromising beginning there sprang the first colonists of Australia.

Convict station at Botany Bay. 1788.

The great continent of Australia had early been discovered, though its exact shape and coastline were not correctly known for a very long time. Australia lies south of the Spice Islands, that centre of ancient trade rivalry, and it was a question whether the Spaniard or the Dutchman would first reach it. Fortune favoured the latter, and early voyagers from the Dutch islands brought news of a great south land. Fired by this news, Van Diemen, the governor of the Dutch East Indies, sent Tasman in 1643 and 1644 to explore. In his two voyages Tasman examined the northern and western coasts of Australia itself, reached New Zealand, and touched at Van Diemen's Land, whose name was afterwards changed to Tasmania in honour of the actual discoverer. Soon afterwards the Dutch were engaged in a long series of wars with England, and their interest in discovery flagged. The English then took up the task, and William Dampier, a buccaneer from the West Indies, touched Australia when sailing round the world in 1639 as a man before the mast: ten years later he returned as an explorer in command of his ship. "New Holland," he wrote, "is a very large tract of

Discovery of Australia.

land. It is not yet determined whether it is an island, or a main continent, but I am certain that it joins neither to Asia, Africa nor America. . . . The land is of a dry, sandy soil, destitute of water, except you make wells." It was only gradually during the eighteenth century that the eastern coasts became known, largely owing to the voyages of the English explorer Captain Cook (1769–1774). He examined New Zealand, and the whole of the eastern coasts of Australia very thoroughly. It is not difficult to understand why this slowly-discovered continent remained so long without settlers: it was a dry and thirsty land where sailors became "scorbutick" looking in vain for water; it offered no riches for trade such as could be found easily in the Spice Islands. Indeed, it was only when England wished to rid herself of a band of undesirables, that it was decided to dump them on the new-discovered eastern coast of this far-off empty land. Such was the strange beginning of the great Commonwealth of Australia.

South Africa

When the King of Portugal declared that the Cape of Storms should be called the Cape of Good Hope, his optimism was soon rewarded, for a few years later his sailors found their way to India. The seventeenth century saw the Dutch and English East India Companies both striving to wrest trade from the Portuguese, and for a long time the Cape was merely a convenient port of call for either nation. There the storm-tossed ships put in before setting out again for the calm seas of the tropics, and there beneath the shadow of the great Table Mountain they scoured out their evil-smelling water-butts, and refilled them with fresh water from the tiny stream which ran down to the sea. There, too, they posted their letters. Hiding them beneath a cairn of stones, and carving the name of the ship and the date upon the neighbouring boulders, they sailed away, trusting that the next ship homeward would find and deliver the mail which they had left to fortune.

This haphazard and friendly arrangement could not last for ever, and as the rivalry between the two companies became intense the Dutch determined to establish a small settlement at the Cape. In 1652 Van Riebeck arrived with some two hundred settlers, who were to build a fort, and cultivate fresh vegetables which would be useful to the company's ships and help to keep away the plague of scurvy. At first the settlement had to face the attack of the Hottentots and the threats of famine, but it was gradually strengthened by fresh settlers whose farms began to stretch away from the Castle at Table Bay. Between 1688 and 1690 a number of French Huguenots, flying from persecution, were settled there by the Company, and though they became merged in the Dutch settlers and lost their own language, they have remained to this day an important element in the population. The settlers were ruled autocratically by the Company's governor from Cape Town, through their local magistrates, and they were only allowed to trade direct with the Company. This stringent control led to much discontent, and the Company refused to make any modification in the system. The law officer of the Cape Government poured ridicule on the colonists' requests. "It would be a mere waste of words to dwell on the remarkable distinction to be drawn between burghers whose ancestors nobly fought for freedom, and conquered their freedom from tyranny (*i.e.* in Holland) . . . and such as are named burghers here, who have been permitted as matter of grace to have a residence in a land of which possession has been taken by the Sovereign Power, there to gain a livelihood as tillers of the earth, tailors and shoe-makers. . . . Now it is clear, and requires no lengthy argument, that for the purpose of enabling a subordinate colony to flourish as a colony, it is not always expedient to apply these means which, considered in the abstract, might be conducive to its prosperity. The object of paramount importance in legislating for colonies should be the welfare of the parent state, of which such colony is but a subordinate part, and to which it owes its existence." Thus the Cape was sacrificed to the supposed welfare of Holland, the Dutch settlers remained in a dependent position, and became ignorant, backward and discontented, while in the inland settlements they sometimes refused to recognise the authority of the Governor at all.

Dutch Settlement. Van Riebeck. 1652.

Autocratic government by Dutch East India Company.

Such was the settlement which fell into English hands during the Revolutionary War. When in 1794 Holland was overrun by France, and set up the Batavian Republic, Britain determined to seize the Cape and to prevent it falling into the hands of the French. Next year a British expedition sailed into False Bay, and the cannon-balls fired by the ships still lie about the sand-dunes which surround the bay. Landing a small force, the British defeated the Dutch at the little hamlet of Retreat. Thus the Cape surrendered, and though it was returned to Holland at the Peace of Amiens (1801) war soon broke out again, and it was easily recaptured in 1806. Finally, at the Treaty of Vienna, the British were confirmed in their possession, and paid the Dutch £2,000,000 as compensation for their claims.

British capture the Cape, 1794, 1806, and buy it, 1814.

BOOKS.—Some of the chapters in W. H. Fitchett's books, *Deeds that won the Empire*, and *Fights for the Flag*, tell in popular style of the great struggles of the naval war. J. Leyland, *The Royal Navy*, and J. R. Thursfield, *Naval Warfare* [Cambridge Manuals], are useful little books. For Canada there are C. P. Lucas, *History of Canada, 1763–1812*, and A. G. Bradley, *The Making of Canada*. For Australia and South Africa see notes to Chapters X and XI.

1788. Convicts shipped to Australia.
1791. Pitt's Canada Act (creates two provinces).
1798. The Battle of the Nile.
1805. Trafalgar.
1812–1814. War with U.S.A. Fighting on the Canadian frontier.
1814. Cape ceded to Britain by Treaty of Vienna.

CHAPTER VII

The East India Company as an Imperial Power [1760–1818]

WE have already seen how England lost her old Empire in America, and how the seeds of a new Empire were planted in different parts of the world, while her fleets gave her ports and stations on every sea. In India, too, a new Empire was being built, for the British were now winning for themselves political power instead of the mere trading rights which they had possessed up to the Seven Years' War. The hundred years between Clive's first conquest of Bengal and the outbreak of the Mutiny saw this vital change. Before Clive's expedition to Bengal the East India Company was a successful trading organisation, owning forts and factories, but enjoying no great territorial possessions: at the time of the Mutiny it had ceased to trade and was merely a government department which administered the whole of India, either directly by its officials, or indirectly by a series of subordinate native rulers. By 1858, then, India had undergone a complete change: externally, for the whole of India was now subject to the Company; politically, for the framework of the modern governmental system had been evolved; and economically, for all the main lines of later economic development had been laid down.

Changes after 1760.

Thus the period is one of steady expansion, during which by wars and by diplomacy the Company gained and extended its political power. This new policy was partly due to the hard logic of facts. The break-up of the Mogul Empire had left a number of warring states, and unless the Company was willing to seize power it could no longer expect to carry on its trade in peace. Besides this, French schemers were often successful in stirring up trouble for the British, and the Company had either to act promptly, and at times to annex the lands of an enemy, or run the risk of annihilation. Some of the governors, too, were men of great ambition, who strove to extend British dominion, believing that it brought great advantage both to the Indians and to the Company. The Directors in England usually disapproved of this policy, but were not able to control their servants effectually. It took a year to send a letter and obtain a reply, and even when an overland mail was established across the Isthmus of Suez, schemes of which the Directors disapproved were often carried out before they could be prevented.

East India Company becomes a political power.

At the same time there was a steady increase of Governmental interference in the affairs of the Company. Parliament became embarrassingly inquisitive about the Company's business, and each time the charter was renewed further conditions were imposed, which brought the Company more closely under the control of the Government. This was partly due to the vast fortunes which men brought home from the East. These nabobs (nawabs) came back to England with sufficient money to buy land, to set up as "country gentlemen," and to bribe their way into Parliament so as to make their influence felt in politics. Stories, too, of various abuses floated home to England, and it was felt that a place where such fortunes could be made, and where men were exposed to such temptations, should not be entirely controlled by a mere trading company, which might abuse its powers of patronage. There was yet another point of view: it seemed wrong to some that a company should exercise sovereign rights over territorial possessions, and Chatham laid this down as an axiom. The fight between the champions of vested interests and private property and those who upheld the claims of the State was long drawn out, but the State won in 1858, when the Company was dissolved, and all its territorial possessions taken over by the Crown.

Development of Parliamentary control.

Four great men played an important part in this development. Clive, the soldier, who laid the foundations of British power in Bengal, but failed to solve the problem of devising an administrative system for his conquests; Warren Hastings, the organiser, who managed, despite the factious opposition of his council, to purify and organise the civil service and the law-courts, and to save the British power in an hour of danger; Wellesley, the conqueror, who extended the British Raj and laid the basis of the British India of to-day; and Dalhousie, whose far-seeing and tireless energy encouraged those new lines of economic development to which India owes its subsequent progress.

The turning-point in the story of the East India Company is marked by the attack of the young Nawab of Bengal, Siraj-ud-Daula, on Calcutta in 1756. For some time there had been friction between the old nawab and the Governor of Calcutta over questions of trade, but the sudden attack came as a thunder-clap, and the ships in the river sailed down-stream, leaving the defenders of the fort to their fate. When the news reached Madras that the British factories in Bengal had been captured, and that most of the prisoners at Calcutta had perished in the "Black Hole," the Governor determined to act at once. Although war with France was threatening, Clive was despatched with some nine hundred Europeans and fifteen hundred natives to re-establish the British power in Bengal. Robert Clive was then only thirty-one: he had come to India in 1744 as a writer in the Company's service, but his bent was always towards a military life, and he had seized the opportunity to become a soldier. He was only a captain when his bold dash on Arcot in 1751 defeated Dupleix's plans, and made his own reputation as a soldier. He was a man of melancholy temperament, and, despite the great riches and success he was about to win, it was his fate to die by his own hand. Clive was chosen to command the expedition over the heads of several of his seniors, and he was confident of recapturing Calcutta. In this he was correct, and his initial success enabled him to make a treaty with the nawab, by which the latter restored the Company's possessions and promised them compensation. Clive now found himself in a difficult position: war with France had broken out, and he feared the nawab would join with these new enemies. He determined to strike first, and falling on the French factory of Chandernagore succeeded in taking it. By June, 1757, he was marching against the nawab once again, and with only three thousand men he defeated over fifty thousand native troops at Plassey. In this campaign Clive had with him the 39th [the Dorset] Regiment, the first royal regiment to serve in India, who still bear on their colours the title, "Primus in Indis." This victory raised British prestige still higher, but it was partly due to the treachery of Mir Jafar, whom Clive now recognised as nawab in Siraj-ud-Daula's place. Clive had more than completed his task, and next year he returned to England loaded with "presents" from the new nawab. His action in accept-

Black Hole of Calcutta. 1756.

Plassey. 1757.

ing these gifts, and bargaining for a yearly pension of £30,000, was severely criticised in England, and it formed an evil precedent which the Council of Bengal were but too ready to follow. We must remember, however, that in the eighteenth century the standard of political morality was lamentably low, and that the frequent attacks on great Anglo-Indians are signs of a better doctrine of financial honesty.

While Clive was in England the state of Bengal went from bad to worse: the Council of Calcutta fomented a series of revolutions in Bengal which they turned to their own advantage, while the Company's officials, great and small, abused their position by claiming exemption from tolls for their private trade. When in despair Mir Kasim, the new nawab, extended the exemption to native merchants, a quarrel arose with the Council, and he and his ally, the Nawab of Oudh, were defeated at Buxar in 1764. Thus when Clive returned as governor a second time, in 1765, he had a difficult problem to solve.

Clive's second governorship. 1765-1767.

The nominal ruler of Bengal was the nawab, but his power really depended upon British support. Clive determined to take over the "diwani," or collection of revenue, while leaving to the nawab the "nizamet," or military power and criminal jurisdiction. Although the Company was nominally responsible for collecting the revenue, it actually employed two natives to organise the work, and this soon led to trouble. From the diwani the nawab was paid a fixed sum, while the Mogul, now a wanderer expelled from Delhi, was to receive a large annual payment: the balance went into the Company's treasury. Clive settled the Mogul at Allahabad, and thus had this phantom power under his control, and was able to obtain grants in favour of the Company. Following up the same policy, Clive made a treaty with the Nawab of Oudh, thus getting a "buffer-state" on the north-west of Bengal, which remained a useful protection until it was annexed by Dalhousie in 1856. But it was the Directors' attempt to purify the civil service by forbidding the acceptance of "presents" that caused most discontent, for it seemed that after Clive had lined his own pockets a similar privilege was denied to others.

Clive's "Dual Government" was a failure from the first,

and the system of revenue collection only led to oppression: the Company wished to make as much as possible, and so the actual collectors, the zemindars, pressed the peasants until they were on the verge of desperation. "It must give pain to an Englishman," wrote one of the Company's servants in 1769, "to have reason to think that since the accession of the Company to the Diwani the condition of the people of this country has been worse than it was before; and yet I am afraid the Fact is undoubted; . . . this fine Country, which flourished under the most despotic and arbitrary Government, is verging towards its ruin." Thus up till now British power in Bengal had been a curse; this was recognised in England, and a deliberate attempt to improve matters was now made.

Failure of Clive's system.

It was the breakdown of Clive's system of government, and the exposure of his doings in India which led to the first definite scheme for extending Parliamentary control to Indian affairs. In 1767 an Act had ordered the annual payment by the Company to the Crown of £400,000, but this was merely a demand to share the plunder. The bad state of affairs was shown when in 1770 the Company had to beg relief from this Act, for abuses were ruining the natural revenue of the country. Things were made worse by the terrible famine of 1770, and at last after much discussion a remedy was proposed by Lord North in his Regulating Act of 1773.

Since Clive's administration Calcutta had become by far the most important British factory in India, and the new Act recognised this by giving its governor the title of Governor-General, with supervisory powers over the governors of Madras, Bombay, and Bencoolen. A Supreme Court was established at Calcutta to administer English law, with jurisdiction over British subjects, whether natives or Europeans. Large salaries were provided for the judges and chief officials, and they were not allowed to trade or to receive presents, while the rights of other civil servants to trade on their own account was strictly limited. Lastly, the Company had to keep the Secretary of State informed of all important letters from the East. In future the Governor-General was to be appointed by the Company and approved by

Regulating Act, 1773.

the Crown, but the first Governor-General was named in the Act, Warren Hastings.

Warren Hastings. 1772-1785. Reforms.

Hastings was a strong man with a keen and sympathetic insight into the state of affairs, and a burning desire to do away with the terrible abuses which had grown up in Bengal. He was a great organiser, and not afraid to act on his own responsibility. He had already been Governor of Calcutta for two years, and introduced great reforms. Thus he quickly recognised that Clive's Dual System was impossible, and saw that as the Company was really supreme in Bengal, any attempt to avoid the responsibility of that position would only end in confusion. He therefore pensioned off the nawab, reducing him to a "mere name," and took the military power and criminal jurisdiction, the nizamet, directly into the hands of the Company. Still Bengal was an Indian province, and Hastings realised that it should be ruled by Indian customs, but he wished to improve and cheapen the legal system. To this end he set up two Supreme Courts at Calcutta, one for civil, the other for criminal affairs, and he also organised local courts and lowered their fees. He made a great attempt to improve the revenue system, which had been growing less efficient as it became more oppressive, and removed the great native deputies who had administered the system for the Company. To protect the ryots, or peasants, he gave them legal contracts stating the amounts which they would have to pay, and this prevented the zemindars from swindling them. One of Hastings' greatest desires was to purify the civil service, and he urged that the Company's servants should have high salaries that they might not be tempted to accept bribes, or engage in private trade. Though he could not carry this proposal, his trade reforms did much to remedy the greatest source of evil. He did away with the multifarious customhouses, and imposed a uniform duty of 2½ per cent., which was paid by native and European traders alike, and even by the Company's goods. Thus he abolished the freedom from duties, enjoyed by English traders, which had been the cause of so much trouble. Hastings abolished also the native agents, who had oppressed the local weaver by various abuses when purchasing goods for the Company, and allowed the Indian craftsmen to sell direct to the Company. This long list of reforms does not exhaust Hastings' activities, for he had another problem to settle : the Mogul, whom Clive had pensioned off at Allahabad, had now fallen into the hands of the Mahrattas, who set up this puppet emperor at Delhi again. Hastings promptly refused to pay the annual allowance now that the Mogul was in enemy hands, and when the Mahrattas threatened to seize Allahabad, he sold that district to the Nawab of Oudh, and also supported him in a war against his northern neighbours, the Rohillas. Hastings concluded a treaty with Oudh, by which that province became a vassal state, and he wished to extend this system. "You are already well acquainted," he wrote in 1777, "with the general system which I wish to be empowered to establish in India; namely, to extend the influence of the British nation to every part of India not too remote from their possessions, without enlarging the circle of their defence, or involving them in hazardous or indefinite engagements, and to accept of the allegiance of such of our neighbours as shall sue to be enlisted among the friends and allies of the King of Great Britain." But it was not till the time of Wellesley that such a policy could be carried out.

Contest with Council. 1774-1776.

Though the Regulating Act seemed to give Hastings greater power, it really limited his activities, for it saddled him with an independent council which could control his policy. He became Governor-General in 1774, and for the first two years of his government under the Act he found himself constantly opposed by his council, of whom the most factious was Philip Francis, the writer of the Letters of Junius. The council undid much of the good work of the last years, and reversed Hastings' policy in many cases; they encouraged accusations against the Governor, and treated the most violent charges as if they were already proved, indeed it was only his devotion to the work of reform which kept Hastings at his post during these "two years of anguish."

The death of one of his counsellors in 1776 gave Hastings control of his policy once more, by means of his casting vote, but he had little time now to think of reforms, for the rest of his governorship was a period of war. Hastings had nominal control of the native policy of the other Presidencies, but his power was really small, and they each succeeded by blunder and mismanagement in involving him in war. In the west, Bombay had in 1775 rashly concluded a treaty with a claimant to the Peshwaship, and this precipitated the long-threatened struggle with the Mahrattas. Hastings condemned in scathing words the policy of Bombay. "The first hostilities against the Mahrattas commenced unknown and unsuspected by our government, and had not even the shadow of a plea to justify them." After an uneasy peace, which was repudiated by the Directors, the war began again in 1778, and dragged on for several years, until the outbreak of a new war in the south forced Hastings to conclude a peace in 1782 which left matters as they were. The question whether the Mahrattas or the British were to be the paramount power in India had yet to be fought out.

War period. 1776-1785.

(1) Mahratta war. 1777-1782.

The hapless struggle of England against her revolted colonies had led to war with France in 1778, and Hastings feared lest French influence should organise once more a great alliance in India. Meanwhile, the Government of Madras had been busy making money by dishonest means instead of attending to the business of the Company; they even imprisoned a new Governor who proved too inquisitive about their evil ways. Thus the ambitious Nizam of Hyderabad was able to mature his plans without interruption: he allied himself secretly with the Mahrattas, and with Hyder Ali, the Mohammedan ruler of Mysore, and planned to drive the English into the sea. In 1780 Hyder Ali burst into the Carnatic, captured Arcot, and even threatened Madras.

(2) War in the South: Hyderabad and Mysore. 1780-1784.

It was a dangerous moment for Hastings: the British were at war with all the chief powers in India, a great expedition was preparing in France to aid his enemies, while England was much too busy to send him any help. Hastings acted with energy and decision; his diplomacy succeeded in dividing the Mahrattas and concluding with them the Peace of 1782. In the Carnatic

(3) The French in India. 1782-1783.

his generals won victories over Hyder Ali, which even the arrival of the French admiral, de Suffren, was unable to reverse. For eighteen months the French and English fleets struggled for supremacy off the coasts of India and Ceylon, and it was not till the arrival of a second English fleet late in 1783 that the command of the sea was definitely regained. Meanwhile the Dutch had thrown in their lot against England, and had quickly lost most of their Eastern stations, including Trincomalee in Ceylon. Thus, when the long-expected reinforcements under de Bussy managed to escape the English fleets and arrive in 1783, the great opportunity had passed. The war ended with an unsatisfactory treaty signed with Tipu of Mysore, Hyder Ali's son, in March, 1784. "The valour of others acquired, I enlarged and gave shape and consistency to the dominion which you hold there; I preserved it." Such is Hastings' summary of his work in India during these eventful years.

Treaty of Mangalore. 1784.

Warren Hastings returned to England in 1785 to "a life of impeachment." In 1788 he was impeached on numerous charges of extortion and misgovernment, brought by his old enemy, Philip Francis, and pushed by the Whigs largely for political reasons. The bitter eloquence of Burke, who led the attack, has given the trial too large a place in the story of Hastings, for we are apt to forget his work of organisation and defence in India, and think only of the charges brought against him. Historians have differed to this day as to the accuracy of some of the charges, for most were withdrawn, but all now recognise his greatness as an Indian administrator. After a trial of over seven years, Warren Hastings was acquitted, and when, many years later, he appeared to give evidence in an inquiry before Parliament, the whole House rose and stood bareheaded as a mark of respect to a great man, who had wrought and suffered much for his country.

Impeachment of Hastings. 1788.

Thus the Regulating Act had proved a failure: the continual friction between the Governor-General and his council had nearly paralysed government, while the control of Calcutta over the other Presidencies was only nominal, and this had led to disastrous wars. Even Parliament's control over the Company needed strengthening: in 1782 the House of Commons had ordered the recall of Hastings, and though the Court of Governors had agreed, the Court of Proprietors (or Shareholders) had reversed the decision, and so he had remained in India. Thus, when the Company's charter came up for renewal in 1783, there was keen discussion as to what new conditions should be imposed. Fox had a scheme for the nomination of all political officers by a Commission, which was to be appointed in the first place by Parliament, but afterwards by the Crown: most people, however, feared that this was merely a gift of vast patronage to Fox and his friends, and the Bill was thrown out by the Lords. The Coalition ministry fell, William Pitt came into office, and next year passed his India Act, under whose regulations the Company continued to exist until its final dissolution. Pitt wished to leave the Company free as a trading institution, but to bring its political activities under the close control of Parliament; to this end, the Act established a Board of Control under a President, who was a Minister of the Crown. The Company had to submit to the Board all letters received from India, and were not allowed to send away any letters until approved by the Board. Thus the Company soon became little more than a machine by which the Board controlled the government of India. To prevent the clash between the governor and council, the number of counsellors was reduced to three, while, a little later (1793), the governor was even empowered to act contrary to the decision of the majority of his council, provided he made a formal minute of his reasons. Two sections of great importance were included in the Act: further extension of British power, or treaties implying assistance to native princes were forbidden, because "to pursue schemes of conquest and extension of dominion in India, are measures repugnant to the wish, the honour and policy of this nation"; and a strict inquiry into the land and revenue system of Bengal was ordered. We must now see in what way these instructions were carried out.

Fox's India Bill, 1783.

Pitt's India Act, 1784.

Lord Cornwallis went to India as Governor-General in 1786: he was chosen as a great and independent nobleman, who had not been through the mill of the Indian service, and so would come unprejudiced to the task of carrying out the principles laid down in the new Act. His great work was the "Permanent Settlement" of Bengal, by which he made a final assessment for all time of the amount to be paid in taxes by the farmers of Bengal. An English landlord himself, he could neither understand nor appreciate the Bengal system by which the zemindars were merely hereditary tax-collectors, and the ryots practically tenants of the State, though tenants with the security of very lengthy possession. Thinking the British system ideal, Cornwallis, by his settlement, made the zemindars into landlords, thus leaving the ryots at their mercy, while, by fixing the taxes permanently, he deprived the State of any share in the increased value which land might have as the country developed. This plan has led to much discussion: it has been praised by some for protecting the tenant against the state, and condemned by others for creating a landlord class, but when other parts of India came under British rule it was not followed, and a system of periodic reassessments was adopted instead. Such, then, was Cornwallis' interpretation of his instructions to reorganise the revenue of Bengal: we must now examine his attempts to carry out a policy of non-intervention.

Cornwallis. 1786–1793.

(1) Permanent settlement of Bengal.

The trouble came from Tipu of Mysore. He was a violent and ambitious man, and, despite his defeat by Warren Hastings, determined to extend his power and his territory. He openly threw off all allegiance to the phantom authority of the Mogul, and assumed the title of Sultan. A bigoted persecutor, he forced great numbers of his Hindu subjects to become Mohammedans, and finally he determined to challenge the power of the British, and began an attack on the state of Travancore, which had but recently been guaranteed by the Company. This was an insult which could not be overlooked, and Cornwallis was forced to act: he tried at first to settle the matter by negotiation, and, when this failed, he determined on war. The Governor-General now recognised the dangers of the policy of non-intervention: it had "the unavoidable inconvenience of

(2) Difficulty of Non-intervention.

our being constantly exposed to the necessity of commencing a war, without having previously secured the assistance of efficient allies." Bound as he was by Act of Parliament not to make alliances, Cornwallis got round the difficulty by making a treaty which should end on the conclusion of the war. Thus he formed the triple alliance between the Company, the Nizam, and the Peshwa, though the latter was very slow in sending help. Tipu was beaten, and, besides an indemnity, he was forced to cede territory to the British: on the west a strip of land which shut him off from the sea, on the east a block of inland territory, which gave the Company the control of the passes leading from the highlands of Mysore down to the protected state of the Carnatic. It was hoped that this isolation of Mysore would make Tipu powerless for the future, for both the Peshwa and the Nizam also gained territory at his expense.

Thus Cornwallis had been forced by circumstances to abandon the official policy of non-intervention, and to substitute a policy of the balance of power. But, when as his successor there was appointed a scrupulous and successful servant of the Company, Sir John Shore, non-intervention was tried once again. Shore merely carried out instructions: he was not sufficiently bold or far-seeing to develop an independent policy such as was needed in India at the time.

Sir John Shore. 1793-1798.

The triple alliance had only provided for mutual defence against Tipu, and when, in 1795, the Peshwa turned against the Nizam, Shore stood by as a spectator, despite the Nizam's appeals for help. The Mahratta confederacy made short work of their enemy, and, by the Treaty of Kurdhla, seized vast territories and forced a heavy indemnity upon their foe.

A return was now made to the policy of sending as Governor-General an independent statesman, and not a servant of the Company: a good man was needed for the post, and the choice fell upon Lord Wellesley. The new Governor-General, who took with him to India his younger brother Arthur, afterwards the Duke of Wellington, was an Irishman possessed of great ability and still greater self-confidence. Though only thirty-seven

Lord Wellesley. 1798-1806.

when he came to India, Wellesley had already distinguished himself in public life, and he threw himself energetically into the task which now faced him. The seven years of his governorship were, for good or ill, to revolutionise the position of the British in India.

The position of affairs in India was difficult, for the British had lost prestige during the governorship of Shore, and were accused of deserting an ally in time of need. The Mahrattas were now the strongest native power in India, but the strength of their loose confederacy was always limited by the internal quarrels of their different chiefs. The four most important rulers were the northern chieftains, Sindhia, Holkar, Bhonsla, and Gaekwar, and of these Sindhia was at the moment quite the strongest. He had succeeded in gaining control over the aged Shah Alam, and thus the shadowy power of the Mogul was used in favour of this chieftain. But his power stretched still further, for he had complete control of the Peshwa also, and it looked as if Sindhia would now make the Peshwa a puppet ruler, just as the Peshwas had done to the descendants of the great Shivaji. Since their defeat of the Nizam, the Mahratta schemes knew no bounds, and they revived old claims to "chouth," or blackmail, over a large part of India. The struggle between the Mahrattas and the Company could not be long delayed.

Position in India.

In the south, Tipu, though beaten by Cornwallis, was dreaming of revenge. He had reorganised his army, and built it up on modern lines with the help of French officers. He even entered into relations with the French governor of Mauritius, and received a body of French troops. This aspect of the situation was what alarmed Wellesley most. England was now plunged into the long war with revolutionary France: Bonaparte had sailed for the Eastern Mediterranean in 1798, and Nelson had sought to catch him in vain. Bonaparte in Egypt was a constant threat to India, and the most alarming rumours spread throughout the country. Indeed, French influence was strong in India at this time, and Bonaparte dreamed of re-creating a French power in the country once again. "Citoyen Tipoo," with his tree of Liberty and his membership of the Jacobin club, was quickly raising a French state in the centre of India, while the Nizam, and also the Mahrattas, had French soldiers to train their armies, and doubtless to lead them against the British. Lastly, there was the bad position into which the British power had fallen: constant changes of policy had discredited the Company altogether. The turning-point had now been reached; either Britain must be the paramount power in India, or she must remain a mere trading company paying blackmail to robber chieftains, and existing practically on sufferance.

This was the position as it appeared to Wellesley, and he set himself to deal with the situation. The most necessary thing to be done was to expel the French agents and their troops, and to prevent their gaining influence in future; this was to be brought about by negotiation, or by the sword. But Wellesley's policy went further: he set out deliberately to make Britain the paramount power in India. This he did partly by annexations and partly by a series of subsidiary alliances. Such alliances had existed before, but Wellesley revised the old agreements, and arranged similar alliances with a number of other states. He tried to bring the whole of India within this system, and practically succeeded. Although differing in some details, the main principle of these alliances was the same. The native state remained independent in its internal affairs, but its foreign relations were controlled by the Company. It received a body of the Company's troops, for whose pay it was responsible, and a portion of land was usually handed over to the Company to provide this allowance. This policy of subsidiary alliances marks an important step in the development of British dominion in India, for the relations between the native states and the British Raj to-day are very similar to those introduced by Wellesley.

Wellesley's plans.

Wellesley had not been long in India before he realised that Tipu was the most dangerous enemy, and so he determined to deal with him first. He aimed at reviving Cornwallis' Triple Alliance, and persuaded the Nizam to dismiss the French officers and their soldiers, and to receive instead a body of English troops. This success was not repeated with the Mahrattas, for

War with Tipu of Mysore. 1799.

they had large claims against the Nizam and were suspicious of the new alliance between him and the Company. Meanwhile, Tipu refused to abandon his French alliance. Mysore was invaded from both sides, British armies moving from Bombay and from Madras, and finally in May, 1799, the capital of Seringapatam was stormed, and Tipu himself was among the slain. This was a great victory, for Wellesley had succeeded in reviving the old alliance, and had destroyed the great power of the south which had threatened the Company for so long. The Governor-General was not the man to underestimate the value of his achievements, and he wrote home to his friends openly hinting that he should receive some startling honour. What he wished for was a Dukedom, what he received was the title of Marquis in the Irish peerage : he was furiously angry, and scoffed at this "double-gilt potato," as he called his new title. But his friends wrote to congratulate him, and to beg for souvenirs from Tipu's palace.

Settlement of Southern India.

Tipu's death was fortunate for Wellesley, for it gave him an opportunity to recast southern India according to his own ideas. Mysore lost a large portion of territory, and a descendant of the old Hindu rulers, whom Hyder Ali had expelled, was set upon the throne. The new rajah willingly made a subsidiary treaty with the Company. The lands taken from Mysore were divided among the conquerors : the southern went to the British, the northern were given to the Nizam for the moment, and some were even offered as bribes to the Mahrattas, though they were not accepted. Meanwhile Wellesley had decided to deal strongly with the Carnatic ; for a long time its ruler, the Rajah of Arcot, had been dependent upon the Governor of Madras, but when Seringapatam fell letters were found there which proved that the rajah had been plotting with Tipu against the British. The rajah had been constantly in arrears with his payments of tribute, and his frequent borrowings from the officials and other Europeans of Madras had led to grave scandals in the government of the Presidency. Wellesley determined to solve the problem by annexing the Carnatic : its rajah was pensioned off, and the land came directly under the rule of the Company. By these arrangements, the whole of southern India was subordinated to the Company, either directly or by subsidiary alliances.

Wellesley continued his policy by negotiating a subsidiary treaty with the Nizam, which guaranteed him from attack by his recent enemies the Mahrattas. To pay for the troops stationed in his territory the Nizam agreed to return to the Company his share of the Mysore lands, and he was the more ready to do this as he had never been able properly to establish his power over them, or to collect his taxes there. In the north a similar policy was carried out with Oudh: here there were constant threats of invasion by the Afghan King Zeman Shah, and the Company was forced to keep a large army in Oudh for its defence, but the nawab's native levies were a continual menace, for they were ill-disciplined and untrustworthy. By the new treaty the border territories of Oudh were ceded to the Company for the support of its troops. Subsidiary alliances were also made with some of the small Rajput states beyond the River Jumna.

Subsidiary alliances.

Wellesley was now faced with the Mahratta problem. He had made several attempts to negotiate a treaty with the Peshwa, but so far he had failed. Now a lucky chance enabled him to carry through his plan. The constant quarrels within the Mahratta confederacy forced the Peshwa to fly in 1802 for refuge to Bassein near Bombay. Here Wellesley was able to come to an understanding with the homeless fugitive, and by the Treaty of Bassein the Peshwa made the usual agreement to maintain a subsidiary force and to cede certain lands for its pay. But this treaty could only become effective when the Peshwa was in power once again, and so the Company proceeded to instal their vassal in his capital of Poona.

The Mahrattas.

The Mahratta chieftains looked on at this game with distrust; they saw their nominal chief a vassal of the British power, but they did not intend to follow in his steps. The Gaekwar indeed had already accepted such an alliance, but Sindhia and Bhonsla laid their heads together and plotted to defeat this new policy, while the Peshwa, now he was safely at Poona again, begged them to save him from his new friends. Holkar, the other chieftain, had but recently been at bitter enmity with Sindhia, and for the moment took no part in the game; he amused himself instead by sending marauding expeditions into the territories of his neighbours. Wellesley knew what was afoot, and was alarmed at the French battalions in Sindhia's army. The Peace of Amiens (1801–1803) was known to be but a hollow affair, and Wellesley on his own responsibility had suspended the restoration of the French factories he had seized: news of the outbreak of war was expected by every ship, and once again there were rumours that Napoleon was planning the invasion of India. Meanwhile, Bhonsla and Sindhia had joined forces, and their refusal of Arthur Wellesley's request that they should retire to their own territories was a declaration of war. In the north General Lake marched straight from Oudh on Delhi; Sindhia's French battalions were destroyed, and the feeble old man who bore the burden of the past glories of the Grand Mogul changed masters once again. The southern armies met at last at Assaye (September, 1803) in the north of the Nizam's territories, where Arthur Wellesley with less than five thousand men defeated a Mahratta army of fifty thousand. The campaign was quickly over, and the Mahratta chieftains suing for peace. This was given them on the usual terms: Sindhia and Bhonsla made subsidiary alliances and surrendered a portion of their territory, and thus Delhi passed into British hands. But Wellesley was not destined to leave India at peace: Holkar, who had kept himself out of the recent quarrel, now made arrogant claims to levy blackmail from British vassals. He succeeded in defeating a British army, and for a moment even seized Delhi, but it was a new Governor-General who had to settle with this adventurer, for Wellesley had been recalled.

Mahratta War. 1803–1804.

The vigorous policy which Wellesley had carried out had long alarmed the Directors. Though at times they had agreed with him in particular cases, they endeavoured to control his plans. This to a man of Wellesley's stamp was an impossible situation: how dare a body of merchants in London attempt to dictate to him, a nobleman, a man on the spot and able to see and understand the needs of the situation? Wellesley's feeling on this matter is well shown in a letter written in

June, 1804, where he begs for "a full disclosure to Parliament of every act of my administration, and of every proceeding of the Court of Directors since I have had the misfortune to be subjected to the ignominious tyranny of Leadenhall Street." That "most loathesome den of the India House," as Wellesley rather impolitely described his masters' office, was destined to have the last word. In 1805 the Directors censured Wellesley for disobedience of the Court's orders and for acting in the greatest affairs without the sanction of the Government at home: they also condemned his lavish expenditure of money.

Wellesley resigns. 1805.

After this Wellesley could do nothing but resign, and he left India in August, 1805. His work was unfinished, for some of the Mahrattas were still in arms, and further campaigns were needed before that

INDIA IN 1805.

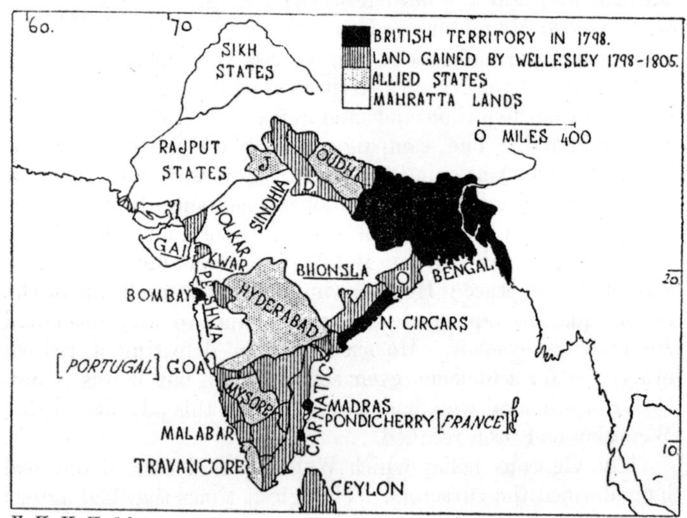

E. H. H. H. del.

J = Jaipur. *D = Doab.* *O = Orissa.*

The names of the Mahratta chieftains who had accepted subsidiary alliances are underlined.

problem was really settled. But the greatness of Wellesley's work can easily be seen if the position of India in 1805 is compared with the state of affairs when he arrived in 1797. It was only forty-five years since Clive's first campaign and the beginning of the Company's authority as a political body, and yet in that short time practically the whole of India had become dependent on the Company. In this great transformation Wellesley had played by far the largest part.

For some eight years after Wellesley left India the policy of non-intervention was carefully followed by successive governors: the treaties with the Rajput states were annulled, and for a time there was even talk of giving up all Wellesley's gains during the Mahratta war. Though this was never done, the change from Wellesley's policy was so marked that every independent ruler raised claims against the British power, and demanded the restoration of territory that had been ceded. This new policy was regarded as a sign of British weakness, and the refusal to intervene to help states as had been promised caused much dissatisfaction.

Reaction from Wellesley's policy. 1806–1813.

This policy came to an end with Lord Hastings, who though he came out to India a confirmed opponent of Wellesley's plans, soon found himself convinced that there would be no peace in India until Britain stood at the head of a league of all the native states. The first trouble came from the north. The little state of Nepal, among the lofty foothills of the Himalayas, was inhabited by sturdy Gurkhas who had conquered the country some fifty years before, and were now busily annexing the northernmost villages of British territory. Remonstrances proved useless, and in 1814 after some reverses the British managed to fight their way into the heart of the country. The Gurkhas were forced to cede a small strip of territory, including Simla, which has since become the summer residence of the Viceroy. Since then there have been good relations between Nepal and the British, and some of the best regiments of the Indian army are recruited from among the sturdy, short-legged Highlanders of Nepal.

Lord Hastings. 1814–1823.

(1) Nepal War. 1814–1816.

A more difficult problem had to be settled in dealing with the Pindharies. These people were marauding bands of freebooters, composed of low-caste or broken men from all parts of India, who joined in mounted robber gangs to plunder the more peaceful villages under British protection. Although not definitely part of the Mahratta armies, they generally made their headquarters in the Mahratta states, whence just before harvest they would swoop down on the luckless villages, to plunder, burn, destroy, and carry off their spoil before news of their deeds could bring vengeance down upon their heads. Hastings determined to stamp out this pest, but he knew that the Peshwa and Sindhia looked on them with friendly eyes, for though the Pindharies might ravage a Mahratta village or two, they would prove useful allies if trouble broke out with the British. Hastings knew the Mahratta princes were plotting against him, but he managed to frighten them into giving him help. Starting with a large army from Madras, he drove the Pindharies northward out of their favourite haunts, and meeting them with a second army from Bengal succeeded in stamping them out, once and for all.

(2) War against Pindharies. 1816–1817.

The destruction of the Pindharies was followed almost at once by the last war with the Peshwa. The Mahratta schemes, though checked by Hastings' policy, were not completely foiled. The Peshwa had increased his army pretending that he was going to help against the Pindharies, but when he saw his chance he attacked a British force. All his plans fell through; the assistance promised by the other Mahratta states failed him, and the Peshwa found himself a fugitive. Hastings had now completed Wellesley's task, he had the Mahratta states at his feet, and he determined to make a final settlement. The lands of the Peshwa were annexed, and the title itself abolished. Thus Hastings destroyed the centre around which all the Mahratta schemes had been woven: there was no longer a chieftain to whom the Mahratta princes owed loyalty and obedience. The other three Mahratta princes, who had either helped the Peshwa with their armies or had only been prevented by British action, were allowed to keep their lands, but their treaties of alliance were revised. Thus by 1818 the British controlled the whole of India except the North-West Territories beyond the River Indus.

(3) Mahratta War. 1817–1818.

Hastings' Mahratta settlement. 1818.

BOOKS.—See note to Chapter IV. Macaulay's *Essay on Clive* may be read, but his *Warren Hastings* is a bitter partisan attack, not an historical statement. G. B. Malleson, *Clive*, W. H. Hutton, *Wellesley* [Rulers of India], and A. Lyall, *Warren Hastings* [English Men of Action] are useful biographies. A. D. Innes, *A Short History of the British in India*, is a text-book, well supplied with sketch maps, that deals chiefly with the period 1760-1853.

1756. Black Hole of Calcutta.
1773. Lord North's Regulating Act.
1774-1785. Warren Hastings Governor-General.
1784. Pitt's India Act establishes Board of Control.
1786-1793. Cornwallis Governor-General. (Permanent Settlement of Bengal.)
1798-1805. Wellesley Governor-General.

CHAPTER VIII

The New Colonial Policy

WE have traced the way in which the seeds of a new Empire were sown by Britain after the disaster of the American Revolution, and we must now see how that new Empire developed. The year 1815 is an important turning-point, for it left Britain supreme at sea, but face to face once more with all those problems which she had failed to solve in dealing with the first colonies. The Empire was still bound together by the old ideal of exclusive trade, secured by the Navigation Laws and a system of preferential tariffs, while the colonies were still governed by the Colonial Office. Most of the American colonies, however, had some form of local Parliament, and it was in Canada that the great contest was to be fought out: the Cape and New South Wales were as yet too unimportant to have local Parliaments, the first a captured post and the second a mere convict station. During the nineteenth century the Empire divides itself into two quite distinct parts: the Dominions, where the government is modelled on the lines of the English constitution, and men rule themselves under a system of responsible government,

The "New" Empire in 1815.

and the dependent Empire, which consists of colonies ruled autocratically by their governors under the control of the Colonial Office. This division is a natural one, for the Dominions are countries with a temperate climate, where white men live in great numbers and make their homes, while the dependent Empire consists chiefly of tropical lands with a large native population ruled by a few white men who always look to England as their home, where they hope to spend the evening of their life.

Growth of responsible government inevitable.

Thus we may say that the growth of a responsible government in the Dominions was inevitable, for it is inconceivable that large numbers of Britons abroad would consent to live under a system of government which they had long rejected at home. But the way in which responsible government came was not inevitable. It might have come with civil war and another breach of Imperial unity, as came American Independence; but instead it came by a series of compromises and a system of give and take, for which we must give credit to the wisdom of British statesmen and to the moderation of Britons beyond the seas.

At first the outlook was not good. In 1794, at the beginning of the great war with France, the new office of Secretary for War was created, and the colonies were soon allotted to its care; thus it was not until 1854, at the time of the Crimean War, that a separate Secretary of State for the Colonies was created. After the American disaster, the Colonial Office became essentially bureaucratic and overbearing, and its control of colonial business was often influenced by party interests in England and by political jobbery. The title of "Mr. Mother Country" was coined to fit this interfering administrative system, where even the very colonial governors were appointed by influence. "The patronage of the Colonial Office is the prey of every hungry department of our Government. On it the Horse Guards quarters its worn-out general officers as governors: the Admiralty cribs its share; and jobs which parliamentary rapacity would blush to ask from the Treasury are perpetrated with impunity in the silent realm of Mr. Mother Country." The manner of dealing with colonial problems, too, was most unsatisfactory: the authority

Over-centralisation of Colonial Office.

of Parliament or of the Secretary was great in theory, but in practice all power fell into the hands of the little group of bureaucrats "in the large house which forms the end of that cul-de-sac so well known by the name of Downing Street." Though "the Office" might be the only place which knew anything about the colonies, its attempt to regulate their affairs minutely was bound to end in failure. The system by which Crown lands were given away, often in vast grants, for a nominal sum, was one of the causes of the great want of labour in the colonies: land was so cheap that every one could become a landowner at once.

Wasteful land grants.

It was fortunate that about this time there arose a number of brilliant men who gave much thought to colonial matters, and fought against this dangerous policy of over-centralisation, striving to set up a more liberal system in its place. The movement for political reform in England, which forced the Reform Act of 1832 through Parliament, had its influence on men's ideas about the colonies. Lord Durham, an extreme Whig who quarrelled with the leaders of his party because of his radical views, was a champion of further reform, and he it was who drew up the great report which recommended responsible government for Canada. Friends of his were such men as Charles Buller, who made the sarcastic attack on "Mr. Mother Country," and Molesworth, who declared "this country should interfere as little as possible in the internal affairs of its colonies." Another famous man was Gibbon Wakefield, who wrote the *Art of Colonisation*, and set forth a scheme of emigration. Labour was unobtainable in the colonies, he declared, because land was so absurdly cheap. To remedy this he proposed that all Crown lands should be sold at a fixed price, so that new settlers should be forced to work for a few years before earning enough money to set up as farmers themselves. With the money so obtained the Government should establish a fund to assist emigration to the colonies, and so supply the much-needed labourers. Though Wakefield's scheme never worked quite satisfactorily, it marks an important step in the theory of colonisation, and the practice, which had sprung up

Imperial statesmen: Lord Durham.

Gibbon Wakefield: "Art of Colonisation."

after 1815, of shipping emigrants overseas haphazard to relieve the distress at home, was much improved and altered. But Wakefield was a practical man as well as a theorist: he went to Canada with Durham: he floated a company to settle South Australia, and then another to send emigrants to New Zealand, and it was very largely due to his exertions that a reluctant British Government was forced to recognise that island as a colony.

There was another movement at work which had then, and still retains, a great influence on the development of the Empire. The growth of a strong humanitarian feeling, at first among the Quakers and other religious bodies, was steadily going on. One of the first objects of their attack was the iniquity of the Slave Trade, and after some eighteen years' strenuous effort the Society for the Abolition of the Slave Trade scored a success by Act of Parliament in 1807. Ever since, Britain has been foremost in suppressing the traffic in slaves throughout the world. Not content with their partial victory, the humanitarians set themselves to work for the abolition of slavery itself: a vigorous campaign was carried on by means of pamphlets and public meetings, but the movement was met by the determined opposition of the slave-owners. Two places were particularly affected by the proposal: the West Indies, where the great sugar-plantations were cultivated by slave labour, and the Cape, where most of the Dutch farmers possessed slaves. The opposition in England was carefully organised by the West Indian planters, but even their arguments failed at last, and in 1834 slavery was abolished throughout the British Empire. The State paid £20,000,000 to the owners of the slaves as compensation, but though this was thought a generous act by many, it was barely half the value of the slaves, and the owners declared that they were ruined. In the West Indies a system of apprenticeship was established as a step between slavery and freedom, but this half-measure was vigorously denounced and soon broke down, and the planters found it almost impossible to get the freed men to work on the plantations for wages, and the speedy

The humanitarian movement.

Slave Trade abolished. 1807.

Abolition of slavery. 1834. Its results.

abolition of preferential sugar duties nearly ruined the islands. In the Cape, the effects were still more important: a little over a million pounds was allotted to that country, though the slaves were valued at three times that amount, and many of the Dutch farmers lost heavily through the method of payment. Angry and disgusted at an interfering country which would not allow them to live under their old customs, many Boers decided to go away and to seek new homes for themselves up country. So began the Great Trek which led to the founding of the two Boer republics. Thus, though the abolition of slavery was a reform long overdue, and on the part of its advocates was an honest attempt to right a most grievous wrong, yet some of its immediate effects were disastrous.

Continued effect of humanitarian ideas.

The influence of the humanitarian movement did not end with the abolition of slavery. All through the century the British Government has been subjected to pressure from religious bodies, missionary societies, and from other humanitarian associations, all striving for the protection of native races from the exploitation of the white settler. As time went on similar pressure came from a different source, and the Labour Party took up the same attitude. Often the missionary has been at loggerheads with the settler or the local governor, while sometimes the ill-advised action of benevolent people at home has led to trouble in the colonies, but on the whole this humanitarian pressure has been a great blessing. It has forced the home government to stand forward definitely as the protector of native races, and it has secured that, throughout the length and breadth of the British Empire, grave scandals of cruelty or exploitation have been generally avoided.

We shall see the same movement influencing British action in India, modifying the powers of the great East India Company, introducing equal law for all, fostering education, encouraging medical charities, and finally taking over the government of the whole of India, with the fixed idea of maintaining peace and good government for the benefit of all. Thus gradually there arose a new conception of Empire: instead of regarding the tropical colonies as mere trading-posts, where money was to be made in any fashion, men saw in them great tracts of land where the white man was morally bound to maintain law and order, to put down the grosser and more evil customs, and to see that trade was carried on fairly and without harm to the native. This was "the white man's burden."

The Liberal movement.

The development of responsible government in the colonies was due to the growth of liberal ideas in Britain after the Napoleonic wars, and to the growing claim of the Canadians to control their own affairs. It was but natural that Canada should be the battle-ground of these new ideas, for Canada was the most well-developed of the colonies. When in 1837 a rebellion had broken out, Lord Durham was sent as governor with large powers and with instructions to report on the whole problem. Durham's Report, presented in 1839, is the most famous enunciation of the theory of responsible government for the colonies. "I rely on the efficacy of reform in the constitutional system by which these colonies are governed," he wrote, "for the removal of every abuse in their administration which defective institutions have engendered." Responsible government meant that the royal governor, like the King, should only chose as his ministers those men who had the confidence of the local Parliament, instead of anyone he pleased: otherwise, as Durham saw, "representative government" was merely a cause of endless strife. This change could be easily brought about; it merely needed a definite order to the governor, and it was done, but it would have vast results. Instead of constant disputes between the assembly and the governor, dissatisfaction would be vented on the local minister, and Imperial ties would be saved the continuous friction of discontent. But even Durham thought that there were some things over which the Imperial Government should keep a tight control; foreign affairs, the regulation of external trade, and the administration of the Crown lands.

Lord Durham's Report, 1839, advises "Responsible Government."

These proposals of Lord Durham, simple as they might seem to carry out, really involved a radical change in the whole conception of the relations between the colony and the home country. The Imperial Government only gradually accepted Durham's doctrine, and it was by a series of despatches and instructions that responsible government was introduced into the various Dominions. Thus, in the Dominions, as in Britain, responsible government rests on custom and common sense, and not upon Acts of Parliament, and this is just as well, for "responsible government" is a hard thing to define, and legal definitions always limit the thing they are trying to explain. Just because it rests on custom alone, responsible government has been able to develop, and is still developing every day. Of those things which Lord Durham considered the Imperial Government should still control, lands and the regulation of trade have already been taken over by the Dominions, while their governments are obtaining an increasing influence in foreign affairs, though the need of a uniform policy makes the question of joint control a difficult problem. The system as it stands is an illogical system, but it has this advantage, it works. The success of responsible government in Canada was so great that it gradually became a panacea for all evils. After Australia had, with some hesitation, been given freedom to choose its own institutions in 1850, responsible government was almost forced on the Cape, where many of the colonists would have preferred to remain dependent on the home country for protection and for finance. Thus responsible government became the keyword of the white man's countries in the British Empire. Its greatest achievement was in South Africa, where the bold experiment was made of granting responsible government to the Orange Free State and the Transvaal in 1906, only five years after the Boer War. No experiment was ever more successful, for within three years the long-dreamt of Union of South Africa had become an accomplished fact.

Responsible government extended to other colonies.

There was yet another radical change in the relations between the colonies and the mother country, and this change was brought about by the growing power of new theories of political economy. Ever since Adam Smith had published his *Wealth of Nations*, in which he attacked the old system of regulating trade by navigation laws and tariff systems, the movement for free

The "Laissez Faire" Movement.

trade had been gaining ground. Men argued that if there were no artificial restrictions on trade the free play of competition would reduce prices, and thus force everything to be made or cultivated in the most economical way. These arguments appealed strongly to the British manufacturers, who were far ahead of the rest of the world with their new systems of factory machinery. They wished to see the price of corn reduced, the duties on raw material removed, and they hoped that the triumph of the new doctrine would open the markets of all the world to their goods, without the burden of a tariff. Thus the Manchester School fought hard for "Free Trade," but found themselves strongly opposed by the Tories, who foresaw that the triumph of such doctrines would mean the decline of agriculture, and a growing dependence on foreign countries for Britain's food supplies. The attack of the Free Traders threatened both the Corn Laws and the Sugar Duties, and in each case colonial interests were involved; for the tariff gave such preference to Canadian corn and British West Indian sugar that they had a large advantage in the British market. Those who opposed Free Trade argued that it would ruin Canada and the West Indies, and it would mean the break up of the Empire no longer surrounded by a tariff wall. They also declaimed loudly against allowing foreign slave-grown sugar to compete with the British sugar cultivated by free labour, though such arguments came ill from men who had but recently opposed the abolition of slavery. They were, however, fighting a losing battle; the argument of the Anti-Corn Law League carried great weight, and in 1846 the Corn Laws were swept away by Peel: the whole system of preferential tariffs also disappeared. At first there was great excitement in Canada, where men saw the United States shipping wheat to England to compete with their corn, while they themselves were still bound by the Navigation Laws which closed the St. Lawrence to all but British and colonial vessels. This grievance, however, was soon remedied, and in 1849 the Navigation Laws were repealed.

Arguments of Free Traders.

Opposition argument.

Repeal of Corn Laws. 1846.
Navigation Laws. 1849.

Now that the home government had been converted to the

new gospel, it determined to force that gospel on the colonies. Durham had considered it the duty of the Imperial Government to regulate colonial trade, while Lord Grey, Secretary of State from 1846 to 1853, declared: "It has always been held to be one of the principal functions of the Imperial Legislature and Government to determine what is to be the commercial policy of the Empire at large. . . . The common interest of all parts of that extended Empire requires that its commercial policy should be the same throughout its numerous dependencies."[1] Following this principle, Lord Grey prevented the colonies from adopting protective measures, and strove to enforce a genuine free trade throughout the Empire. But here the new economic doctrine was faced by the other principle of responsible government, and the latter won the day. Once again the struggle came to a head in Canada. In 1859 the Canadian Parliament passed a Bill increasing heavily a number of import duties. Lord Newcastle, the Secretary of State, regretted "that the experience of England, which has fully proved the injurious effect of the protective system . . . should be lost sight of." But the Canadian Government replied, justifying their bill, and declaring that they could not "waive or diminish the right of the people of Canada to decide for themselves both as to the mode and extent to which taxation shall be imposed." Thus another step was taken in the development of responsible government, and since then all the self-governing colonies have adopted a system of protection, but have generally conceded to the mother country treatment on the basis of the most favoured nation, although their goods compete in her market on equal terms with those from other countries.

Attempt to force Free Trade on Colonies.

Canadian tariff. 1859.

Thus by about 1860 all the old bonds of Empire seemed to have disappeared. Tariffs and Navigation Laws had gone, and with them the idea of a self-dependent Empire: in their place there stood Great Britain inviting commerce free from all the world, and her colonies gradually building tariff walls. The old system of

Position of Empire. 1860.

[1] Quoted by Egerton: "A Short History of British Colonial Policy."

centralised control had gone: Canada enjoyed responsible government, and was quickly widening the first meaning of that phrase. Australia had chosen the same system, while the Cape had representative institutions, and was fast following Canada on the path towards the same goal. The sight of these rapid changes staggered men, and they wondered where events were leading. It seemed to many that the Empire was fast breaking up, the old ties had gone, and at first few perceived those stronger ties which still held the Empire together. There were many who wished deliberately to hasten the process, and eagerly looked for the day when the colonies should "cut the painter" and set up as absolutely independent states. To the logical free trader, who often took nothing into consideration but abstract economic laws, the colonies were a mere encumbrance; since Britain had lost control of their financial policy, it was a nuisance to retain any connection with them at all. They would offer just as good markets if they were independent states, and Britain would prosper better, for there would be no risk of her having to spend money for their protection. Men of this school worked to bring about this end; they encouraged responsible government, not as the natural way to govern Britons overseas, but as the necessary step to the "hiving off" of the colony which they so much desired. The general belief was expressed by Sir F. Rogers, who was for long the Permanent Under-Secretary for the Colonies. "I had always believed," he wrote in later life, "that the destiny of our colonies is independence; and that in this point of view the function of the Colonial Office is to secure that our connection, while it lasts, shall be as profitable to both parties, and our separation, when it comes, as amicable as possible." Similar ideas made statesmen shun the undertaking of fresh burdens; followers of the Manchester School hated the idea of new tropical possessions, and much of the vaccillating policy in South Africa was due to the conflict between these ideas and the views of men on the spot.

Reaction against "Laissez Faire."

Events were at work, however, which were to alter the whole aspect of the colonial problem, and with the bid of Germany for colonial world-power, begun at the Berlin Conference of 1884, Britain began to understand that both dominions and tropical colonies were of greater use to her than she had realised.

We have been discussing ideas and their effects on the development of the Empire, but we must not lose sight of the influence of the great inventions which revolutionised industry and travel. When it took six months for a good ship to reach India, and several weeks to get across the Atlantic to the American colonies, it was very difficult for statesmen at home to keep in touch with what was going on abroad. But distance is only relative, and with the invention of steam, ships were no longer dependent on the chance of the winds, and the colonies were, for practical purposes, brought much closer to the home country. At the very time when the old system of Empire was breaking up, and the new ideas were getting to work, there were being founded, in London and Liverpool, those shipping companies which have bound the colonies yet closer to the Mother Country. The invention of electric telegraphy, too, did much to shorten distances: the first submarine cable was laid between England and France in 1851, but it was not till 1858 that communication was established with America, though after that progress was rapid, and British cables soon began to link the colonies with the Mother Country. Ashore the railway played a great part in developing the new countries, and in making possible the union of far distant settlements into one state. This is best seen in Canada, where Durham recommended the linking of the maritime provinces to Canada by a railway, while the price of British Columbia's agreement to join the Dominion in 1871 was the speedy completion of a railway to the Pacific Coast: thus the Canadian Pacific Railway became the spinal nerve of Canadian life. In South Africa, too, the need for a uniform railway system was one of the greatest forces which brought about the Union of 1909, while, in Australia, a great railway has just been finished to link Western Australia with the Eastern centres of civilisation. This gradual improvement of communications, both by sea and land, brought the various parts of the Empire closer together, and did much to remove misunderstandings and to secure unity of control over large territories. We must now

Improvement in communications.

trace the development of the Dominions, and see how they have prospered under the new conditions of responsible government.

BOOKS.—A. B. Keith, *Select Documents Illustrative of British Colonial Policy* [2 vols., World's Classics], is essential to the study of the development of the Dominions. C. H. Currey, *British Colonial Policy, 1783–1915*, is a handy little book which brings the story up to the Great War. Portions of G. Wakefield, *The Art of Colonisation*, should be read, and also Adam Smith, *Wealth of Nations* [Everyman], Book IV., Chapter VII., on "Colonies."

1776. Adam Smith's "Wealth of Nations."
1807. Abolition of Slave Trade.
1834. Abolition of Slavery.
1839. Lord Durham's Report on Canada.
1846. Repeal of Corn Laws.
1849. Repeal of Navigation Acts.

CHAPTER IX

Canada

When William Pitt passed his Canada Act in 1791, which established the provinces of Upper and Lower Canada, he had two aims in view. He hoped by separating the British and the French to do away with the constant friction between them, and he believed that the new constitution with its representative assembly would act as a safety-valve for discontent. In each of these aims he was disappointed, for in less than fifty years both of the provinces were in rebellion.

Canada Act, 1791.

The trouble in Quebec was racial rather than constitutional. Despite a liberal constitution, and the protection given to their language and religion, the French Canadians found that they had only the shadow of power, and not the real thing. The British lawyers and traders, who had come into the province to the cities of Quebec and Montreal, still remained there, and the Governor chose his ministers and nominated the members of his council from the British and not from the French inhabitants. This angered the French, and, urged by their priests, they began to draw together into a strong political party under the leadership of Papineau, who founded, in 1806, a newspaper called *Le Canadien*, with the object of binding the French together. In granting a constitution to the French Canadians, Pitt had tried a great experiment, for the French were not accustomed, as were the English, to the working of representative institutions. Soon after the war with the United States, the French party, predominant in the elective assembly, began to wage war against the British ascendancy in the council. Thus the racial quarrel took on a constitutional form, and the assembly strove to gain control of the "royal" revenues which were raised by authority of Acts of the Imperial Parliament, and to obtain the right of voting an annual budget. Papineau used violent language, and, after a bitter attack on the Governor, that officer refused to accept him as a Speaker of the House. In 1834 the assembly passed a series of resolutions, urging the need of an elective council, but a body of commissioners reported against this suggestion. The assembly then refused to renew an agreement with Upper Canada, by which the duties collected on the St. Lawrence were shared between the two provinces, and the Imperial Parliament was forced to step in and pass the necessary legislation. Feeling was now very high, and in 1837 a rebellion broke out under Papineau. This was soon suppressed after a little fighting, but Papineau became a national hero, and was hailed as a martyr who had suffered in the cause of constitutional reform.

Quebec: Racial Movement under Papineau.

Revolt of 1837.

Meanwhile, in Upper Canada, different causes had led to a similar result. Here there were not two nationalities to complicate the problem, and the colonists were accustomed to the use of representative institutions, for the loyalist settlers had shared in the government of their colonies before the Revolutionary War, while the newcomers from Britain found a miniature reproduction of what they were familiar with at home. But it was just between these newcomers and the loyalists that the trouble arose. All offices were held by a clique composed of the earliest settlers and their friends, the legislative council was packed by their nominees, and they absorbed the medical and legal professions. As new settlers arrived a reform party grew up under Mackenzie, an able but passionate Scotchman, who was ready to use every means to attain his ends. The reformers began to make themselves heard by founding newspapers and agitating in the assembly; they claimed that some of the land which Pitt had set apart for endowing the Protestant Church should be given to Scotch Presbyterian ministers, but this was opposed by the party in power, who were all supporters of the Church of England. The reformers also desired responsible government, and sent a deputation to England to urge their views on the Colonial Office (1832). Here a new and liberal policy was at work, and some reforms were promised, but the trouble was brought to a head by the indiscreet behaviour of the new governor, Sir Francis Bond Head. This man was entirely out of sympathy with the reformers, and, by representing to the Province that Mackenzie wished to join the United States, he succeeded in obtaining the election of an assembly favourable to the ruling clique.

Upper Canada. Mackenzie's Revolt. 1837.

Mackenzie was furious at this trickery and resorted to force, but here he quite misunderstood the feeling of the province: only a few of the reformers followed him, and when the rebellion broke out in 1837 it was promptly crushed, though for some time a filibustering war was carried on with the leaders who had fled across the American border.

Lord Durham governor. 1837.

Such were the circumstances under which Lord Durham was sent out as Governor-General, with instructions to report on the future constitution of Canada. Anxious to "know nothing of a British, a French, or a Canadian Party," and to prevent the bitter hatred caused by political executions, he granted a general amnesty, but deported certain rebel leaders to the Bermudas by his own proclamation. For this unconstitutional act he was attacked by political enemies in the House of Lords, and though an Act of Indemnity was passed, he immediately resigned and returned to England. Yet Durham had been long enough in Canada to study the situation carefully, and in his Report he pointed out two main causes of friction; the racial and the constitutional. In Quebec, Britain had deliberately allowed the French settlers to develop their nationality, and they were now threatening to oppress the British minority in that province. To deal with this difficulty, Durham proposed that the two provinces should be united, so that a definite British majority might be secured. "I entertain no doubt as to the national character which must be given to Lower Canada; it must be that of the British Empire, that of the majority of the population of British America, that of the great race which must in no long period of time be predominant over the whole North American Continent." The only solution of the constitutional problem was the grant of responsible government. "We are not now to consider the policy of establishing representative government in the North American colonies. That has been irrevocably done, and the experiment of depriving the people of their present constitutional power is not to be thought of. To conduct the government harmoniously in accordance with its established principle is now the business of its rulers; and I know not how it is possible to secure that harmony in any other way than by administering the government on those principles which have been found perfectly efficacious in Great Britain."

His Report. 1839.

(1) Union to absorb the French.

(2) Responsible government.

Of these two recommendations, the first was quickly adopted, though the second only came gradually. In 1840 Lord John Russell carried the Act of Reunion, which gave Canada a nominated council, and an elective assembly consisting of an equal number of members from each province. The English language only was to be used for official purposes. Responsible government, however, was not so easy to introduce: it was a veritable revolution, and it was difficult to see how a governor could play the part of a constitutional monarch, acting on the advice of his ministers, and yet pay attention to the instructions sent to him from the Colonial Office. For several years the governors were encouraged to maintain amicable relations with the leaders of the assembly, and yet to act independently when necessary, but this was a half measure which did not really solve

Act of Reunion, 1840.

the problem, and until it was solved there was always the possibility of grave trouble. It was Lord Elgin, Durham's son-in-law, who really introduced responsible government into Canada. The great test case was the Rebellion Losses Act of 1849, which gave compensation to all who had lost property during the rebellion of 1837. This Act caused a great outcry, the ultra-loyal party claiming that it gave subsidies to rebels, but Elgin felt it his duty to give the royal assent to the Act, since it had passed the Canadian Parliament. A violent riot ensued, Parliament House at Montreal was burnt, and Elgin's life was in danger, but his calm and dignified attitude created a great impression, and, since then, responsible government has been the unwavering practice of the Canadian constitution.

Lord Elgin. Rebellion Losses Bill, 1849.

Thus both of Durham's suggestions had been adopted, and responsible government proved a great success, but the attempt to break up the French party by uniting the provinces was a failure. Indeed, as time went on the French Canadians gained yet greater strength. They stood firm by their party leaders, cherishing their language, religion, and customs, and the French vote soon became all important in politics. Although the population of Upper Canada steadily increased, that province still had only the same number of representatives as Quebec, and any attempt to alter the proportions was opposed by the French. Politics gradually reached a deadlock: the balance of parties was so nice that one or two votes could oust a government, and this led to short-lived administrations, and a general stoppage of business. Statesmen sought for some solution of the problem, and this they found in a federal constitution.

Causes of the Federal Movement.

Other causes also drove men to wish for a federation. When Britain adopted Free Trade in 1846, the Canadians found the Americans competing with them there on equal terms, though the markets of the United States were closed to them by a tariff wall. A slump at once occurred in Canada; property fell in value, and men began to look with longing eyes on the excellent markets just over the border, and a movement for political annexation gained ground. Lord Elgin saw that economic distress was at the back of this movement, and in

1854 he succeeded in negotiating a Reciprocity Treaty, by which raw materials were admitted to either country duty free. As Canada produced much raw material needed by the States, this treaty was very useful to her, and trade at once revived. During the American Civil War, relations were very strained between the Canadian Government and the northern states, and at last in 1866, in anger at Britain's friendly attitude to the Confederates, the Federals repealed the Reciprocity Treaty. They hoped by this measure to force Canada to join the Union, and a bill to arrange this was actually introduced into the American Senate. But the repeal of the Reciprocity Treaty, hard as it hit Canada, had very different results from those which Americans expected. Far from driving Canada to join the Union, the fear of American aggression, and the desire to create an inter-provincial trade, gave additional strength to the federal movement. The Canadians believed that a federal state would be stronger in defence, while some looked yet further and hoped that the whole of the vast territories of the Hudson's Bay Company would be taken over by the new state.

Reciprocity Treaty. 1854.

In 1864 two leading statesmen, Sir John Macdonald and Sir George Cartier, a French-Canadian, formed a coalition government to draft and carry through a scheme of federation. While this matter was being discussed, they heard that the maritime provinces, who were cut off from Canada both economically, and by almost impassable forest land, were themselves considering the question of a local federation. The position of the maritime provinces had been prejudiced by the final settlement of a lengthy dispute concerning the boundary between New Brunswick and the State of Maine. The interpretation of the old Treaty of 1783 had long been in dispute, and affairs had come to such a pitch that the Government of Maine had seized on the disputed territory, and fighting had nearly broken out between the state and the colony. Finally in 1842 the question was dealt with by arbitration, and the Ashburton Treaty gave all the land under dispute to the States, much to the disgust of Canada. Thus the maritime provinces found themselves almost isolated from Canada by a great wedge of the state of

Coalition Government. 1864.

Maine. Fired by the idea of a larger union, the Canadian statesmen invited the maritime provinces to discuss the question with them, and this was done behind closed doors at the Quebec Conference of 1864. Since its sittings were secret, men could say what they really thought, instead of merely talking to the newspapers, and so after much discussion a plan of federation was agreed upon. The Parliament of Canada voted for the new scheme by large majorities, but the case was not the same in the maritime provinces; here the inhabitants feared that they might be swamped by their larger neighbours, and it took much persuasion and some parliamentary jugglery before New Brunswick and Nova Scotia were willing to accept the scheme. Even then little Prince Edward Island stood out for several years, while Newfoundland still remains outside the federation. A number of Canadian statesmen went to London to help in drafting the bill, and in 1867 the British North America Act was passed, and the Dominion of Canada came into being.

British North America Act, 1867.

Under the new constitution Canada itself was split up again into two parts, Ontario and Quebec, and these, with New Brunswick and Nova Scotia, formed the first four provinces of the Dominion. They were given their own local parliaments, which were competent to deal with certain local matters. Both in the province of Quebec, and in federal business generally, French and English were recognised as official languages, and all documents were to be printed in both: thus Durham's plan for absorbing the French had failed. To ensure better comuunication between the maritime provinces and Canada, an inter-colonial railway was begun, and though for many years it did not pay its way, this railway was the price of federation. In framing the Bill, the statesmen of Canada had the example of the United States before their eyes: they had just seen a disastrous war between the north and south over the question of slavery, and they judged that the individual states had too much power under the Constitution. Determined not to make a similar mistake, they limited the power of their provinces very carefully, and gave all the residue of authority to the Federal Parliament. This parliament was framed on the

The Federal Constitution.

English model—a Governor-General to represent the King, and two Houses. The assembly was elected, and the number of members was to be re-distributed after each census as the balance of the population altered. The Upper House, or Senate, instead of being elected as was the Senate of the United States, was nominated for life by the Governor-General. On the whole this has been an unsuccessful arrangement, for the nominations were used by party leaders as rewards for political service : the best men did not get into the Senate, and its influence and value was therefore very small. It was intended that this new constitution should be worked by the cabinet system, and with responsible government, but as usual nothing was said in the Act of Parliament about it. It was left free to develop as custom should show to be best.

Expansion of the Domininion. (I) Boundary fixed by Oregon Award. 1846.

Thus in 1867 there came into being the Dominion of Canada, and within four years it stretched right across the continent from ocean to ocean. Beyond the Great Lakes, and right away up to the Rockies, swept the country which belonged to the Hudson's Bay Company: beyond the Rockies was yet another settlement—British Columbia. The boundaries between these lands and the United States caused much dispute until they were finally settled. The United States based their case on the vague claims of the Spaniards to the Pacific lands of America, which the States had acquired in 1819. The Americans, who were just beginning to realise the great possibilities of their western territories, made vast claims to the north-west. "Fifty-four forty or fight" was the war-cry of the excited crowds, but saner counsels prevailed ; the matter was referred to arbitration, and in 1846 the line 49° north was accepted as the frontier.

In the early days the Hudson's Bay Company had to face the competition of the French Company, but every year when the warmth of the summer melted the ice, and ships were able to get through to York Factory on the Bay, they found a valuable cargo to take home. Even after the capture of Canada by the English the old Company still had a rival, for in 1783 a number of Scotch adventurers founded the North

L

West Company, with their headquarters on the St. Lawrence at Montreal. Making use of the numerous French and Indian half-breeds, who were born trappers, the North West Company was really a revival of the old French Company under another disguise. The new Company pushed its efforts far and wide, its forts and posts were planted on every important river, and and its servants did great work as explorers of the unknown west: the Fraser, the Thompson, and the great River Mackenzie, all recall the heroic deeds of dauntless explorers who pushed on yet further, crossed the barrier of the Rockies, and reached the Pacific. The competition between the two Companies became so keen that the old Company could scarce pay its dividends, while their servants came to blows when they met on expeditions. At last in 1821 the two Companies agreed to unite, and this new Company obtained a fresh charter, and set itself to make dividends once more. It had been the settled policy of the Companies not to speak of the great Lone Land in which they won their wealth, to discourage settlement, and to disparage the usefulness of the land itself. Despite this practice, stories of the great possibilities of the north-west leaked through to Canada, people began to grumble at the Company's monopoly, and to talk of uniting the whole of its territories to Canada, and in the British North America Act provision was made for accepting the land from the Company. This territory was not entirely without settlers, for when the old Company was hard put to it for funds, it had leased some land to the Earl of Selkirk, who had planted a colony of Scotchmen on the Red River, near where Winnipeg now stands. This settlement had many ill adventures, and was attacked by a rival party of French half-breeds, protégées of the North-West Company; but after the amalgamation the Red River settlement still continued. By 1869 Canada had agreed to buy out the Company's governmental rights, but to leave it as a trading concern. An Act was passed for the government of the territory when taken over, and surveyors were sent to examine and lay out the land. The French half-breeds had done their best to destroy the Red River settlement, they looked with suspicion on the new negotiations, and they realised that all possibility of a

(2) Hudson's Bay Company.

French-Canadian nation of the north-west would disappear if once British immigration began. The sight of the surveyors made them fear that they would be turned out of their lands, and they rose in revolt under the leadership of a fanatic named Louis Riel. For nearly a year Riel held his position, while the Canadian Government strove in vain to deal with the matter by fair words instead of by force, even going so far as to send for the Roman Catholic Archbishop Taché from the Vatican Council at Rome to plead with the rebels. At last a small expedition under Wolseley came down to the Red River; the rebels fled across the frontier, and the rebellion was at an end. Meanwhile, the Canadian Government had been listening to the grievance of the Red River settlers, and it was decided to admit them to the Dominion as the province of Manitoba, while the remainder of the Company's land was left for the present as the North West Territory, to be administered by the Lieutenant-Governor of Manitoba and a council.

Manitoba a province. 1871.

We have seen how the explorers of the North West Company pushed over the Rockies, and down to the Pacific, and how the boundary question between Canada and the United States was settled by arbitration. The development of British Columbia, however, was not due to the initiative of a far-reaching trading company, but to the discovery of gold. British Columbia had first been reached from the Pacific, and it was the energy of Captain Cook at the end of the eighteenth century that made the country known in England. Hence, when it was first settled, it was settled from the Pacific, for British Columbia and Canada are back to back: they have the huge Alpine range of the Rockies between them, and it is only the indomitable pluck of man and his engineering skill that have at last driven the railway through the mountains, and so linked those two very different countries together. At first British Columbia was merely administered as part of the Hudson's Bay Territory, but as settlers came pouring in with the rush for gold, the Imperial Government wished to obtain closer control over the country, and so in 1858 British Columbia became a Crown colony, ruled by a governor and nominated council. By 1871 arrangements

(3) British Columbia.

were made for its incorporation in the Dominion. The bargain which induced the new province to join the Dominion was the promise that within two years a railway should be completed between Canada and Vancouver. This was eventually done, after many difficulties; but for a long time the construction and management of the Canadian Pacific Railway was one of the most bitterly disputed questions of Canadian politics. Thus by 1871 the Dominion stretched across the continent from sea to sea. Since then it has had only one addition, when Prince Edward Island joined the Dominion in 1873. The growing trade of Canada with the West Indies has increased her interest in those islands, and in 1911 a proposal was made that she should take over some of the islands, but it came to nothing. Within the Dominion itself, the development of population has led to the formation of the new provinces of Saskatchewan and Alberta.

(4) Prince Edward Island. 1873.

The notion we get of Canada from a glance at an ordinary map is very misleading: it appears an illimitable country, nearly the size of the United States. But besides the shrinking of the land towards the north, for most maps make the northern territories look much larger than they really are, we must remember that great stretches of the land are covered by difficult mountains and almost impenetrable forest, while the further north we go, the colder and less hospitable becomes the climate. In some parts, such as in the prairie provinces, there is ample room for northward expansion, but in other places the country is sterile and of little use. At present the population is spread out in a belt of about one hundred miles wide along the frontier, stretching along that spinal cord, the railway line. In old Canada, besides the busy towns, the land is split up into little farms which have been hewn out of the forest, where the Canadian is forced to carry on general farming much as the Englishman does at home. In the maritime provinces the work is similar, though here many of the inhabitants are sailors and fishermen, earning their living off the banks of Newfoundland. Further west when we come to the prairie provinces, with their rolling

Geographical divisions of Canada.

down lands, we find another type of farming. Here in recent years the vast numbers of immigrants have begun to raise excellent wheat from the virgin soil of the prairie land, though towards the Rockies, where the rainfall is more precarious, careful irrigation has had to be undertaken. Once over the Rockies, we are in quite a different country again. Little valleys, generally heavily timbered, run up into the high mountains and here the saw-mill and lumber-station clear

CANADA.

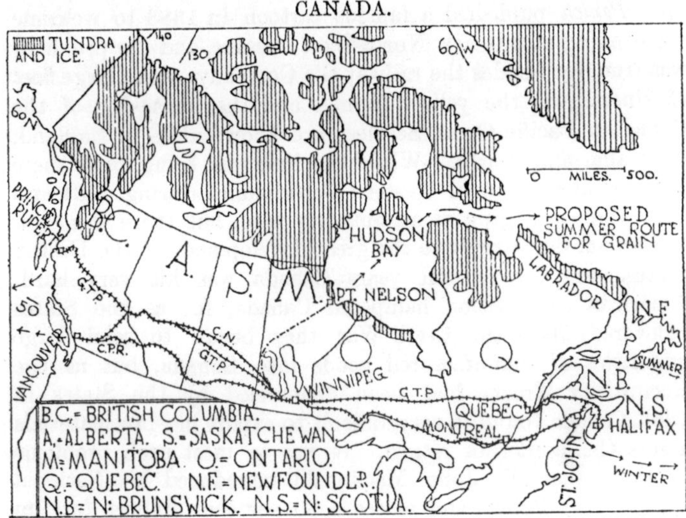

E. H. H. H. del.

The River St. Lawrence is open for seven months of the year, the Hudson Bay route for about three. Notice what a large part of Canada is covered with tundra and ice; much of the rest is still forest-clad.

away the forest, and make room for the farm. Here too there is gold-digging, salmon-fishing, fruit-farming, and stock-raising, but the farms are small and unambitious, for labour is very scarce, and Asiatic immigration is very strictly controlled. Thus, scarcity of labour is one of the problems of British Columbia, as it was in Australia in the early days.

One of the bargains made when British Columbia joined the Dominion was the building of a trans-continental railroad. The Conservative party, under Sir John Macdonald, set themselves to carry through the scheme, though they were vigorously opposed by the Liberals, who pointed out that the railways already built were not paying their way. It was not till 1886 that with the help of Lord Strathcona, and with a guarantee of money from Britain, the great work was completed. It has since become a triumphant success. Vancouver City, the Pacific port, has grown from 30,000 inhabitants in 1900 to more than 100,000, while all along the line the prairie provinces have been opened up. *Punch* published a famous cartoon in 1888 to welcome the opening of this new North-West Passage, and the prophecy was true, for besides the railway the Company owns a large fleet of liners, and the yellow funnels and the house-flag of the Canadian Pacific Ocean Services are known alike in England, Australia, and Japan. While the line was being built there was a sudden boom in Western Canada, and during 1881 and 1882 Winnipeg grew at an amazing pace, but there was soon a reaction, due largely to the great development of the United States, and for several years Canada was hit very hard. American competition hampered Canada, for as the States recovered after the Civil War they began to send large quantities of manufactured goods into Canada, but as the Reciprocity Treaty had been denounced by the States in 1866, Canada found it very difficult to export her raw materials across the border in return. It was to meet such problems as these that Sir John Macdonald introduced his National Policy, and placed a 30 per cent. import duty on manufactures, hoping to encourage Canadians to make their own goods. At first this policy was very unpopular among many of the Liberals, while some people carried on an agitation for commercial union with the United States, believing that a political union would follow in due time. A leader of this school was Goldwin Smith, an English Professor of History, who emigrated first to the United States and thence to Canada and became a great champion of Free Trade and American Union. His caustic phrases and logical analysis, together with the scorn he poured on the fictions of the Dominion constitution, carried weight, but when the Liberals came into power under Sir Wilfrid

Canadian Pacific Railway.

Macdonald's National Policy. 1879.

Laurier in 1896, they found the country so prosperous that they deemed it best to leave the tariff untouched.

Opening up of north-west. 1898-1914.

It was towards the end of the 'nineties that the development of modern Canada commenced : the work of preparation began to tell, and a careful policy of assisted immigration and land-settlement began to open out the fertile prairie lands of the West. Instead of Canadians crossing the border and settling in the States, Americans who realised the value of the virgin soil of the prairie began to pour across into Canada, and to settle down as farmers in the Dominion. This seemed to put the final seal of excellence on the prairie provinces, and helped by a good system of banking and finance the wheat country began to develop at a prodigious rate. From Europe came parties and groups from different countries, Germany, Russia, Ireland, Scotland and elsewhere, who settled down together in the new country. Townships sprang up like mushrooms, while the Missionary Societies found it almost impossible to keep pace with the demand for ministers. New railways too were pushed on to open up new routes across the continent: the Canadian Northern and the Grand Trunk Pacific, both aiming for the further ocean. Besides this, new industries were begun, new mines were opened, and the whole country offered an ever-increasing market for Canadian goods. This vast growth in population can be seen from the census returns: in 1901 there were $5\frac{1}{3}$ millions in Canada ; ten years later the population was more than $7\frac{1}{5}$ millions. The annual immigration return rose from 67,000 in 1901 to 402,000 in 1912.

Reciprocity Treaty. Liberal defeat. 1911.

Such was the state of Canada when at last the Liberals determined to take up a new line on fiscal matters. Laurier negotiated a Reciprocity Treaty with President Taft, but discovered that he had made a bad tactical mistake, for his party was hopelessly beaten at the General Election of 1911. The case was not fought merely upon its merits, for the question of the Imperial tie, and of the future development of Canada, was mixed up with the more theoretical discussions of economic doctrine. The defeat of 1911 was largely the result of that feeling of Canadian nationality which has been growing so fast during the last thirty years, for any policy which seemed to threaten that nationality, however indirectly, was bound to be regarded with suspicion. As late as 1891, Goldwin Smith could write with almost arrogant assurance, "Canada will never contribute to Imperial armaments at her own expense. . . . Let the War Office ask the Canadian High Commissioner whether he thinks that Quebec would, under any conceivable circumstance, send contingents or subsidies to British armaments, or allow the Dominion, which is controlled by the French vote, to send them." Yet only ten years later, when Great Britain found herself at war in South Africa, Laurier, a French-Canadian Premier, was forced by public opinion to send men to fight for the general cause. But lately the voluntary act of the Dominion sent a great army to fight in France for freedom, and on the fields of Flanders Canadian nationality found itself once again. The opening up of the West, a development which has only just begun, is altering the whole balance of power in Canada, and threatens to upset the old arrangements of political parties, for the farmers are beginning to organise directly, and to run their own candidates independently of the older parties. This change also threatens to diminish the importance of the French-Canadian vote, for though they still remain a separate nationality, the day when their vote was strong enough to control the whole of Dominion politics seems to have gone for ever. Power, with wealth, is steadily moving westward. Thus Canada is on the eve of great decisions: the events of recent years, and the development of the Dominion itself, have raised problems which must soon be faced and settled. Her native question is small, for the Indians are but few in number and peacefully inclined, and her racial problem, difficult as it once appeared, is now a minor matter. But the question of first-rate importance is that of her relations to the great English-speaking republic to the south and to the Mother Country and the Empire as a whole.

Development of Canadian Nationality.

Growing power of the West.

BOOKS: J. G. Bourinot, *Canada under British Rule, 1760-1905*, and W. L. Grant, *History of Canada*, are useful text-books. A. G. Bradley, *Canada* [Home University Library], is a fascinating little book. Documents can be studied in Keith's *Colonial Policy*, where the extracts from Durham's report should certainly be read. It is edited in full by C. P. Lucas. The ideas of Goldwin Smith can be seen in his book, *Canada and the Canadian Question.*

1791. Pitt's Canada Act [forms two provinces].
1839. Durham's Report.
1840. Act of Reunion.
1867. The Dominion of Canada [British North America Act].
1870. Red River Rebellion.
1879. Macdonald's "National" Policy of Protection.
1911. Reciprocity Treaty with U.S.A.; fall of Laurier Government.

CHAPTER X

South Africa

The population of South Africa.

THE story of South Africa is a record of the conflict between the white man and the black, but it has been complicated by another racial problem, for the British and the Dutch did not quickly settle down side by side, and so present a united front to the native. There are thus three important elements in the population of South Africa: the native, the Dutch settler, and the later British immigrant. When the Dutch first settled at the Cape, they found there savages of a very low type of civilisation, though these yellow-skinned Bushmen and Hottentots were few in number and of little importance. But while the white man was pushing upward from the Cape, South Africa was being invaded from the north by a type of man very different from the Bushman. The dark-skinned Bantu-speaking negroes came flooding southward, sweeping over the land and claiming it for their flocks and herds. Strong and vigorous, a large portion of the Bantus were by nature men of war and readily submitted themselves to the strict discipline of their soldier-kings. Of these the most terrible were the Zulus, whose well-trained impis would scour the countryside, carrying fire and slaughter wherever they went. The more peaceful Bantus, such as the Mashona, who were ready and desirous of living quietly and tending their flocks, served only as a prey to their more vigorous neighbours, and were frequently reduced to a state of servitude. We can easily understand the constant clash between black and white in South Africa if we realise that it was but the meeting of two steady streams of invaders spreading over the country, from opposite directions.

The Dutch Company discouraged the settlement and development of their station at the Cape; thus when it was captured by the British there were only some 20,000 Europeans in South Africa, though they were spread thinly over a large territory, with its centre at Cape Town. The inland farmer, or Back-veldt Boer, was ignorant and impatient of restraint, the control of the Castle at Cape Town was irksome to him, and when the British seized the country in 1795 some of the Boers were actually in rebellion against their own government. Unlike the French in Canada, who had cleared their little farms with infinite difficulty out of the enveloping forest, the Boers had sprawled across the country and occupied what land seemed good to them. For the Boer it was easy to pack his goods and move away across the veldt to another piece of land; for the French-Canadian, even had he wished so to do, such a thing was impossible. The British who came to the Cape, either as governors or colonists, did not quickly fraternise with the older settlers and there was a good deal of friction between the two races, but the chief quarrel of the Boers was with the British Government for interfering in their manner of life and upsetting their relations with the natives. Things soon came to such a pass that some of the Boers preferred to move away and form new homes for themselves where they could live without foreign control.

Causes of the trek.

The Cape had been captured by force of arms, and the first British governors were soldiers: there was no attempt to apply to the Cape those broad principles of statesmanship which proved so successful in Canada, and the Boers soon began to fear that their new masters had determined on a definite policy of Anglicising the whole colony. The first step which caused them alarm was the planting on the eastern borders of the colony, in 1820 and 1821, of a number of British settlers. This plantation was part of the scheme of colonisation organised to relieve the distress in England after the Napoleonic wars and to develop the colonies. On the whole it was a success; the districts of Albany and Somerset East were named in honour of the scheme, and a hardy band of frontier farmers soon proved their worth, both as a defence against Kaffir attack from the east and as a nucleus of the British element in South Africa. But the Boers were alarmed, especially when English was declared the official language of the colony and an English system of magistrates and law-courts was organised to take the place of the old Dutch courts and local officers. Another great cause of ill-feeling was the emancipation of the slaves. Slavery had been begun in South Africa by the Dutch East India Company, who brought a number of Malays as slaves from their settlements in the Spice Islands; besides this, the Boers had Hottentots and other captured natives as farm slaves. The Boer, who saw everything from a severely practical point of view, could not appreciate the ideals which were behind the anti-slavery agitation. He could hardly be expected to recognise the vote of compensation as generous, for in any case it fell far short of the ascertained value of his slaves, while, as payment was made in London and speculators took a large share, it was difficult for him to obtain the amount to which he was entitled. The Act of Emancipation arranged that the slaves should work for their masters for five years as apprentices, and should obtain their freedom in 1838. In a new country the question of labour is always a difficult problem, and it was not easily solved in South Africa. A gloomy picture was painted by a contemporary: "Masters saw . . . the whole of their farming pursuits and plans destroyed: no bribe, nor entreaty, I believe, did avail in one single instance to induce any one of these now free persons to stay over that day . . . in the eastern country districts, this (wages) was impossible, and the agriculturalists there found themselves totally deprived of every vestige of labour to improve or cultivate their farms, or even to superintend or herd their flocks."

There was yet another thing which stirred the Boers, and finally drove them to action. Beyond the Fish river there was ever the threatening danger of the warlike Kaffirs: one war had already been fought in 1819, and now another broke out suddenly when it seemed that peace and friendship had been concluded with the natives. The sudden attack at Christmas, 1834, took all men by surprise, and it was only after heavy fighting, in which Boer farmer and British settler fought side by sight for the security of the frontier and the safety of their farms, that peace was at last restored. The British governor, Sir Benjamin Durban, determined never to be caught in such a way again. To prevent the danger of a sudden raid he proposed to organise two zones beyond the eastern frontier, the nearer settled by Europeans holding their land by military tenure, the further occupied by friendly natives; thus the colony would have two thick skins between its unprotected farms and the Kaffirs. The home government, however, saw matters very differently: looking through a mist of humanitarian sentiment, they lacked the sharpness of vision of the men on the spot. Forgetting that the war had started with a deliberate and unprovoked raid upon peaceful settlements, they blamed the Cape Government for attacking the Kaffirs. The extension of frontier was considered an uncalled-for aggression, and was forbidden. This reversal of Durban's policy was the last straw for the Boers of the eastern provinces: the trek began.

Kaffir War. 1834–1835.

Packing their household goods and their families into their huge waggons, and rounding up their flocks and herds, they started for the north, where they might found new homes for themselves free from the short-sighted interference of the foreigner. Slowly across the rolling plain, or up the steep passes of the mountains, creaked their cumbrous ox-waggons, while mounted or on foot the Boer trudged along keeping a sharp look out for game or for a possible enemy. By night they would form laager, parking their waggons in a square, and camping within the shelter of its hollow. At first they had but little trouble with the natives, for the Zulus, away in what is now Natal, had become a terrible scourge to their fellow blacks. Led by a military tyrant, Chaka, the

The trek. 1835–1838.

Zulus had exterminated vast numbers of other tribes. But after crossing the Orange river the Boers met with opposition and left a memory of their trek in Winburg, or Victory-town, where they conquered the Matabele. Then turning south they crossed the Drakensberg into Natal, and here the Place of Weeping (Weenen) still recalls a terrible tragedy where a detachment was attacked and massacred. At last, however, they gained a great success ; treated treacherously by Dingaan, Chaka's successor, the Boers won a famous victory over the Zulus, and Dingaan's Day is still celebrated as an annual festival throughout the Union of South Africa. Meanwhile, other farmers had been trekking from the Cape, and in Natal the Boers were joined by more of their fellows.

When first the Boers began their trek to the north the Government did not know what to do : there was no law to prevent a British citizen leaving the country, and as the Government did not wish to extend its limits indefinitely throughout South Africa, for a time nothing was done. When, however, the Boers after the defeat of Dingaan declared the Republic of Natalia (1839), the problem was different. British ships frequently called at Port Natal, and the few settlers there had asked in vain to be annexed, but now that this port might fall into other hands the Government determined to act. Troops were sent to garrison the place, and when besieged by the indignant Boers, they were reinforced again from Cape Town. Reluctantly the Boers withdrew across the Drakensberg again, and in 1843 Natal was formally annexed ; for a few years it remained a part of the Cape, but in 1848 it was made into a separate colony.

Natal annexed. 1843.

The home government was now beginning to wake up to the difficulty of the South African question, and the many new problems which the treks had created. Almost against their will they had now two settlements, the Cape and Natal, instead of one, and these settlements were separated by a large stretch of land inhabited by semi-hostile tribes. Besides this, the Boers across the Orange River were a serious problem ; legally they could not divest themselves of British citizenship, practically their treatment was a thorny question, for the whole safety of the white races depended on their showing a united front in facing the blacks, while the possibility of the Boers developing into an independent state had many elements of danger. On the other hand, no British statesman of that day could look with equanimity on the extension of British responsibility so far to the northward, in an almost unknown country where communications were of the worst.

In this difficult state of affairs it was decided to appoint as governor Sir Harry Smith, an energetic and successful Indian administrator, and to give him very large powers to deal with the problem. The new governor settled the native difficulty along the lines which Durban had proposed and the Imperial Government now adopted a policy which it had roundly condemned but a few years before. The country eastward to the River Kei was declared a Protectorate, under the title of British Kaffraria, and British agents were placed among the native tribes to secure peace and good order. In dealing with the Boers, Sir Harry Smith decided that their existence as a separate state was dangerous for the whites in South Africa, and so in 1848 he annexed the newly established Orange Free State, and reorganised it under the title of the Orange River Sovereignty. As a result of this action all the whites were again under British control, but this state of affairs did not last long. Although many Boers were glad to feel that they were under British protection, and could count on outside aid if needed against the natives, there were others to whom absolute independence seemed the more vital need. To them it seemed that where-ever they went the clutching hand of Britain reached out to drag them within its grasp. Fired by these ideas they rose in revolt, and when defeated at Boomplats withdrew northward across the Vaal River, there to try once again the difficult task of organising a state: for a time they were not recognised by the British Government [August 1848].

Sir Harry Smith. 1848-1854.

(1) British Kaffraria.

(2) Annexation of Orange River Sovereignty.

We now come to one of those sudden changes in Imperial policy which have had such a disastrous effect on the history of South Africa. Distance, difficulty of communications, and failure to appreciate the true significance of events, all contributed their part to this change ; but we must look rather deeper for the real cause. The growing policy during the first half of the nineteenth century was, as we have seen, the policy of *laissez-faire*, of allowing the colonies to develop on their own account, and expecting that they would quickly break away from the Imperial connection. The Imperial Goverment now realised that despite these general principles they had been steadily extending their power in South Africa, and at the same time incurring far-reaching responsibilities. It was the difficult and expensive Basuto war of 1851, into which Sir Harry Smith had been led through trying to enforce the claims of the Boers for compensation for stolen cattle, that really brought about the crisis. The Imperial Government decided to cut its losses, and to get out of the difficulty as quickly as possible, with small regard either to its own obligations or to the wishes of the settlers beyond the Orange river. Already, in 1852, Sir Harry Smith had been forced by the threats of the Transvaal Boers at a critical time to recognise their independence. This was done by the Sand River Convention of 1852, which reserved to Britain a general right of supervision, and bound the Boers not to re-establish slavery. Now after the Basuto war the Imperial Government determined to adopt a similar policy in the Sovereignty. By the Bloemfontein Convention of 1854 the management of affairs was thrust on a not very willing committee of farmers, who were left to face the problems of native hostility which the British had failed to solve.

Sand River Convention. 1852.

Bloemfontein Convention. 1854.

The policy of 1854 marks a turning-point in South African history : the British power withdrew into its shell south of the River Orange, agreeing to make no treaties with native chiefs to the northward. Thus there were now two independent Dutch republics to the north, but the seeds of future trouble were planted in abundance. The relationship between the republics and the British power was but ill-defined : no arrangements had been made for a joint policy with regard to the natives, and the vital but little-appreciated question of northward expansion was likewise left undetermined. For the moment Britain withdrew : she was frightened of herself.

At the same time it was decided to grant representative government to Cape Colony, and this became responsible government in 1872. The rule of military governors with their executive council came to an end with the appointment of Sir George Grey, who met the first parliament at Cape Town in 1854. Grey had won his spurs as Governor of New Zealand, and during his time in South Africa from 1854 to 1861 he did great work in pacifying the Kaffirs and teaching them the rule of law. A man of great personality himself, he realised the value of personality in dealing with natives, and he set himself to stamp on the mind of the Kaffirs the greatness and justice of the Queen. They were much impressed by his picture of the authority of the law: a couple of policemen could turn away the whole Queen's army, if ordered so to do by a magistrate. But in other things too Grey was ahead of his time: he realised the dangers involved in the policy of 1854, and believed that the true remedy lay in a scheme of federation.

Representative government at Cape Town. 1853.

"In effect I was recalled from South Africa," he wrote later, "on account of proposals I had made towards federation in that part of the realm. I planned to federate, for common action, Cape Colony, Natal, our other territories, and also the Orange Free State. Further, I had virtually asked the co-operation of the Transvaal Republic, with the government and people of which I was on very friendly terms. There was to be no change anywhere; simply, a federal parliament would manage affairs that were of concern to all parties. I have little doubt that I could have brought about federation, only I was not permitted to go on. Much as my proposals were supported in South Africa, I could get no hearing for them from my superiors at home." It was most unfortunate for the history of South Africa that Grey's schemes did not find favour at home, for when a few years later the Imperial Government wished to bring about a federation of South Africa, they had no winning personality like Grey to carry through their plans, and the whole situation had been prejudiced by events in the Transvaal.

Sir George Grey. 1854-1861.

The policy of non-intervention begun in 1854 lasted for some sixteen years, when the discovery of diamonds gave a new impulse to expansion, and completely altered men's ideas of South Africa. Instead of a distant and little-known country, where a scanty living could be made by hard farming, or adventure sought in the frequent Kaffir wars, it became a romantic country where fabulous fortunes might be made in a little time ; a stone worth thousands of pounds might be found among a child's play-things, or bought for a few shillings from a wandering Kaffir. After scrambling along the banks of the Vaal and scratching in the mud for chance stones, the prospectors discovered a regular supply in the "blue earth" found in curious, funnel-shaped holes, in a spot to the west of the Free State and north of the Orange river. A sudden rush of miners took place ; Kimberley, a little town of shacks, sprang up, and a furious race for wealth began. As time went on different methods of mining had to be introduced, and in place of the small separate claims where the individual prospector scraped the surface of the earth, great companies were formed who bought out the smaller claims, and driving deep shafts and tunnels mined in underground diggings. The diamond country was promptly claimed by both Republics and by England. It was annexed to the Cape Colony, a sum of money being paid as a compensation to the Free State, but the dispute with the Transvaal remained for long unsettled.

Discovery of diamonds. 1869-1870. Kimberley.

Meanwhile, in England, a change of ministry had brought Beaconsfield into power, with Lord Carnarvon as his Colonial Secretary. Carnarvon had recently succeeded in carrying through the federation of Canada, which promised to be a great success, and he was anxious to apply the same remedy to South African affairs. His first attempts proved a failure, while events in the Transvaal made matters yet more difficult. The Boers there had not been so successful as the Free State burghers : quarrels among themselves had paralysed the state, the taxes were not paid, the laws were disregarded, while disputes with the natives had resulted in a nearly chronic state of war, and the country was bankrupt. It was under these circumstances that the governor of the Cape, anxious to preserve order, and fearful lest the native troubles should spread to the British colonies, rode into

Annexation of Transvaal. 1877.

Pretoria one day with thirty policemen, and declared the Transvaal annexed. For the moment, his action restored confidence, and quietened the fears of native attack, but there quickly grew up in the Transvaal a reaction against British interference which ruined Carnarvon's scheme for federation.

The Imperial Government was pressing on with its plans. An Enabling Act was passed to empower the local states and colonies to frame a federal scheme, and Sir Bartle Frere was chosen as Governor of the Cape to carry through the necessary negotiations. An honest man and a skilful organiser, few men have been dogged with greater ill-fortune in South Africa, that grave of reputations. Misfortune after misfortune fell upon him, until he was recalled before he had been able to carry out his instructions. No sooner had he set foot in the Cape than he was summoned eastward to face a Kaffir rising, which he successfully confined to a small area, thus preventing a general outbreak. Next he was called north to arbitrate between the Transvaal Boers and the Zulus. The latter claimed that the Dutch had occupied some land that rightly belonged to their tribe, and Frere upheld their claim, but at the same time demanded that the Zulu king Ketchwayo should disarm his forces, for the military power of the Zulus and the ambition of their kings were a standing menace to Natal and to the Transvaal alike. When Ketchwayo indignantly refused, a disastrous war began which opened with the annihilation of a British force at Isandlhwana and the gallant defence of Rorke's Drift on the Tugela, which saved Natal from the horrors of a Zulu invasion. It needed the despatch of a large number of men before the Zulus were beaten and disarmed. It might seem now that Frere could turn his attention to his work of federation, but here, again, he was defeated. The movement among the Boers for regaining their independence was steadily growing in the Transvaal, and deputations under Paul Kruger had twice visited England, to ask for autonomy. Signs of hope were seen in the probability of Gladstone's victory at the next election, and the Boers of the Transvaal, declaring that independence must come before federation, persuaded their Dutch friends to throw out the proposals for a conference

Sir Bartle Frere. 1877-1880.

when moved in the Cape Parliament. Meanwhile, in England, Gladstone had been returned to power, and Frere was recalled. In the Transvaal the independence movement quickly broke out into violence, and a British battalion was suddenly attacked at Bronkhurst Spruit and the relief force wiped out at Majuba. During his Midlothian campaign Gladstone had already condemned the annexation of the Transvaal, and now, despite Majuba, he determined to right what he regarded as a wrong. It was, however, unfortunate that what the Imperial Government considered as an act of justice was delayed until after the outbreak of violence, for the act thus lost its grace. Many of the Boers obtained a wholly false idea of the strength of Britain, while to the native imagination it seemed that Britain had been forced to give way. By the Pretoria Convention of 1881 the independence of the Transvaal was restored and its boundaries settled. Thus, once again, in 1881 we see two independent Dutch republics, the Transvaal and the Orange Free State, and the British power withdrawn within the boundaries of the Cape and Natal.

Pretoria Convention: Independence of Transvaal. 1881.

The story of South Africa now becomes more and more the story of the dreaming and doing of Cecil Rhodes, a man who has had more influence on the development of that country than any other single person. Going out to South Africa as a young man, he soon made a vast fortune by amalgamating the diamond mines at Kimberley, and turned his attention to the politics of Cape Colony. A great organiser, Rhodes knew how to deal with men, and well understood the power of money in attaining his ends. Though he was a practical man, Rhodes was no mere materialist, he was a seer of visions and a man of ideals. Sitting on his stoep at Groote Schuur, he would gaze at the scarp of Table Mountain shimmering in the heat, and dream of the day when Briton and Boer should join hands to push forward the work of civilisation, and when those vast lands northward from the Transvaal should provide homes for a people yet to be.

Cecil Rhodes.

It was about 1880 that there began in Europe that outburst of colonial activities which led to so many annexations in Africa and elsewhere. The growth of trade demanded fresh markets abroad, and places from which European countries could draw their raw material. It seemed that traders were more secure if the parts of Africa to which they went were controlled by their own country, and so began the "scramble for Africa." The sight of the French in Tunis and the British in Egypt gave fresh life to the demands of the German Colonial Party, for several years Bismarck had refused to claim land beyond the seas, but in 1883 the pressure became too strong for him, and he annexed German South-West Africa.[1] This step came as a great surprise both to Britain and to the Cape: consistent to their principle, the British Government had several times refused to extend their protection over this country, but now that another power had done so they felt disturbed. The question of the possession of the inlying territory of Bechuanaland at once became important. British agents who had been living among the Bechuana had been withdrawn in 1881, after the Pretoria Convention, but Rhodes had early realised that Bechuanaland was the gateway to the north. He had attempted to secure that gateway in 1881, but the Cape Parliament had refused to support him. Now the whole outlook was different: the German annexation and Boer schemes threatened to close the northward way entirely. So in 1884, when the London Convention amended the terms of the earlier settlement of the Transvaal, it was agreed that Bechuanaland was under British suzerainty, and a Protectorate was at once proclaimed. This action was only just in time. Despite the terms of the Conventions, which limited the Transvaal boundaries, Boers were flooding across into Bechuanaland and declaring themselves independent republics: it needed a special expedition, sent out in 1885, to establish British authority. This was done successfully without any fighting.

Germans annex South West Africa. 1883.

London Convention. 1884.

The gateway was now secure: Europe was parcelling up Africa into Protectorates and spheres of influence, and it behoved England, who had done so much for the exploration of Africa and the destruction of the slave trade, to see she was not left out in the cold. Rhodes' plans now came to fruition, and he was able to negotiate a treaty and obtain concessions

[1] See Chapter XVI.

from Lobengula, the Matabele chief. An old instrument of English colonising enterprise, the trading company, was once again called upon to play its part in colonising and developing new lands. In 1889 the British South Africa Company was formed under a royal charter, and, in the parcelling out of Africa, it received a large area of inland territory to develop. Unlike the earlier companies, the Chartered Company did not propose to limit or monopolise trade, but to encourage settlement and commerce in the new country: profits were looked for from mineral concessions, but for a long time the Company had to be heavily financed by Rhodes from the diamond industry. Rhodes was now both Premier of Cape Colony and a director of the Company, and he gave a solemn promise that if ever his duties clashed he would resign office: it was the neglect to keep this promise that led to his downfall.

British South Africa Company. 1889.

The new country was quickly occupied under the direction of Jameson: farms were built, railways were begun, and a system of mounted police organised. For a time the Matabele were suspicious, despite the friendly attitude of their chief, but a small rising in 1893 did not really hinder the growth of the country. The great crisis was brought about by a mad gamble, whose evil results were destined to stretch far into the future. As we shall see, fresh trouble had arisen in the Transvaal, and in 1895 Jameson, now Commissioner for the British South Africa Company, made a raid into the Transvaal with the Company's troopers, which soon ended in a disastrous defeat. The results were immediate: Rhodes, who had been privy to part of the scheme, fell from power in the Cape, while war broke out in Rhodesia. The Matabele saw that all the troopers had left the country, they knew in some vague way that the great white man was in disgrace, and, smarting from their previous defeat, they determined on a last attempt at revenge. All through 1896 a devastating war went on; the natives burnt farms and houses and all the first-fruits of the settlers' toil, and it was only towards the end of the year that they were rounded up in the Matoppo hills. Here Rhodes, who had been fighting as a trooper, met the indunas, unarmed, heard their complaints, and made a lasting peace. His bravery and frankness at this meeting, the way in which he listened to their complaints and chid them for their foolishness in making war, all had the greatest effect on the indunas. They still believe that their great father's spirit watches over his people, and they still recount the story of this parley, sitting at his grave. For here, some six years later, Rhodes at his own wish was buried, that he might rest in the heart of the country which his energy had made ready for the white settlers of the future.

Rhodes's death, 1902.

It was while the difficult question of Bechuanaland was being settled in 1884–1885 that those discoveries of gold were made in the Transvaal which entirely altered the condition of that state. Before gold was discovered there were only some 50,000 Boers in the Transvaal—less than the population of an English town the size of Reading. The Republic was a backward country, dependent on an unprogressive system of agriculture. Now immigrants poured into the country, intent on making their fortunes at the mines, and in a few years these newcomers were nearly as many as the Dutch inhabitants themselves. The barren ridge of the Rand was a scene of bustling activity, and soon for mile on mile against the sky could be seen the pit-head gears and the dumps of the various mines. Gold-mining was no easy business, and large companies were formed to bear the many expenses of driving shafts and erecting machinery. The mushroom town of Johannesburg sprang up, and quickly attained an irritating predominance in the state. Thus within a few years the whole political situation within the Republic had been revolutionised. Vast crowds of Uitlanders—British, American, German, and others—had crowded into the country, and the Boers had quickly to make up their minds what they intended to do with these new settlers. The mines meant a great increase of wealth to the Transvaal, and the Uitlanders claimed that they should have some say in the manner in which that money was spent. Thus there arose a demand for a quick and simple method of admission to citizen rights.

Discovery of gold in the Transvaal, 1884-1885.

The Boers, however, were very suspicious of their new neighbours: they had watched with alarm the extension of

British power in Bechuanaland, and northward in Rhodesia, and they feared lest the enfranchisement of the Uitlander should involve a change in the customary policy of their own Republic. Led by Kruger, the reactionary party not only refused reform, but began a policy of repression: the franchise was limited, and a series of vexatious monopolies were granted to Hollanders. After several years of agitation the Uitlanders determined to assert their claims by force, scheming to overthrow the reactionary government and replace it by a more liberal system, but declaring their adhesion to the Republican flag. To this movement Rhodes adopted a friendly attitude, and Jameson arranged to cross the frontier and co-operate with the insurgents. The whole plan miscarried: Jameson was defeated and captured, the Uitlanders were forced to hand in their arms, and found themselves in a worse position than ever, while Rhodes' political career was ruined. But the effects of the Jameson Raid were more far-reaching still. In the Transvaal the moderate Boers, who stood for an understanding with the Uitlanders, were discredited, while Kruger's reactionary policy gained a new lease of life. Emboldened by success, and trusting to German help, Kruger became more uncompromising than ever. On the Continent, and even in America, the British position was misunderstood, and Rhodes' complicity made most nations believe that Britain was merely using the Uitlanders as a stalking horse. Hence, when war broke out general sympathy was felt for the Boers.

The Jameson Raid. 1896.

The end of the miserable story must be briefly told. Before the raid a friendly settlement was possible, after that disaster war was almost inevitable. Sir Alfred Milner was sent out as High Commissioner to attempt an agreement, and though he was the first governor since Sir George Grey who had troubled to learn Dutch, he failed to reach a settlement. Kruger adopted a hectoring attitude, demanded the immediate cancelling of orders for troops moving to South Africa, and when this was refused, declared war. Neither side had realised the strength of its opponent: the Boers, remembering Majuba, and hoping for continental aid, expected a speedy victory, while the British

South African War. 1899-1902.

despised an enemy who had no regular army, and were surprised to find that the Orange Free State joined the Transvaal. At first the honours went to the Boers: marksmen from childhood, clothed in dun-colour which melted into the background of the veldt, and mounted on their sturdy horses, they were more than a match for the British. Indeed, the British found themselves in much the same position as had the English soldiers in the old days in America, fighting against backwoodsmen and Indians. It was only after large reinforcements had been received, backed by troops from the Dominions, and after many corps of mounted infantry had been organised, that the Boers began to find themselves outmanœuvred at their own game. In June, 1900, Lord Roberts captured Pretoria, and the main part of the war was at an end, but it still required months of the organisation of blockhouses and entanglements, accompanied by great drives, before the guerilla war was brought to an end. At Vereeniging, in May, 1902, peace was made and the promise given to the Boers that "as soon as circumstances permit, representative institutions, leading up to self-government, will be introduced."

The pacification and economic reconstruction of the Boer states was quickly carried out. A grant of money, accompanied by loans, was made by the Imperial Government to assist the Boer farmers, and Lord Milner's tact and judgment did much to settle the country. The Boers loyally performed their part of the bargain, and by 1906 it was possible to carry out the terms of Vereeniging by granting full responsible government. At the time this seemed a hazardous step, but once again the British statesmen determined to rely on the panacea of responsibility, and they were not deceived. The best proof of the success of this policy is the fact that within three years the colonies had drawn up and sent to the Imperial Parliament an Act to federate South Africa. Thus, after so many mistakes and so much suffering, the vision of the prophets had come true, and the Europeans of South Africa had joined together willingly to found one great state.

Responsible government to Boer States. 1906.

The Union of South Africa is, as its name implies, a single state rather than a federation of separate states.

Realising the need for unified control of their railway system, and for common action on many points of great importance, the different states determined to sink their local claims, and to become provinces of one single state. The powers of the provincial councils were strictly limited, and the Union Parliament was given large authority. The Act was a compromise, based on mutual concessions. Thus both Dutch and English are official languages, and all records are kept in duplicate. The claims of different cities to be chosen as the capital were settled by making Cape Town the seat of parliament, Pretoria the seat of executive government. Since then the Union has grown steadily, and is a power whose influence is felt far beyond the borders of South Africa.

Union of South Africa. 1909.

The great development of South Africa in recent years, and its growing importance in the counsels of the world, have been largely due to the wealthy mining industries. But apart from the mines, the economic development of South Africa has been slow, and great problems of improvements have yet to be faced. A large proportion of its exports has been in mineral wealth, and agriculture generally is in a backward state. This is partly due to the nature of the country, for large tracts of land are actual desert, while most of the country needs scientific cultivation and careful irrigation to make it really fruitful. For this type of cultivation the Boer farmers were not very ready; intensely conservative and wedded to their old methods, they looked with distrust on anything that was new, but a change has come over the country, for the Department of Agriculture is steadily encouraging the adoption of more scientific methods. An example of unsuccessful methods is given by the wine industry: vines were early introduced into South Africa, and grow readily in the Cape, the fruit being cultivated on low bushes. The Cape wines are of excellent quality, and yet but little is exported. An important industry is sheep-farming, and it is to British enterprise that this is largely due. Soon after the capture of the Cape, special breeds of sheep were introduced by the English settlers, and since then the export of wool has steadily increased, though it is by

Economic development.

no means so important as the Australian clip. Ostrich-farming is a typical South African enterprise, but it was only after long and patient endeavour that the ostrich was successfully domesticated. Now, however, it is a wealthy industry, and one whole district of the Cape is noted for its ostrich feathers. Despite a policy of protection, South Africa has but few manufactures, and indeed has but few large towns ; hence manufactured goods of every kind are imported, chiefly from Britain, and paid for by the export of precious metals and raw materials. At present the wealth of South Africa is hardly touched ; large areas of gold are still unmined, while northward there is a vast supply of copper, coal too is there in abundance. The development depends largely on the growth of railways : this Rhodes knew well, and planned to run his line from Cape to Cairo—a dream which is now well on its way towards completion. As in the United States, so in South Africa, the control of the railways by different states in what was economically a single country was a cause of constant trouble, and this as much as anything brought about the Act of Union in 1909. South Africa has now free trade within the Union and a single railway system, and her successful economic development seems now to be assured.

The native problem.

A still greater problem that the Union has to face is the question of the natives. There are some million and a quarter whites in South Africa, and about five million natives, and the latter are increasing more rapidly than the whites. Though there is not the same bitterness of feeling which exists in the United States, where the curse of slavery has borne much evil fruit, there is in South Africa a strong colour bar and a policy of denying political rights to the native. The only province in which natives had the vote before 1909 was the Cape, and there the electoral laws of the old colony have been preserved, though only a white man can be elected to Parliament. In the old Transvaal constitution it was laid down that "The people shall admit of no equality between white and black in either State or Church." Rhodes, on the other hand, wished to make civilisation, irrespective of colour, the test for political rights. Between these two policies there is still an active fight, and the question is complicated by economic considerations. The black man works for less money than the white, and for a long time there has been a strong objection to teaching natives a trade, and the Kaffir College, established by missionaries at Lovedale in 1841, has frequently been criticised. Recently an attempt has been made in the Union to separate the native and European landholders, and to relegate natives to definite reserves. Besides the natives in the Union, there are the Protectorates of Bechuanaland, Swaziland, and Basutoland which still remain under Imperial control, and a special charter to secure their rights, if handed over to the Union, has been incorporated in the Act of Union. Rhodesia, too, still governed by the Chartered Company, has a vast number of natives whose future relation to the whites is a serious problem.[1] The native question of South Africa is one of the most difficult with which a dominion has ever had to cope, and its successful handling calls for great tact and statesmanship.

Yet another problem faces South Africa, and that is the question of its political development. The steady growth of a South African nation was hindered by the Boer War, which accentuated the racial differences, for most of the Dutch in the Cape sympathised with their comrades across the frontier. Later developments, however, tended to heal that gap, though a body of irreconcilables led by De Wet broke into open revolt in 1914, and were defeated by Union forces under Botha. There is, however, a Nationalist party which embitters the relations of the two races, and seeks either for complete separation for the Orange Free State from the Union or the "independence" of the Union as a whole. There are two other great parties in the State. The South African party, led by General Smuts, represents the moderate and progressive side of the Dutch Afrikander people, who accept loyally the establishment of the Union, and are determined to work for the growth of South Africa along the lines of dominion development. The other is called the Unionist party, and is largely composed of the British element, who agree with the main ideas of the

Political parties.

[1] The white population of Southern Rhodesia have petitioned for responsible government.

South African party. Both these parties have now united under Smuts to oppose the movement for reunion. At present the Labour party is small, but it has grown of recent years. Thus the future of South Africa depends upon the reasonableness of its party leaders and the extent to which they can think broadly on the great questions which will inevitably face them as time goes on.

BOOKS.—W. B. Worsfold, *History of South Africa* [Temple Primers], is a useful little book. See also the volumes in Lucas' Historical Geography. The documents in Keith should be read. The chapters in H. H. Johnston, *Britain Overseas: Africa*, are very interesting. A small and readable biography of Cecil Rhodes is that written by T. E. Fuller. The South African War of 1899–1902 called forth a mass of literature, some of it written under the influence of strong party feeling.

1835-1838. The Trek.
1848. Sir Harry Smith proclaims the Orange River Sovereignty.
1854. Reversal of Imperial policy: Bloemfontein Convention establishes Orange Free State.
1881 Pretoria Convention restores modified independence to Transvaal.
1889. Rhodes founds British South Africa Company.
1899-1902. South African War.
1906. Responsible government given to the Boer States.
1909. The Union of South Africa.

CHAPTER XI

Australasia

AUSTRALIA

THE little settlement at Sydney was at first merely a penal station, and contained only the convicts and a guard of soldiers to watch them, but a change quickly came over the little society. Even Phillip, the first governor, realised the hopeless task of trying to build a colony of such poor material. "The sending out of the disordered and helpless clears the jails," he wrote, "and may ease the parishes from which they are sent, but it is obvious that this settlement, instead of being a colony which is to support itself, will, if the practice be continued, remain for years a burthen to the mother-country." But the Government in England were not interested in the future of Sydney; they were content to find a place where they could get rid of all the undesirable characters from England.

Society at Sydney soon divided itself into distinct classes. There were the convicts; either worked in government gangs, or else "assigned" to settlers for work on their farms. Though liable to severe discipline and often harshly treated, the convict who worked well might hope to obtain his freedom. Those who behaved badly were sent away to prison stations further along the coast. Many of the convicts were the lowest types of humanity, confirmed criminals who never reformed, but others were educated people sent out for a technical offence, or political prisoners who were transported by the Government. Thus there were doctors, lawyers, merchants, and even parsons among the convicts—all ready to take their part in the life of the new colony.

Sydney society.

When a man had served his sentence, or was allowed his freedom for good behaviour, he was called an emancipist. These men settled down as farmers or merchants, and some became very wealthy, but their treatment in this growing society was a delicate question. The governors generally held that the emancipist was as good as the freeman, but those who had never been in prison disliked to meet them. The officers of the regiment were most particular, and once when the governor brought an emancipist friend into the mess, all the junior officers rose and walked out. Besides the emancipists there were a growing number of free settlers, either retired officers or men attracted to the colony by the prospects of farming or trade. Of these the most famous was John Macarthur, a strong impetuous man, who quarrelled with governor after governor, and led the movement for constitutional reform. Macarthur did a great work for Australia by bringing a special breed of merino sheep from the Cape, and breeding a very fine stock of sheep for wool. His work laid the foundations of the great wool-producing industry of Australia, and soon men began to plot out great runs along the countryside, and New South Wales became famous for its wool. At the top of colonial society were the officers of the special New South Wales Corps, but they soon got out of hand. The officers obtained monopolies in the trade of various necessaries, they made vast sums in smuggling rum into the country, and finally matters came to such a pass that, on Macarthur's suggestion, they actually deposed Governor Bligh. Soon after this the corps was broken up; regular soldiers were sent out instead, and the beginnings of constitutional government were given to New South Wales.

When Sydney was founded but little was known of Australia: men were not even sure that New South Wales, which Cook had discovered from the eastward, was one land with the western coasts traversed by Dampier. From the very first adventurous spirits set themselves to solve these various problems. Shut in between the Blue Mountains and the sea, the settlers soon tried to make their way inland, but for several years the steep precipices foiled them, and it was not till 1813 that a party succeeded in pushing through, and so discovered the fertile and well-watered plains that lay on the further side. A road was made by convict labour through the mountains, and settlement began to spread across to the new lands. By 1818 Lord Sidmouth declared "the dread of transportation had almost entirely subsided, and had been succeeded by a desire to emigrate to New South Wales." This was the result of the new discoveries and the growth of sheep-farming. Another set of discoveries were made by sea. Two friends, Bass and Flinders, made some daring voyages in their little boat, the *Tom Thumb*. Together they proved that Tasmania was a separate island by sailing round it in 1798, while some years later Flinders explored the southern coasts of Australia, and thus showed that it was all one great continent and not a series of islands, as had been suggested. As soon as the Blue Mountains had been crossed, another field lay open for the bold explorers. Rivers were found, rising in the Blue Mountains and flowing westward. Where did they go? For many years explorers

Further exploration.

tried to solve this problem ; they followed river after river, only to find them disappear in great swampy pools or reedy morass. At last, in 1830, Sturt managed to follow one of these rivers down to the great River Murray, and thence to the sea. Thus it was gradually shown that all these rivers were part of one great system which drained into the sea at Encounter Bay, in what is now Victoria.

While these discoveries were going on, new settlements were being made along the coast. At home in England the Government were steadily averse from extending their responsibility in Australia, but step by step they were forced to take action. In New South Wales the growth of a large free population made it necessary to distinguish between the well-behaved convicts and those who seemed incorrigible, and so new stations were needed where the latter could be sent under stricter discipline. Besides this, there was the fear of French competition: when Flinders reached Encounter Bay in 1802 he found a French scientific expedition there, and when the name Terre Napoléon appeared on French maps men became anxious. Thus in 1802–1804 several small English settlements were made, and again in 1824–1827 when the restored monarchy in France began to interest itself in colonial schemes. In England, too, the news of the various discoveries stirred the imagination: men dreamt of great fortunes to be made by farming in a fertile country where land could be had for the asking, and so land companies were formed which pushed the reluctant Government to new schemes. Wakefield's plans for emigration gained great support, and the desire to find a colony where they might receive a fair trial led to the founding of South Australia.

Causes of new settlements.

The first of these new settlements was made in Van Diemen's Land in 1803, where two points were occupied to secure the land against French settlement. As a penal settlement Van Diemen's Land had a sad history: it was first used as a place for sending specially vicious characters, and their treatment in the island was too brutal to describe. An even worse fate befell those wretches who were condemned to the special horrors of Macquarie Harbour, where the worst

New Settlements: (1) Van Diemen's Land (Tasmania). 1803.

ruffians laboured under the gaoler's lash, exposed to all winds of heaven. It is little wonder that escapes were frequent, and that bands of desperadoes terrorised the country. These bushrangers in time became so insolent that they claimed to rule the island: expecting no mercy, they showed none, and the whole island was appalled by their cruelty and outrages. Governor Arthur (1824) set himself to stamp out this pest, and though he could not capture all the villains, he managed to reduce their numbers. But Arthur had to face another trouble: the aborigines, a very primitive race of blacks, were friendly to the settlers, but the outrages of the bushrangers, and indeed of many of the early settlers, bred such ill-feeling that a war of extermination began. Arthur tried to organise a vast drive, and so to confine them to one part of the island, but the skilful natives slipped through his beaters. It was the honesty and Christian behaviour of a Methodist workman, George Robinson, that finally secured peace. Alone and unarmed, he went fearlessly among the savages, explained that the white man wished peace to the black-fellow, and thus persuaded them to settle in Flinders Island. Despite the care of various friends, the few survivors of this race soon died out, but the behaviour of Robinson stands out as a bright spot in a terrible story. Though Van Dieman's Land was separated from New South Wales in 1825, and even received some form of constitutional government then, it was still mainly a penal settlement, and when the transporting of convicts to Sydney was stopped in 1840, the whole flood of crime and misery was diverted to Van Diemen's Land. Into this little island convicts were shipped at the rate of four thousand a year, and it was not till 1853, when responsible government was granted to Van Diemen's Land, that the system ceased, and the new name of Tasmania was then adopted to mark the beginning of a new and brighter period.

(2) Western Australia: Swan River.

The next colony to be founded was Western Australia, though it was first called Swan River, a name given by an old Dutch sea-captain who had found black swans there, and for long commemorated by the stamps of the new colony. Alarmed by the rumours of French schemes, Governor Darling had sent a small settlement to King George's Sound (Adelaide) in 1827, and had written home to urge the planting of a colony in the far west, at Swan River. The Imperial Government were anxious not to spend more money, but Sir Robert Peel's cousin, Thomas Peel, was fired with the idea of becoming a great colonial patron, and, if possible, of making some money out of the business. He floated a company, obtained from the Crown a grant of land at Swan River, engaged a number of labourers for his own land, and in 1829 set out with many other emigrants on his great adventure. Peel's schemes, however, fell to pieces; he landed his party on Garden Island, and then began to explore the countryside for suitable places to settle. But difficulties had been greatly underrated; the work of clearing land, building houses and barns, and laying out the farms was too hard for many of the colonists, and they slipped away, some to the other settlements, and some back to England. Peel gave up in despair, but the colony was saved from disappearing altogether by its governor, Stirling, who for many years strove hard to make the place a success, and gradually established a small settlement along the banks of the river. For a long time, however, the colony remained a very small place. It was cut off from the other Australian settlements by hundreds of miles of nearly impassable bush and great waterless deserts; it produced nothing which those colonies would want, and so its whole trade and interests were much more closely bound up with London than with Australian ports. Indeed, when the Commonwealth was discussed, Western Australia for long remained unfriendly, and only decided to join the scheme after the Act had been already passed by the Imperial Parliament. The fortunes of Western Australia long hung in the balance; even in 1850 there were only five thousand people in the colony, and the need for labour was insistent, as but few people would emigrate willingly to a place with such poor prospects. Almost in despair the colonists determined in 1849 to ask for convicts to be sent to the colony, and from 1850 to 1867 convicts were regularly shipped to Western Australia. At the same time the Imperial Government sent a corresponding number of free settlers, and thus the colony was gradually set upon its legs, though the

Peel's colony. 1829.

other Australian colonies looked with much disfavour upon the system. It was, however, the discovery in 1872 of great gold deposits which really made the modern colony. Miners came flocking in from the Victoria gold-fields, and though for some time the old landowning oligarchy strove to keep them out of political power, their influence finally triumphed by forcing Western Australia to join the Commonwealth. The long-promised railway to link this western state with the prosperous eastern towns has just been completed, and thus communication by land has at last been established.

Gold discoveries, 1872.

When Western Australia was founded in 1829, the parallel 129° E. was made the division between the new colony and New South Wales, and so, for the first time, English authority was extended over the whole of Australia. Thus, when a new colony of South Australia came to be settled, it had to be carved out of the boundaries of New South Wales. South Australia is a colony founded specially to test a scientific theory of colonisation, and it attracted a great deal of interest at the time. Wakefield's scheme to raise an immigration fund by the sale of public land at a fixed and "sufficient" price, was looked upon as a solution of the difficulty of finding labour in the colonies, and the recent disaster to Peel's colony on the Swan river was quoted as a case in point where the absurd cheapness of land had turned all the labourers into landowners. Thus Wakefield and his friends pressed for a colony where they might put their theory into practice. Just at this time came news of the discovery of the Murray river, and here seemed an ideal place for a new colony. Wakefield had formed a colonisation society in 1830, but the Government poured cold water on the scheme. "The Secretary of State does not feel at liberty at the present moment to hold out any encouragement to schemes which have for their object the extension of the number of His Majesty's settlements abroad, and which, whether formed in the outset by individuals or the Government, are always liable to end in becoming in some way or other a source of expense to the revenue of this country." But Wakefield's persistence won the day, and in 1834 an Act to found South Australia was

(3) South Australia. 1834.

passed, and a board of commissioners was appointed to sell the land at not less than twelve shillings per acre, using the proceeds as an immigration fund. But the home Government did not intend to spend money on the scheme: the commissioners had to deposit a sum of money as a guarantee, and to raise this money a society was formed which really colonised South Australia. As little forethought was exercised in founding this scientific colony as in Peel's settlement on the Swan river. No surveys were made; the first shiploads of emigrants had to shiver on Kangaroo Island, while their leaders went to find the best site for the settlement. Adelaide was soon chosen, and a town began to grow up on the spot. In England the promoters did their part, ship after ship was sent out, and colonists poured into the country. It seemed at first that the scheme was working splendidly, for there was an abundance of labourers, but things soon went awry. Instead of cultivating their new land, the owners preferred to speculate; they gambled in buying and selling estates, and by 1841 of nearly 300,000 acres which had been sold, only 2500 were under cultivation. To provide work the governor, Gawler, began great public works in Adelaide, and to pay for this he had to issue paper money. For a while there was seeming prosperity, but when news reached the colony that this paper money would not be honoured in England, there was a sudden panic, and it seemed as if South Australia would end in a worse disaster than Swan River. But luckily for the colony the new governor, George Grey, proved a man of great foresight and keen enthusiasm, and his statesmanlike policy saved South Australia. Though only twenty-eight, he was already famous as the explorer of the north-western coasts of Australia. He set to work vigorously to cut down expenditure, a task which at first made him very unpopular, and to encourage the settlers to cultivate their farms, but he also determined to force the Government to honour Gawler's paper money. The very rumour of this attempt quickly improved matters, and when Grey left South Australia in 1845 to become Governor of New Zealand, he was already famous as a skilful and energetic administrator, and he left the colony well on its way to success.

Governor George Grey. 1841–1845.

The two other colonies in Australia, Queensland and Victoria, were out-settlements of Sydney, which, after much clamour, succeeded in separating from New South Wales. But the separation of Victoria is connected with several other important movements, which we must now trace. As the humanitarian movement of the nineteenth century grew, the custom of transportation seemed more and more barbarous and disgraceful; a committee examined the system and exposed its horrors, and so, in 1840, it was ordered that transportation should cease except to Van Diemen's Land. Meanwhile the movement for prison reform had resulted in an attempt to substitute for that deadening system a new method which might give the prisoner a chance of reform. After a certain period of confinement in the special prison at Pentonville, the well-behaved prisoner would be sent abroad with a "conditional pardon." Thus for several years Australia still found itself flooded with criminals, who were no longer under the old restraints of the convicts. Meanwhile, feeling in Australia had been growing, for although the land-owners might like a system which gave them cheap labour, the general population hated the whole policy. Matters came to a head in 1849, when the Government tried once more to send convicts to Australia. A huge public meeting at Melbourne refused to allow the convicts to be landed, threatening armed rebellion; the ship sailed on to Sydney, there to suffer the same fate. Thus, the convict system came to an end in Australia, though it lasted till 1853 in Tasmania: the colonies gained their freedom by their own vigorous protests, for the Whig statesman Lord Grey thought that England "was perfectly justified in continuing the practice of transportation to Australia, the colonies being only entitled to ask that in the arrangements for conducting it their interests and welfare should be consulted as far as possible."

Economic changes.

Meanwhile, the colonists had been growing rich both as sheep-farmers and as agriculturists. Macarthur's breed of sheep had made Australian wool famous, and other sheep-farmers began to breed for mutton as well as for the fleece. Vast areas of land in New South Wales were marked out as sheep-runs, and settlers "squatted" on these runs, paying a small fee to the Government. At first this development of sheep-farming meant a great growth of wealth for the state, but after a time it was found that these vast runs, especially when near to towns, were a hindrance to further settlement, and steps had to be taken to break them up. Besides sheep-farming, agriculture developed too ; new classes of grain were evolved which were better able to stand the dry climate of the land, and Australia gradually became an important wheat-producing country. Soon the harvest became so great that it was difficult to find labourers to gather it, and mechanical reapers were invented. The Australian "stripper," invented in 1843, became the forerunner of the automatic harvester, and Australia led the way in large-scale agriculture, for the wealth of the Canadian prairie land was as yet unknown.

It was the desire to find new lands for sheep-farming that led to the settlement of Victoria. Colonists from Swan River, disgusted with the failure there, came and squatted in the new land, while other settlers crossed the strait from Tasmania, and, making friends with the black man, acquired land. At first the Governor of New South Wales tried to expel these squatters, but he was forced to take over the settlement and to appoint a magistrate there in 1836. Here Melbourne was founded on a beautiful spot, chosen with shrewd foresight by the first squatters, and here there quickly developed a wealthy colony of sheep-breeders. Thus the Port Phillip settlement became rich and important, and looked with ill-favour on the control exercised from Sydney. The sudden growth of this settlement was due to the discovery of gold about 1850, and the fame of the fortunes to be won at Bendigo and Ballarat brought floods of miners from all over the world. Beginning in the early 'fifties, the rush to the mines brought men from California and China, and from all the countries of Europe. Here a future Premier of England rubbed shoulders with an Italian exile, and the failure of the great revolutionary movement of 1848 in Europe sent idealists and conspirators, republicans and visionaries to seek their fortunes in Australia. This inrush of men of advanced ideas had a great influence on Australian development ; it strengthened the growing movement for self-

Squatters in Victoria.

Discovery of gold. 1850.

government, and was responsible for the keen and democratic tinge that politics took on.

The original military government of New South Wales had been modified by Acts of 1823 and 1828, which limited the powers of the governor by giving him a nominated legislative council, but it was early felt that some form of election was necessary for Britons living overseas. So in 1842 it was arranged that the councils of New South Wales and Tasmania should each of them contain a certain number of elective members. Port Philip settlement was specially provided for, as it was given a certain number of representatives on the council of New South Wales, but the settlers there felt that they were unfairly treated and clamoured for separation. To draw attention to their grievances they solemnly elected members of the English Cabinet as their representatives on the Sydney Council. The Imperial Government now decided to have done with the difficult problem once for all: if they could not find something to satisfy the colonies, the colonies must choose for themselves. So by the Act of 1850 Port Phillip was created an independent colony under the name of Victoria, and the colonies were empowered to draft constitutions for themselves, and to submit them to the home Government. No more liberal Act has been passed in the British Parliament, and this Act shows the extent to which the doctrine of responsibility was carried by British statesmen. Within the next few years all the Australian colonies except Western Australia set up for themselves representative government with two houses, and obtained the rights and duties of responsible government. It was not till 1890 that Western Australia had developed sufficiently to be given a similar constitution.

Constitutional development.

Act of 1850.

Victoria a separate colony.

The early settlements on the coast to the north of Sydney were used as convict stations, though they were afterwards abandoned: even Gladstone's plan of 1847 to found a special colony here for the Pentonville probationers was cancelled six months after it was launched. But the real development of Queensland was due to squatters who were pushing north across the Darling Downs, and in 1853 the Governor of New

South Wales determined to appoint a resident. Settlers came quickly, and soon began to agitate for separate government; by 1859 they succeeded in their plans, and the new colony of Queensland was granted responsible government. Founded so late, after the system of transportation had become discredited, the Queensland farmers found themselves hard put to it to obtain labour; the northern part of the colony, too, was of a tropical climate, and whites found it difficult to work on the land. The planters, therefore, looking about for labourers, began to entice the natives from the islands of the Pacific. These Kanakas were brought as indentured labourers to Queensland, where they worked on the sugar plantations for a number of years and were then sent back to their homes with a trumpery reward. Treated well or ill, according to the honesty of their white masters, many of these Kanakas were little better than slaves, and the labour traffic soon got an evil name for brutality and dishonesty, and even the stringent legislation of the Queensland Government did not entirely solve this problem.

Queensland a separate colony. 1859.

Thus by 1860 Australia was divided up into six separate colonies, all except Western Australia possessing responsible government, and all faced with a large number of problems both social and economic. It did not take long for statesmen to realise that for some purposes at least the colonies would do better if they acted in common; but between the different colonies there was keen rivalry, and it was many years before a satisfactory plan was evolved. The statesmen in England had included in the Bill of 1850 a proviso for the election by the local parliaments of a Federal House of Representatives but this clause was struck out. By 1885, however, the need for common action, especially in the Pacific, was very great, and so an Act was passed by the Imperial Parliament enabling the various colonies to create a Federal Council. This plan, however, proved a failure, for New South Wales, the most influential colony, stood aloof from the scheme, and the council when it met had but little authority. It had no executive power, nor could it impose a single tax—it was little better than a

Federal Council. 1885.

debating society. Henry Parkes, the Premier of New South Wales, had worked for the Federal Council although his colony threw over the plan when it had been established, and he now set himself once more to work for federation. Through his influence a convention was called in 1891, which was attended by all the colonies, as well as by New Zealand, and here was drafted a scheme of federation. Again it was Parkes' colony of New South Wales that spoilt the plan,

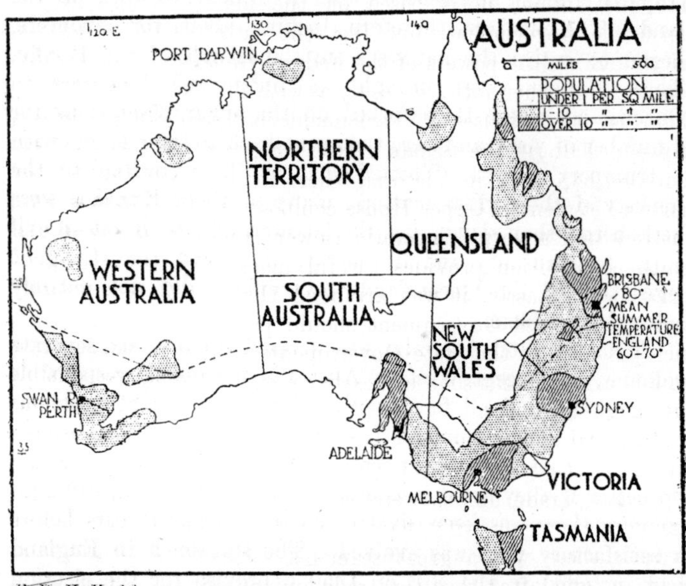

E. H. H. H. del.

All lands north of the dotted line have a mean summer temperature of 80° Fahr.

fearing to give up its great position and influence as premier colony by becoming merely a part of a federation. Now, however, public opinion began to run in favour of the movement: meetings were held all over Australia, and it was determined to call a new convention formed of ten delegates from each colony, who should be elected directly by the people. This second convention met in 1897, and was attended by all the Australian colonies except Queensland :

it drew up a constitution, which was submitted and passed by the people at a referendum, though the fears of New South Wales led to amendment and a second referendum, at which the new constitution was carried by a vast majority. The new constitution was passed by the Imperial Parliament in 1900, and came into operation on New Year's Day, 1901.

Commonwealth of Australia. 1901.

The Commonwealth of Australia is a compromise between the constitutions of Canada and the United States. Like the former it is based on the idea of responsible government, but like the latter it strictly defines the powers of the Federal Government, and all other authority remains with the separate colonies. There are two Houses of Parliament, both elective, though only one half of the Senate retires at a time. Warned by what had happened in Victoria, where there had been violent quarrels between an Upper House composed of an oligarchy of squatters and a very democratic Lower House, the Commonwealth constitution provides careful machinery for avoiding a deadlock. Lastly, it was arranged that for a number of years the Federal Government should pay from the taxes so much per head to the State Governments for their exchequers, but this arrangement soon comes to an end and a new scheme must be thought out.

Labour Party.

Many great changes have come over Australia since 1900, and one of the most important is the rise of the Labour Party to power. Trade unions were early formed in Australia, and were in close touch with the unions of London. In 1890 there was a great seamen's strike in Australia, and after that the trade unions determined to try to obtain political power, so that they might then gain social and economic reform. The political Labour Party soon gained ground, and after the founding of the Commonwealth it held the balance between the other parties; finally in 1910 it attained power with a clear majority of its own. The most important social legislation is the attempt to prevent strikes by compulsory arbitration; special courts were set up, whose findings were authoritative, and strikes were to be punished by the State. But this was not a complete success: there were still some workers who would only accept the finding if in their own favour. Even a Labour Government found it difficult to prevent a strike by force. So attempts have been made along another line, and wages boards consisting of masters and men have been created to settle disputes. The Commonwealth has adopted a policy of protective tariffs; all the colonies except New South Wales had such a tariff before 1900, and the great squatters of New South Wales were forced to swallow Protection as the price of Union. It was generally agreed to give a five per cent. preference to British goods, and since 1906 that has been the rule. But the Labour Party have tried to use Protection for direct social ends; they have placed a heavy duty on foreign sugar, and have given bounties on Queensland sugar grown by white labour. This is part of the policy of "white Australia," which aims at keeping Australia for the European, and preferably for the British race. There is a smaller admixture of other nations in the population of Australia and New Zealand than in any other Dominion, and the "white Australia" policy aims at keeping this distinction. This is done in three ways. Indentured labour is discouraged. The influx of Asiatics is prevented by an education test which is so framed as to exclude Orientals, though this policy leads to delicate questions with Japan, and especially with India. For Indians claim that they too are citizens of the Empire, and object to being excluded from Australia. Lastly, the inflow of Englishmen is encouraged by a system of assisted immigration: the flaring posters and the many-coloured pamphlets, with their fascinating pictures of sheep-shearing and dairy-farming and with their enticing maps, are all a part of this campaign. About 1906 this policy came into full swing, and great numbers of Englishmen went to find new homes in Australia, though there were some people at home who grumbled at the growing depopulation of the British country-side.

White Australia.

To find land for these immigrants a policy of "closer settlement" was adopted, and both New South Wales and South Australia arranged to resume large sheep-runs, where necessary by compulsion, and to break them up for small farms for the newcomers. Money was

Closer settlement.

advanced by the State for the stocking and preliminary working of the new farms, and the price of the land could be repaid on easy terms. Thus the sheep-breeders were pushed further afield, and the land near the towns and railways was to become farm land.

Yet another important result of the Commonwealth was the reorganisation of Australian defence. The Australians realised that if they had these great plans for their future they must be ready to defend their country if necessary; hitherto they had depended on British sea-power for their safety, now they aspired to possess fleets of their own. Thus, after a careful survey by Lord Kitchener, the Commonwealth adopted a scheme of compulsory training for a national militia. They arranged also to build up an Australian fleet unit which should be stationed in the Pacific in peace time, but in war should pass under the authority of the Admiralty in England if necessary. The Commonwealth had assumed large liabilities, for in 1911 it took over the Northern Territory which had previously been administered by South Australia. Five years earlier it had relieved Queensland of responsibility for Papua (British New Guinea). This territory had been annexed by the Imperial Government in 1884 on the urgent advice of the Queensland Government, who feared lest a German colony should be established so near their shores.

Defence.

Australia's future depends on the power of organisation and statesmanship which her citizens can bring to the various tasks which await them. She has begun great experiments in the control and direction of business undertakings by the State, and all the world will look with interest to see how they develop and to learn from her experiments how to solve their own great problems. Australia has still vast tracts of land which will repay cultivation, and as scientific irrigation is applied to her country-side, and the system of artesian wells developed, much land that is now regarded as arid desert may yet become fertile. The policy of "white Australia" must thus be justified by the continued development of the resources of the great continent.

New Zealand

New Zealand lies some thousand miles to the east of Sydney, and is a land of high mountains and beautiful scenery, plentifully watered by many lakes and rivers. Its inhabitants were Maoris, men of the very best type of the Polynesian race, who had attained a very high civilisation, and preserved with pride the traditions of their race and the story of how they came from across the sea to settle in their new home.

The early European explorers did not find New Zealand, and even when Tasman reached the islands in 1642 he learnt but little of their shape and size, and it was really Captain Cook who first made a careful examination of their coasts in 1769. From the early days of the nineteenth century Europeans began to visit New Zealand; whalers called there and made the place a depôt, shipwrecked crews and escaped convicts squatted where they could, traders arrived and soon got on friendly terms with the Maoris, though unscrupulous men were ready to barter firearms, or even to lend their ships and help in native blood feuds, and this soon led to reprisals. But while the riff-raff of civilisation was gradually collected in the islands, another set of men were at work striving to show the Maoris a different side of European civilisation. Mission stations sprang up, and the energetic type of practical man who went as missionary to New Zealand did a great work among the Maoris, and always stood for honest dealing with the natives.

The Governor of New South Wales was watching this development with anxious eyes, and felt that such a disorderly crew of settlers needed some control, but the Imperial Government was loth to extend its authority any further. Moved at last by vague stories of what was going on, the Crown extended the Governor's jurisdiction over the settlers in New Zealand, and in 1833 a resident magistrate was even appointed.

New Zealand annexed, 1839. A separate colony, 1840.

Things were brought to a head in 1839. It was known that a party of French colonists intended to settle in New Zealand and doubtless claim the country for France, while in England the energetic Wakefield, not content with his venture in South Australia, was busily organising a company to acquire land and colonise New Zealand on the basis of his famous theory. His brother had actually set out for the new land, and it was certain that if no steps were taken to control the Company, trouble with the Maoris would certainly ensue. New Zealand was, therefore, annexed to New South Wales, and Hobson sent out as deputy-governor; next year (1840) it became a separate colony. Hobson had a difficult task, for the North Island was full of Maoris, who were deeply suspicious of the arrival of the white men, but he succeeded in making friends with them and persuading them to agree to the Treaty of Waitangi. By this arrangement they recognised the sovereignty of the British, and in return the possession of their lands was guaranteed to them for ever.

Treaty of Waitangi. 1840.

For the first twelve years of the life of the new colony there were two conflicting authorities in the islands: the Governor representing the Crown, and the Wakefield Company representing a powerful moneyed interest in England. This division of authority nearly ruined New Zealand, for despite the efforts of the Governor the Company bought land direct from the natives, and this quickly led to disputes. The Maoris held that land belonged to the tribe and not to the individual, and so refused to recognise land sales made to the Company by individuals, even if they were chiefs. As soon as Wakefield arrived, he made large purchases, while close on his heels came the first batch of settlers clamouring for the land which had been promised them. Wellington and New Plymouth were founded by the Company in the North Island, and Nelson in the South Island, while Hobson founded Auckland as the seat of government. Meanwhile, a special commissioner had been appointed to inquire into the purchase of land, and he limited Wakefield's concessions very severely: it was also ordered that no purchase should be made from the Maoris except through the Government. This sound policy, however, was not strictly carried out, for Hobson's successors were not strong men, while the Company was very powerful in England. The Maoris were alarmed at the whole proceeding, and blood had already been shed when George Grey was sent from

New Zealand Company. 1841.

NEW ZEALAND.

Walker & Boutall sc.

Longmans & Co. London & New York.

South Australia to undertake the government of New Zealand.

The new Governor threw himself heart and soul into the problems which faced him. He worked hard to prevent the fraudulent transfer of land from the natives in the North Island, and by a series of skilful purchases in the South Island, where there were but few Maoris living, he was able to make room for fresh colonists without disturbing the natives. Thus there sprang up two new settlements in the South Island, Otago, founded by Scotch Presbyterians, and Canterbury, a Church of England settlement promoted by Selwyn, the first Bishop of New Zealand. With the Maoris, too, Grey won a great success. He set to work to learn their language, studied their customs and ideas, and was thus able to meet their chiefs and discuss in person their complaints. By this means Grey gained their entire sympathy, for they respected a man who was both firm and just, and who showed not the slightest trace of personal fear or private ambition. Indeed, their love for him went so far that a native chief whom he had once imprisoned petitioned the Queen that Grey should be made perpetual Governor of New Zealand. The Governor showed his courage in yet another way, for when in 1846 a paper constitution was granted to New Zealand, which seemed to him too elaborate and quite unsuited to the needs of the colony, he simply refrained from putting it into force. In England the ministry recognised its mistake, and Grey and his council were asked to suggest a suitable form of government. Meanwhile, in 1851, the New Zealand Company had been dissolved, and this cleared the ground. Next year a constitution was granted to the colony, based on the Governor's recommendations. The six chief settlements became provinces, with councils for local affairs, while over all there was the Governor with a Federal Council and Assembly.

George Grey, Governor, 1845-1853 and 1862-1867.

Federal constitution. 1852.

But the British colonists and the Maoris were not destined to settle down side by side without further strife. With the removal of Grey's influence, by his transference to the Cape in 1853, trouble soon began, and in 1860 a dispute over a land purchase led to war. The tribe which refused to recognise the sale appealed for help to a semi-independent Maori "king," whom some of the tribes of the North Island had recently proclaimed, and the Governor foolishly declared that he was going to abolish this "king-state." Grey was sent post-haste from South Africa to save the situation. He urged the restoration of the disputed territory, and it seemed at first that he would succeed in pacifying the island, but a treacherous attack by some Maoris made war break out again (1863). The Maoris were fighting a losing battle, for Grey's influence obtained help from friendly Maori tribes. But the war was prolonged by the disputes between the Governor and the military authorities; the control of Maori affairs had by now been handed over to the colonists, and the Imperial troops were gradually withdrawn. In 1866 Grey declared that peace had been restored, and soon after, his term of office expired. A few years later there was another outbreak, but it was quickly suppressed by colonial militia. After the war a policy of conciliation was adopted: tribes were allowed to return to their lands, while roads and railways began to open up the country, and the memory of the struggle gradually passed into the background.

The Great Maori War. 1860–1870.

Except for the Maori War, and for the fact that convicts were never sent to the country, the social and political development of New Zealand was similar to that of Australia. But New Zealand is not so hot a country as Australia, for its climate is more like that of England. Sheep-farming early became an important industry; with the invention of cold storage, mutton as well as wool was exported to England, and "Canterbury lamb" reminds every one of this fact. Dairy-farming was also a profitable occupation. Though the constitution of 1852 did not contemplate responsible government, the idea was in the air; the colonists claimed the right to govern themselves, and in 1856 the first responsible ministry was formed, though the control of Maori affairs was not handed over till some years later. In 1870 the old system of provincial governments was abolished, and New Zealand became a unitary state: a few years earlier the capital was

Economic development.

Responsible government. 1856.

moved from the northern town of Auckland to the more conveniently situated Wellington on Cook's Strait. Since then New Zealand has developed a strongly democratic government, and has enjoyed the strange experience of seeing one who had but lately been her Governor play the part of responsible minister, for the versatile Sir George Grey had not finished with New Zealand when his second term as Governor expired. He returned to the colony and soon became famous as a Radical premier.

New Zealand has been a pioneer in democratic and social legislation. She soon adopted universal adult suffrage and the payment of members, and her social legislation led the way in regulating the conditions of labour, both in the workshop and on board ship. She early tackled the problem of big estates, and successfully adopted the plan of breaking them up for closer settlement by small farmers. A wide scheme of Government loans to farmers, and a policy of retaining the ownership of land in the hands of the State, has also been tried; while State-aided immigration has been in operation for many years. The aim is to make New Zealand a preserve for the white man and to develop in the Dominion an ideal system of social life by means of a vast scheme of State regulation.

The Maoris' position.

The position of the Maoris in New Zealand is unique. Ever since the end of the Maori War they have been recognised as full citizens of the State: the New Zealand nation consists of the Europeans and the Maoris. The Maoris possess special representation in the Dominion Parliament, electing four members of their own, Maoris sit in the Senate, they assist in the administration of the Native Land Court, and control their local councils. Thus the Maoris seem definitely to have decided to accept the new civilisation and to become part of a modern state. During the great war, when New Zealand supplied her share to the famous Anzac Corps, the Maoris insisted on taking their part in the risk and honour of the war. Thus the native question in New Zealand has ceased to be a difficult problem, as it still is in South Africa, but the political future of the country is of great interest. New Zealand is

New Zealand and the Pacific.

naturally interested in the control of the Pacific, and some groups of islands have already been handed over to her control. She has not, however, been able to decide on joining the Commonwealth of Australia, although negotiations were on foot in 1900, but despite the similarity of interests she prefers at present to continue her development as a separate Dominion within the Empire.

BOOKS.—R. Jenks, *A History of the Australasian Colonies*, and E. Scott, *A Short History of Australia*, are useful text-books. W. P. Reeves, *The Long White Cloud*, tells the story of New Zealand up to the end of last century in a fascinating way, and is illustrated. C. G. Henderson, *Life of Sir George Grey*. C. G. Wade, *Australia*, describes recent experiments in social legislation in Australia.

1788. **Convict settlement at Botany Bay.**
1829. **Swan River (Western Australia) Colony.**
1834. **South Australia founded by Wakefield's influence.**
1839 **New Zealand annexed. (1840. Treaty of Waitangi.)**
1850. **Act of Parliament (1) separates Victoria; (2) allows colonies to choose their own form of government.**
1901. **Commonwealth of Australia.**

CHAPTER XII

The Commonwealth of Nations

THE development of responsible government in the colonies, and the adoption of a free trade policy in Britain, were accompanied by a general feeling that the inevitable result would be the complete separation of the colonies from the Mother Country. When the Dominions rejected the new-found gospel of free trade and built tariff walls to foster their own manufactures it seemed as if the last straw were added; the sooner the Dominions became independent states the better, for then the Mother Country would no longer run the risk of being dragged into war for any local quarrel.[1] This

[1] The Canadian tariff of 1859 marks an important step in this development. See pages 135, 136.

attitude was very general at home, though in the colonies men were not over-anxious to cut themselves off from the protection of the all-powerful British fleet. But despite the economic doctrines of the day, there were not wanting, even in Britain, men of wide imagination, who could not think that the Empire must split up into separate and possibly warring nations; with no very clear idea of the future, they yet believed that some future development would link the Dominions and the Mother Country together for common action and common defence. As the nineteenth century went on, this feeling gradually developed. The separation of the Colonies from the War Office in 1854 marked a step in the right direction, while the founding of the Royal Colonial Institute provided a rallying point where statesmen and administrators from different parts of the Empire could meet in London and exchange ideas with others interested in Imperial problems.

Reaction against idea of Imperial dissolution.

The new ideas gained ground during the 'eighties, and the interest in Imperial affairs was stimulated by the writing of some famous books. Both at Cambridge and Oxford there were teachers of history who appreciated the romance of British development: Seeley's lectures drew crowds of students, and his *Expansion of England* re-told the story of the eighteenth century in a new and fascinating way; Froude visited South Africa and Australia, and related his experiences in *Oceana;* while Sir Charles Dilke, a thoughtful statesman, had already coined a new word to express a new development; his fascinating book, *Greater Britain*, did much to teach people that there were real problems worthy of careful thought. In the colonies, too, there was growing up that sense of nationality which made men feel that the word colonial was an insult, Canadian or New Zealander should be used instead. But this very feeling emphasised the unity between colony and home country; the same tongue, similar institutions, and a similar culture drew men closer, despite the growth of marked differences. At the same time, the reluctance of the home Government to undertake new Imperial responsibilities, as in the case of New Guinea or South West Africa, made the colonies feel that they needed a closer co-operation for the purpose of influencing British foreign policy. They could not afford to set up as independent states, at least for the present, but they did wish to use the might of the British Empire to gain their own ends. The sudden scramble to divide out the ends of the earth, which began in 1884 at the Berlin Conference, made all the parts of the Empire draw together for common support. Nor were the various inventions and improvements in communications without their part in linking the Empire together, by improving the transit of news and of private messages, and by enabling visits to be paid to friends in distant lands. Train, steamer, telegraph, cable, post, all helped to dispel that placid ignorance which is the basis of prejudice and ill-feeling.

The result of this reawakening interest was an examination of the various problems of Empire, and an attempt to find solutions for them. The constitution of the Empire was then, as it is to-day, largely the result of custom and common practice, and much of it seemed illogical. The very fact that the constitution could grow and develop without elaborate machinery, was a source of strength, but some of the absurdities needed alteration. It was obviously ridiculous, for instance, that a man who had been naturalised in Canada, and might even be a Minister of the Crown, should be merely an alien if he came to England! Many other laws needed to be adjusted so that they should have the same effect throughout the Empire, but there were even graver problems to be settled.

The year 1887 was the jubilee of Queen Victoria's accession, and it was decided to take the opportunity of the visit of many statesmen from various parts of the Empire to London to hold a conference of representatives from the different colonies. Though this conference did not produce any very great results, it was an important step in the development of the Empire. It was quite obvious that the delegates, though not ready to draft any formal scheme of union, did not hold the old idea that the future of the Empire was speedy separation. The Conference of 1887 was but the beginning of a series of conferences: it is another example of the way in which the British constitution evolves to meet the needs of the day, without relying on formal written constitutions. Seven years later the Canadian

Conferences at London, 1887 and 1897.

Government called a conference at Ottawa to discuss the trade relations of the Empire, and recommended a system of Imperial preferential tariffs. At the diamond jubilee in 1897 the second Conference was held at London, and representatives of the colonial governments discussed a number of questions with Joseph Chamberlain, the Colonial Secretary, and parted with the recommendation that periodic conferences should be held.

There were three main problems which came up for discussion at these conferences, and they are still important problems in Imperial organisation. The first was the question of Imperial trade. The various colonies had adopted a system of protective tariffs, but they wished, if possible, to encourage and develop trade within the Empire. They dreamt of binding the Empire together again by ties of economic interest, such as had existed in the days of the "old" Empire. But, instead of the British Parliament creating the system and forcing it on the Colonies, it was to be built up by the joint authority of the British and Colonial Parliaments. Thus, the colonies desired a system of preferential tariffs which should keep trade within the Empire by only allowing foreign goods to be imported after paying a high import duty. This was the scheme at which the Ottawa Conference aimed, while the matter was raised again in 1897. But here the economic ideas of the Mother Country and the colonies were directly opposed. The adoption of Free Trade by Britain had been followed by a period of great prosperity, and statesmen did not wish to tamper with the system. Though willing to leave the colonies absolutely free as to their tariff policy, and to negotiate for their relief from old treaties made by England, which still bound them in this matter, the Imperial Government would not alter its own system.

Problems: (1) Preferential tariffs.

The second great problem concerned the relations between the colonies and the Mother Country. In England a society had been formed for encouraging Imperial federation, but statesmen were shy of handling the matter. When the question was raised in the Conference of 1897 the colonies were diffident; the problems to be solved were so great, the success of any formal scheme was so questionable, that it was decided to let well alone. Although

(2) Imperial federation.

in theory a scheme of federation may look very simple, in practice there are often unexpected and even alarming developments, as may be seen from the history of the United States, or any federal constitution. The Dominions were jealous of their autonomy, and feared that any new central authority would encroach on their local powers. Then, again, there were obvious difficulties. How were the states to be represented? If on a population basis, Britain would swamp the Dominions; if on a basis of states, then they would outvote the Mother Country: and neither arrangement promised a satisfactory solution of the problem. And there was yet another difficulty. Representative institutions seem to need party organisation, and with party government comes all the dust and clamour of party strife, the lies and abuse of the party press, and the trickeries of electioneering. Any change might prejudice the relations of the home country with the Dominions, and spoil the calm spirit of the conference where Labour premier can meet Tory statesman, and French Canadian talk with Dutch Afrikander in honest confidence and truth. Thus, for a time, the question was dropped.

The problem which interested the Imperial Government most, and which it was most anxious to get the colonies to tackle, was the question of Imperial defence. This problem was of increasing importance, for though the grant of responsible government implied that the colonies were responsible for their own defence, their real security depended on the supremacy of the Navy, and the British control of the sea. As science developed, the cost of material and upkeep continually increased, and this burden was borne by the Mother Country alone. Though the grouping of the distant fleets by the Admiralty should be based only on strategic considerations, yet each colony wished to see as large a squadron stationed off its shores as possible. The colonies were growing quickly both in population and in wealth, and it seemed but fair that they should help to share the burden of naval defence. This question involved two other problems: the old principle of no taxation without representation loomed in the background, while it was obvious that if the colonies helped to keep the Navy, they

(3) Imperial defence.

should have some share in controlling foreign policy, and so in deciding the ultimate issues of war and peace. But this was a very difficult question, and little progress was made in the matter. The Australian colonies, however, promised in 1887 an annual subsidy to the Pacific squadron; they renewed the guarantee in 1897, while the Cape and Natal also gave an annual subsidy in that year.

The influence of Joseph Chamberlain had a great effect in encouraging the growth of Imperial sentiment. A man of large ideas, self-reliant and of vigorous personality, he deliberately chose what had previously been regarded as a minor office that he might show how important he considered Imperial affairs, and might give full play to his schemes. While Colonial Secretary from 1895 to 1902 he took special interest in developing the Crown colonies, and wherever he went he left his mark in some improvement, or some new undertaking. He was the guiding spirit at the Conference of 1897, and though his explanation of the problem of Imperial defence did not at the time obtain great results, he was soon recognised as a true prophet. When the Boer War broke out in 1899, and the British were so hard pressed in South Africa, the Dominion of Canada and all the colonies of Australia sent troops to fight for what they felt was the common cause. The sight of their nodding plumes and clattering horses, as they came up the sunny streets of Cape Town, was a cheery sight in a very anxious time, and a visible pledge of Imperial unity. This was not the first occasion that a self-governing colony had sent aid to an Imperial expedition, for New South Wales had sent troops to assist in the Sudan campaign. But it was the first time that troops from all the self-governing colonies had fought side by side, and it emphasised both the need for some common scheme of Imperial defence, and for some method for the joint control of foreign policy.

South African War, 1899-1902. Help from the colonies.

In 1902, at King Edward VII's coronation, there met the next Colonial Conference: again there was an exchange of ideas, but little definite work accomplished. Despite Chamberlain's suggestions, federal union was not supported, while the unanimous desire of the Dominions for a

Conference of 1902.

scheme of preferential tariffs was courteously refused by the Imperial Government. But now there came a dramatic turn of events. Chamberlain declared himself a convert to the policy of Tariff Reform; he resigned from the Government, and stumped the country on behalf of Colonial Preference. His campaign was a failure, the country did not respond; he split his party, and at the next election in 1906 the Liberals gained a sweeping victory.

The development of the Empire during the last twenty years has been conditioned by the German menace, and the steps that had to be taken in defence; just as after 1884 the Empire began to draw together in self-defence, so lately the need of mutual protection has driven the different units to common counsel and common action. Things were made easier for Imperial statesmen by the federation of Australia in 1900 and the union of South Africa nine years later, for thus there were two large states with which to deal instead of many conflicting colonies. For a little while interest in Imperial matters was somewhat hidden by the development of foreign affairs. A great movement for substituting arbitration for war was quickly gaining ground; led by Britain and America many countries had agreed to submit their disputes to arbitration, and treaties to that effect had been signed almost throughout the world. Though the Conferences at the Hague (1899 and 1907) had failed to bring about a reduction of armaments, much good work had been done, and men looked forward to a better future. Britain, too, had set herself to improve her international relations: by the Entente of 1904 she had settled her outstanding quarrels with France, and three years later a similar arrangement was made with Russia. Fired by this plan, the Liberal Government of 1906 set itself to come to an understanding with Germany, and thus to remove the one cloud on the sky-line. Here, however, failure was to come.

Movement for international arbitration.

The Colonial Conference of 1902 had arranged for the holding of such Conferences at four-year intervals, and the next Conference met in 1907. It can be easily understood that the usual subjects of discussion were out of place: the Liberal Government were pledged to

Conference of 1907.

a policy of Free Trade, the question of federation did not appeal to either party, while elaborate schemes of defence seemed absurd at a time when all efforts were being turned to disarmament and international good feeling. The Conference, therefore, spent its energies in organising its own machinery, and arranging the procedure for future meetings. It was decided that the Conference should in future consist of the Premiers of the Dominions, with the Colonial Secretary and the British Premier, who was to act as chairman. A permanent staff was appointed to prepare the agenda for business, and to collect information. The Conference also resolved that, if necessary, special conferences should be called to deal with any urgent question that might arise.

The first of these special conferences was summoned within two years. The German naval preparations were so alarming, the avowed hostility to the British Empire so open, that the Imperial Government was forced to call a special Conference in 1909 to discuss the very question of defence which it had not considered necessary to examine in 1907. At this Conference the momentous decision was adopted that the Dominions should set up local navies as branches of the Royal Navy. Although the ideal from a purely strategic point of view was to have one fleet under one centralised control, distributed over the seas of the world as seemed best for the needs of the moment, the growing desire of the Dominions to have local squadrons under their own control led to a compromise. South Africa and New Zealand preferred to continue a system of subsidies, but the Dominion and the Commonwealth both undertook to raise and maintain separate fleet units, which should be armed, disciplined and trained on the same lines as the Royal Navy. Thus in war-time it would be possible, if desired, to place these fleet units under Imperial control. Australia carried out her plans, beginning her fleet with the *Sydney*, which did such good work in destroying the German cruiser *Emden* in 1915. In Canada the fall of the Laurier government in 1911 led to a change of plan: Sir Robert Borden, the new Premier, did not approve of the policy of separate fleet units, and preferred to continue a subsidy.

Special Defence Conference, 1909.

Besides these naval preparations, plans were made to train and organise the Dominion citizen forces on similar lines to the Imperial troops, so that co-operation in case of need should be easy and effective.

The important decision to create Dominion fleet units showed that the question of the control of foreign policy could not much longer remain undecided. Thus when the next Conference met in 1911 this question came quickly to the fore. It was pointed out that the British delegates to the Hague Conference had received instructions which were drafted without consultation with the Dominions, while the Declaration of London, an agreement modifying International Law as to sea-warfare, had been made without their previous knowledge. The Imperial Government willingly promised to consult them as to future instructions to representatives at the Hague, and about the negotiation of treaties. Sir Wilfrid Laurier, however, was anxious about this latter promise; he did not wish Canada to find herself bound to fight in any future wars because of any responsibility for British diplomacy. But the most important step was to come. At a secret meeting the Foreign Minister, Sir Edward Grey, made a full and confidential review of the whole international situation, and thus for the first time the Dominions were taken into the confidence of the Imperial Government, and were in a position to appreciate the storm-clouds which were gathering in the sky.

The Imperial Conference of 1911.

The outbreak of the war with Germany in 1914 showed that the Empire, loosely knit as it might seem politically, could yet act together quickly in a crisis. The time and thought which had been spent on the question of Imperial defence were now repaid, and not only all the Dominions, but India and also the dependent Empire sent willingly to help in a common cause. The local fleet units were placed under Imperial control, and played their part in the keeping of the seas. The Commonwealth seized New Guinea and the other German possessions in the Pacific, while men from Australia and New Zealand won immortal fame, and created the charmed word of Anzac. Thence they fought in Egypt, and took part in the great drive through Palestine. Union troops swept through the desert land of German South West Africa, and, led by Botha and Smuts, rounded up the enemy by a brilliant campaign in a difficult country. Later they took part in a still more trying business, and helped to beat the tropical forest and bush-covered mountains of East Africa. From Canada came help at the most critical time, and the first Canadian Division took its place in the line in Flanders early in 1915, and a constant stream of men, both new divisions and drafts, came steadily until the war was won. "The Australians at the Dardanelles, and the Canadians at Ypres," declared a French general, "fought with supreme and absolute devotion for what to many of them must have seemed simple abstractions, and that nation which will support for an abstraction the horror of this war of all wars, will ever hold the highest place in the records of human valour."

The Dominions and the War. 1914-1918.

As the war went on another development took place in the relations of the Empire. The usual conference which should have been held in 1915 had been postponed because of the war, but it was now felt that a special conference should be held, both to decide on closer co-operation during the war itself, and to discuss the terms on which peace could be made when the time should come. The Coalition Government, which came into power under Lloyd George in December, 1916, decided to form an inner "War" Cabinet to press on the conduct of the war, and promptly invited the Dominions to a special War Conference. A new step was taken by including the Secretary of State for India in the invitation. This Conference met in the middle of March, 1917, though an Australian representative could not be present for the moment owing to a general election. Meanwhile, it was decided to invite the Dominion premiers to sit as members of the War Cabinet to deal with wide Imperial affairs. Thus without any special constitutional legislation the Dominions were given a share in the responsibilities and executive authority of the Imperial Government. So successful did this experiment prove, that when the members of the Conference returned to their

War Cabinet: Dominion premiers included 1917.

Dominions, General Smuts remained as a member of the War Cabinet. The Conference itself passed a resolution before dispersing, that an Imperial Conference should be called after the war to consider the readjustment of constitutional relations upon the basis of "a full recognition of the Dominions as autonomous nations of an Imperial Commonwealth, and of India as an important part of the same." It should "recognise the right of the Dominions and India to an adequate voice in foreign policy and in foreign relations." This resolution is of fundamental importance, as it lays down the claims of the Dominions in clear and unmistakable terms.

It was not long before these claims were definitely recognised. When the terms of the Peace came to be discussed, the Dominions were for the first time officially represented at a Peace Conference, and for the first time they signed a Peace Treaty as "smaller nations." Under the stress of war a spirit of idealism had grown up, for only high ideals could justify such terrible sacrifices, and from this spirit of idealism sprang the Covenant of the League of Nations, an attempt to organise an international league for the prevention of war, and the encouragement of disarmament and arbitration. In the scheme of the League of Nations the Dominions were recognised as smaller nations, having their seats on the Assembly, but with special arrangements as to voting power; to this proposal America has objected, claiming that such a representation unfairly outweighs her own position.

Dominions sign Treaty of Versailles. 1919.

In joining the League of Nations both Great Britain and the Dominions have been willing to submit to restraints, and to undertake obligations far more onerous than they were ready to bear for any scheme of Imperial union before the war. This shows what a strong appeal is made by the attempt to find some practical international machinery. The success of its working must depend on the honesty with which the new scheme is handled. The present position of the Empire is illogical, and the League has made it more illogical than ever, but the British people have never troubled themselves about logicality; their concern has always been with the practical working of institutions. The essential facts of the situation are these. There is spread throughout the world a friendly fellowship of six English-speaking nations. The four Dominions and Britain herself are legally subject to one Crown, the sixth is the great independent Republic of the United States. These nations have the same great story to look back upon, the same literary heritage, similar ideals, a similar type of institution and of culture. They are responsible in one way or another for the welfare and protection of over five hundred million people. The future alone can show how these nations will develop, but their destiny lies safe in the keeping of the coming generation.

BOOKS.—See Note to Chapter VIII. Most of the literature on this subject is political and discusses the possible developments of the future. An interesting book is G. L. Beer, *The English-speaking Peoples.*

1854. Office of Colonial Secretary established.
1887. Jubilee Conference in London.
1909. Special Defence Conference: fleet units established.
1917. Imperial War Conference and Imperial War Cabinet.
1919. Dominions sign Treaty and join League as "smaller nations."

CHAPTER XIII

The End of the East India Company, 1818–1858

LORD HASTINGS' settlement of the Mahratta problem in 1818 decided that there should be one effectively supreme power throughout India. The Directors, however, were reluctant to accept this inheritance, but all their wishes and express instructions to their servants could not alter the fact that peace could only be secured by the existence of one great power ruling India from North to South. That power was to be the British Raj. Indian history is made up for the next forty

British expansion. 1818–1858.

years of a series of wars arising out of this unsatisfactory state of affairs, followed by periods of reaction when the Directors strove in vain against an almost inevitable development.

The British power advanced in two directions: on the north-west towards the Himalayas, until a more definite frontier was reached with the wilds of Afghanistan, and eastward in Burma across the Bay of Bengal. Another factor complicated the situation. Just as Wellesley was always alarmed lest French influence should supplant the British in India, so during the nineteenth century the advance of Russia through Central Asia was a continual nightmare to British statesmen. Diplomatists dreamed of Russian schemes of invasion through the passes of Afghanistan, while soldiers were for ever considering the best lines of defence if war should come. After the Treaty of Vienna in 1815, Russia had become one of the reactionary powers in Europe, and Britain, frightened of her schemes, supported Turkey throughout the century for fear lest Russia should gain influence over the Ottoman Empire, and so control the Mediterranean and menace India.

Burmese War. 1825-1826.

Hastings' wars had been denounced in England, and his successor, Lord Amherst, was expected to continue the old policy of non-intervention, but the fates were against him, for he at once found himself faced by a long-standing quarrel. For some time there had been disputes between Burma and the British over the question of political refugees who had fled for British protection: and the Burmese Government had invaded British territory, while extending their power in Assam. Thus Amherst found himself forced into a war against his will. The Burmese intended to invade Bengal by land, but a British expedition took them by surprise and landed men at Rangoon, who quickly defeated the army which opposed them. Next year an advance was made up the river towards Ava, the capital, and the Burmese were so alarmed that they quickly made peace. Besides an indemnity, the inland province of Assam and the seaboard provinces of Arakan and Tenasserim were ceded to the British. The great port of Rangoon and the whole of Upper and Lower Burma were left untouched.

After this long series of wars there followed again a period of non-intervention. The Governor-General, Lord William Bentinck, was not only personally inclined to such a policy, but he had very definite orders on the subject from the Company. Bentinck was a typical Liberal of his day, and in many of his schemes a forerunner of that other great reformer, Lord Dalhousie: his attack on the practice of widow-burning (sati) and the hereditary system of highway-robbery (thagi) was a forecast of Dalhousie's methods. In his dealings with native states Bentinck determined to interfere as little as possible; but he gradually realised that this policy had its limits. The alliance guaranteed a native prince protection from external attack, but it was quite impossible for the British Government to stand by and watch a devastating civil war, or a deliberate policy of cruelty and oppression. In several cases Bentinck found his patience strained to the limit, and particularly in the case of Coorg. Here the rajah carried out a series of ghastly brutalities, and when warned he declared war on the British Government. After his defeat his people begged that he might be sent away and Coorg annexed, and Bentinck was forced to comply.

Lord William Bentinck. 1826–1835. Internal reforms.

The end of Bentinck's government coincided with the growth of suspicion against Russia, which turned men's attention to the north-west frontier of India. Here the British power extended, by alliances with the Rajput states, to the bank of the River Sutlej. North of the river, in the Punjab, dwelt the Sikhs, a vigorous and warlike aristocracy who professed a religion that was a type of reformed Hinduism. These stalwart people were now ruled by a great soldier-statesman, Ranjit Singh, the "Lion of Lahore." This man had reorganised the Sikh army, trained and disciplined it with the help of some of Napoleon's officers, and had established his power against the Afghan claims to his borderland. In 1809 he had made the Treaty of Amritsar with the British, by which the Sutlej was recognised as the common frontier, and Ranjit Singh loyally

The North-West Frontier.

abode by the agreement all his life. But the Sikh power with its well-organised army was a standing menace to British rule, and its situation on the route to Afghanistan and the great passes made it yet more important.

Yet further east the vast wall of the Himalayas shut off the mountain country of Afghanistan. Here the strength of the State depended on the strength of the individual ruler, and at the moment the country seemed in danger of breaking up. Dost Mahomed held Kabul, but the Persians were threatening his western frontier, while another claimant to the throne, Shah Shuja, was a fugitive in India. To the south of the Punjab lay the barren land of Sind; important since it controlled the route to easy passes into Afghanistan, and because the Indus with all its commerce flowed through its territory.

When Lord Auckland came to India in 1836 English jealousy of Russia was very great, and the new Governor-General soon began to hear rumours of Russian negotiations in Afghanistan. He felt that the present ruler, Dost Mahomed, was not favourable to British interests, and so devised the ill-planned scheme of placing the feeble old man, Shah Shuja, on the throne instead. Ranjit Singh, though an ally of the Company, would not allow the passage of a British army through the Punjab, and so arrangements were made to march through Sind. At first all went well, Kabul was occupied, and Shah Shuja placed on the throne, but soon a reaction set in. Kabul rose and murdered the British resident; the army withdrew under a safe-conduct, but was treacherously attacked and destroyed in the Khyber Pass. Only one single man escaped to tell the story. Auckland was too unnerved by the disaster to do anything, but fortunately his successor, Lord Ellenborough, was a man of action. He determined to avenge the treachery, and so to restore British prestige, but he realised the absurdity of attempting to force an old and feeble ruler on an independent race of mountaineers; so after recapturing Kabul, he withdrew from Afghanistan and left the Afghans to their own devices. Issuing a bombastic proclamation, Ellenborough tried to cover the failure of the adventure by pomp and pageantry: he even brought back with

Afghan War. 1839–1842.

great solemnity a set of gates which the Afghans had carried off many years before from a Hindu temple. It was quickly rumoured that these gates were forgeries, and the bombastic Governor-General found himself a general laughing-stock.

Though the Afghan policy had been a failure, British power was soon carried up to the mountain wall, the natural frontier of India. Ellenborough had been annoyed at the behaviour of the Amirs of Sind, and he quickly quarrelled with them, accusing them of breaches of various agreements. But the real reason for the attack on Sind was Ellenborough's great desire to do something to restore British prestige after the Afghan fiasco. After a short campaign Sind was annexed, and a violent controversy broke out as to the truth of the story that the Amirs had been guilty of intrigues against British power.

Capture of Sind. 1843.

The Punjab, however, as long as Ranjit Singh was alive, remained on friendly terms with the British Government, and even after his death in 1839 peace continued for some time. But as soon as the strong hold of Ranjit Singh was removed, trouble began in the Punjab: quarrels between rival leaders, and palace revolutions, weakened the state, while the army got completely out of hand. Committees of five in each regiment, elected by the soldiers themselves, controlled all their officers, and finally in November, 1845, the so-called government encouraged the army in an attack on British territory, in the hope of ending the anarchy. The Sikh army was by far the best native army in India, and had its leaders been faithful to the cause it might have done serious damage. As it was the war was short, but very bloody; within eight weeks no fewer than four pitched battles had been fought, but the victory of Sobraon (February, 1846) was really the end of the war. In settling the Punjab Lord Hardinge determined against annexation. He recognised Kashmir, which had been conquered by Ranjit Singh, as a separate state, and made an alliance with its ruler. But the Punjab itself was to remain an independent state: the Sikh army was disbanded, and a British force was only left there for a year, on the urgent request of the Sikhs themselves. Hardinge explained his policy to the Sikh leaders. "The

First Sikh War. 1845–1846.

P

British Government does not desire to interfere in your internal affairs . . . you will become an independent and prosperous state. The success or failure is in your own hands." The attempt, however, ended in failure, for the disbanded army were eager to seize any opportunity of reasserting their power, while the weakness of a regency allowed the local Sirdars to become very independent. At last, in 1848, the trouble came to a head, a Sirdar named Sher Singh revolted, and was helped by the disbanded army of the Sikhs and by the Afghans. Early in January the British Army fought a dearly-won battle at Chillianwallah, and a month later destroyed the Sikh army at Guzerat. Lord Dalhousie, who was now the Governor-General, determined at once to annex the Punjab, and within a few years it became the model province of British India.

Second Sikh War. 1848-1849.

With the final settlement of the Punjab, British power in India extended nearly as far as it does to-day; but besides this external expansion there had been going on a less obvious movement, but one that was quite as important for the future of the country. By the time of Wellesley's conquests, men had begun to realise that, for better or worse, the British position in India had entirely altered. The British power now extended over many millions of Indians, and thoughtful men began to ask themselves what principle should guide Britain in her treatment of the natives? Now that this great power had been acquired, how was it to be used? In India this problem was faced by a group of energetic servants of the Company, who were constantly brought into touch with the natives during great inquiries made for settling the land revenue in different conquered territories. These statesmen realised that no good was to be gained by sweeping away wholesale native customs and native laws; and they showed a sympathetic attempt to understand the native point of view which recalls the best days of Warren Hastings. In England, too, the charter of the Company was only granted for a term of years, and on each application for renewal the whole policy of the Company was critically examined and new principles of government laid down. The liberal ideas of the early nineteenth century

New problems to be faced.

influenced this development, and statesmen in India tried to translate these principles into practice.

Thus in 1813 the Company was authorised to make provision for education from its surplus funds, but there was a lengthy delay in carrying out this policy, for a dispute arose as to whether English or a classical Eastern tongue, such as Sanskrit, Arabic or Persian, should be used in the teaching. The latter proposal was upheld by several famous civil servants, who objected to a policy of Anglicising India, but it was opposed by Indians who were interested in educational work. English was at last adopted, and it has become a *lingua franca* for educated Indians throughout the world. Thus there were established government secondary schools and colleges, which later developed into Universities, though it is but a very small fraction of the vast population who are reached by this means. The true pioneers of education, however, were the missionaries, both Scotch and English, who were flocking into India, and their colleges are still an important part of the Indian educational system. In 1833 a legal member was added to the Governor-General's Council, and he was instructed to codify the law. Macaulay was the first holder of this post, and the Act instructed him to show due regard "to the rights, feelings, and peculiar usages of the People."

Education.

Law.

Meanwhile, the degrading customs which had long been practised by the Hindus had called for attention. Although it was feared that there might be strong opposition, Lord William Bentinck boldly decided to put down the cruel practice of sati, or the burning alive of the widow on her husband's bier. Bentinck argued that sati was no part of the original Hindu worship, and in this he was supported by the more enlightened Indians themselves. Thus a policy of quiet suppression was begun which proved successful.

Sati.

But broader questions still were being discussed. In 1824 Sir Thomas Munro, the Governor of Madras, recorded his opinion as follows: "We should look upon India, not as a temporary possession, but as one which is to be maintained permanently, until the natives shall . . . become sufficiently enlightened to frame a regular government for themselves, and to conduct and preserve it." The actual trend of affairs was turning the Company more and more into an instrument for the new government of India—an instrument checked and supervised by Parliament. In 1823, when renewing the charter, Parliament abolished the trade monopoly of the Company except in tea and in the China trade, and thus British traders were allowed to go freely to India. Ten years later the great Act of 1833 abolished the Company's trading powers altogether. This Act also regulated the selection and training of the Company's civil servants, and gave to the Governor-General the new title of "Governor-General in India." But more important still, it defined the relation of Indians to the machinery of government. No native shall "by reason only of his religion, place of birth, descent, colour, or any of them be disabled from holding any Place, Office, or Employment under the said Company." This regulation must be read in conjunction with the statement made by the Parliamentary Committee in the same year, when they declared it "an indisputable principle that the interests of the Native Subjects are to be consulted in preference to those of Europeans, whenever the two come in competition." However far actual accomplishment may have fallen short of these two statements of principle, they stand as reasoned declarations of the ideal at which British rule in India should aim.

Act of 1833. Company ceases to trade.

Lord Dalhousie was only thirty-five when he became Governor-General in 1848, but he had already made his mark in politics at home. A Scotchman of tireless energy, and with a vigorous and far-seeing intellect, he was to leave his stamp on India; during the seven years of his rule he worked himself almost to death, striving to bring the benefits of Western civilisation to the East. His famous saying at the outbreak of the second Sikh War is characteristic of the man: "The Sikh nation has called for war, and on my word, sirs, they shall have it with a vengeance." At the end of the war he annexed the Punjab, and threw himself into the task of developing his conquest with equal zeal: he

Dalhousie. 1848-1856.

(1) Punjab annexed and organised. 1849.

chose John Lawrence, the most famous of the Lawrence brothers, to organise the new territory. Under Lawrence the Punjab became a model province; a great road was carried right across to the frontier town of Peshawar, while canals for irrigating the country were quickly undertaken. The whole of the civil administration of the province soon became the great example of efficient government; the land tax was reorganised and reduced, while transit duties were abolished. "Jan Lawrents" himself became famous for his impartial justice. In Burma, too, Dalhousie showed his efficiency. The continual insults and ill-treatment given by the Burmese Government to British merchants led in 1852 to war, and the whole expedition was so well organised that the campaign was quickly over. Pegu, or Lower Burma, with its great port of Rangoon, was annexed, and here Dalhousie found further scope for his energy.

(2) Burma annexed. 1852.

In his treatment of the native states Dalhousie introduced a new policy. To such a logical mind, impatient of half-measures, Wellesley's policy of the subsidiary alliance was an obvious evil. To Dalhousie it seemed that the protection of the native rajahs merely left them free to squander their revenues on self-indulgence and to ill-treat their subjects. He thought it an obvious advantage to the Indians that they should be under British instead of native rule, and to this end he developed the doctrine of lapse. Instead of following the ancient custom of allowing a native ruler to adopt an heir, he held that when a prince died childless his state "lapsed" to the British rule. In this way he acquired the Bhonsla rajah's state of Nagpur, the state of Jhansi, and the petty state of Satara. He also limited the pensions already granted by the Company to deposed rulers. All this caused much ill-feeling, while his refusal to recognise the ex-Peshwa's adoption of Nana Sahib, and to continue the pension, made the Nana a violent enemy of the British during the days of the Mutiny. Dalhousie even proposed to abolish the title of Mogul, when the old Bahadur Shah should die; but this suggestion seemed so dangerous that he modified it by arranging for the next Mogul to leave the ancient palace at Delhi and to

(3) Doctrine of lapse.

live in the country. Shortly before leaving India Dalhousie deposed the Nawab of Oudh, and annexed that state. This step was forced on the British by the vicious behaviour of the Nawab and the constant misgovernment and disorder in Oudh itself: Dalhousie wished only to assume the administration of the country, but annexation was ordered by the Directors. This was very unpopular with the great landlords, who had been enjoying a feudal independence, and next year Oudh became the hotbed of the great Mutiny.

(4) Oudh annexed. 1856.

But Dalhousie's chief work in India consisted in the introduction or development of Western means of progress, and laying down the lines along which modern India has developed. A mere list of his achievements would be a lengthy one. Above all, he set himself to improve the communications of the country: the Grand Trunk road was pushed on until it stretched right across Northern India, linking Calcutta with the far-distant town of Peshawar just below the Khyber Pass. A great scheme for railway building was drawn up, and work begun, to link the great towns together, while the telegraph was quickly stretched between town and town, until all the important centres were in touch with one another. The post was reorganised, and a letter could now be sent anywhere within British India for less than a penny. The development of river transport was encouraged, harbour works begun, and great canals for transport and for irrigation were constructed. To make sure of a steady supply of competent men, a number of schools of civil engineering were instituted. Nor did Dalhousie neglect agriculture. Tea was introduced into Assam, and the Governor's forecast of its great development has since been amply justified. Forest conservation was begun, while systematic surveys for coal and iron were made.

(5) Social and economic progress.

In social matters, too, Dalhousie was a great reformer: he set himself to improve the state of the prisons, and appointed special inspectors for this purpose. In educational affairs he endeavoured to encourage and improve the vernacular schools, while he started the inquiry which led to the establishment of the first universities. He carried on Bentinck's fight against sati, and declared that the thags had been practically exterminated: the only thags now known to exist had given up their evil ways and were peaceably employed in making fabrics, some of which had been exhibited in the Great Exhibition of 1851.[1]

Dalhousie left India in 1856, and within a year there broke out the famous Mutiny of the sepoys in the Bengal Army of the East India Company. Although it would be quite wrong to say that the mutiny was wholly due to Dalhousie's policy, there is no doubt that his reforms had much to do with the general unrest which was growing in India. During recent years India had been forced along the road of Western development at a rate which was very alarming to the conservative mind of the Oriental. Vague rumours were afoot, and the employment of sepoys in Afghanistan, or across the seas in Burma, was very unpopular. It was commonly reported that the Government intended to break down the system of caste and to force all men to become Christians. The recent attempt to abolish the custom of sati was regarded by many as part of a general attack on the Hindu system. Dalhousie's policy of lapse was another cause of alarm: not only were the ruling families enraged at losing power in the annexed territories, but their vast crowds of retainers, and all who had hoped to gain profit by their rule, looked askance at the new system. This was especially the case in Oudh, where the local landowners considered themselves very harshly treated by the strict inquiry into titles which had been begun. The very development of mechanical inventions caused alarm, and as men saw the telegraph and the railway line spread their grip on India they shuddered and whispered in awestruck tones about this new magic which the British were introducing into India. The general feeling of discontent was kept alive by rumours in every bazaar of British defeats during the Crimean War, and it only needed some spark to set the fire alight. This came with the story of the greased cartridges.

Causes of Mutiny.

The army of the Honourable East India Company was composed partly of European regiments and partly of sepoys.

[1] See Dalhousie's famous Minute in Muir's *Making of British India*, p. 352.

The Indian battalions were recruited from Hindus and from Mohammedans, and had both native and British officers, though the huts of the latter were always separated in cantonments from those of the Indians. There were also Imperial troops stationed in India, but at the outbreak of the Mutiny there were only some 43,000 European troops as against 233,000 Indians. This was not Dalhousie's fault, for he had asked in vain that the regiments which had been called away to the Crimea should be replaced. A new rifle was issued to these troops in place of the old Brown Bess, with a cartridge which rumour said was greased with the fat of cows and swine: as the men had to bite the cartridge before loading, both Hindu and Moslem would be defiled. Feeling grew quickly, for the sepoys saw in the new ammunition part of a deliberate attack upon their caste, and in several places there were threats of trouble.

It was at Meerut, a great military station near Delhi, that the first serious outbreak occurred. Here, on May 10th, 1857, the sepoys mutinied, murdered indiscriminately any Europeans they could find, and set off for Delhi. The hesitation of the commander at Meerut, who had several European regiments, with cavalry and guns at his disposal, allowed the mutineers to reach Delhi unpursued and to persuade the sepoys there to join their cause and proclaim again the puppet Mogul as ruler of India. Thus a military mutiny had now become a political revolution: its success would depend upon how far the Moslem princes would rally to the Mogul. Meanwhile, at Lucknow, the capital of Oudh, a similar mutiny had broken out; the sepoys there joined with the discontented townsfolk to besiege Sir Henry Lawrence, who had collected all the Europeans behind the walls of the Residency. The whole of Oudh, led by the discontented landowners, was in rebellion. At Cawnpore a ghastly tragedy had been enacted. The local mutineers had been persuaded by Nana Sahib, the adopted son of the old Peshwa, to return and besiege the small European garrison. By treachery the Nana massacred the British soldiers, who were being sent down the Ganges under an armistice. The women and children he retained as hostages, only to murder them with orrid

Mogul proclaimed at Delhi. 1857.

brutality when an advancing column under Havelock threatened Cawnpore.

To meet this terrible crisis men were sent from Ceylon, from the Cape, and from England; but before they arrived the mutiny was already in hand. Canning, the Governor-General, at once realised the importance of Delhi, to which centre mutineers were making their way from all parts, and he sent what troops he had to attack the place. At first they were too few, but when John Lawrence was able to reinforce them with men from the Punjab, the city was carried by storm. This was really the turning-point of the Mutiny: once again the Mogul was in British power, but this time he was deposed and sent away into exile as a state prisoner.

Recapture of Delhi. 20th Sept., 1857.

The heroic garrison at Lucknow held out awaiting relief, and this was brought by Henry Havelock. A poor man, who was unable to purchase promotion, Havelock had grown grey as a subaltern officer, but at last his service and skill had brought him to the front: he was a fine soldier and a good Christian, and won a great name both for himself and for his "saints," as men called his regiment with humorous admiration. With but 2000 men Havelock fought his way to Cawnpore in the heat of summer, and then crossed into Oudh, but was forced to fall back on Cawnpore by the sickness of his men. Reinforced there by Outram, who, though his senior officer, volunteered to serve under his command, Havelock fought his way on to Lucknow, and after desperate street-fighting in the suburbs managed to reach the Residency. But the relieving force was too few to carry away the beleaguered garrison, and for some weeks they had to await the arrival of another column. Meanwhile Sir Colin Campbell, a veteran commander sent out from England, pushed on to Lucknow, and after six months of gallant and desperate defence the brave garrison were at last taken to a place of safety. The stamping out of the Mutiny was now only a question of time. Campbell undertook a thorough campaign in Oudh, where he broke up the mutineers and restored order. Sir Hugh Rose, starting from Bombay, had marched through the difficult hill country of Central India. Just as his task seemed completed, one of Nana Sahib's generals persuaded the Mahratta army of Sindhia to revolt and to proclaim the Nana as Peshwa. This definite bid for Mahratta support might have proved very dangerous, but it was quickly crushed by Sir Hugh Rose.

The Mutiny was thus a military revolt which took on a political significance by the proclamation of the Mogul at Delhi, and by the claims of Nana Sahib to be recognised as Peshwa of the Mahrattas. It failed chiefly because of the attitude of the native princes of India: the Mahratta chieftains gave the Nana no support, and Sindhia even fled from his capital rather than join his treacherous army. In South India, too, the Nizam and other rulers remained loyal to the Company. But the loyalty of the Punjab, which had only been conquered some eight years before, was of the greatest importance. Under John Lawrence's bold and tactful handling the sepoy regiments were disarmed, the Sikh population remained quiet, and Lawrence was soon able to send those much-needed reinforcements to Delhi which made possible the recapture of that great city. The Amir of Afghanistan, too, remained true to his treaties, and the north-west was secure; while from Nepal came contingents of Gurkhas, those hardy hillmen who proudly claim to be brothers-in-arms of the English rifle regiments. There is yet another important reason for the failure of the Mutiny: England was fortunate in possessing a number of able soldiers at her call, while the mutineers had hardly a leader of distinction, and though they were well trained and excellently armed, they failed before the attack of British troops. Thus the great Mutiny came to an end, and with it ended the Company, for the Imperial Parliament decided to take over direct control of India and to dissolve the East India Company.

BOOKS.—See Note to Chapter IV. W. W. Hunter, *The Marquis of Dalhousie* [Rulers of India]. Personal reminiscences of the Mutiny in Lord Roberts' *Forty-one Years in India.* Other Mutiny records are available in Nelson's series, *e.g.* G. W. Sherer, *Havelock's March*, etc.

1823. East India Company trading monopoly abolished.
1833. East India Company ceases to trade but remains a governing body.

1839–1842. First Afghan War.
1848–1849. Second Sikh War. [Punjab annexed.]
1848–1856. Lord Dalhousie Viceroy: great reforms.
1857. The Mutiny.

CHAPTER XIV

India since the Mutiny, 1858–1920

Results of Act of 1858.

The Act of 1858, which dissolved the East India Company, was merely the end of a long series of Acts limiting the Company's powers, and did not disturb the administrative system in India itself. In this sense the change was more apparent than real, but in some ways the change was fundamental. While the Company still existed it was subjected, every time that its charter was renewed, to a most searching inquiry by an independent body, a committee appointed by Parliament. Under the new system this was altered: instead of a periodic inquiry there was to be rendered annually by the Government of India a report on the Material and Moral Progress of the Country. Such a report was bound to become more and more formal, and the disappearance of inquiry by non-officials has been a great loss.

The Act created a Secretary of State for India, to take the place of the President of the Board of Control, and gave him a Council with duties of advice and assistance which replaced the old Court of Directors. In India the Governor-General became the Viceroy, but his higher title did not endow him with greater powers. The disappearance of the Company meant that the Viceroy had one master instead of two: he could no longer play off the Board of Control against the Directors. Indeed, the improvement of communications and the telegraph brought India much nearer to London and the Viceroy much more under the thumb of the Secretary. In England the new arrangement gave greater powers to the

Secretary: he could act direct, instead of through the Company, and although he was supposed to consult with his Council on all important business, this was no effective check, and some secretaries are said to have treated their Council in a very autocratic way.

Under the Company the Civil Service had become a most efficient department, and after the early reforms of Hastings had developed an increasing tradition of purity and honest administration. The men it produced obtained a name throughout all India for their just and upright dealings, and it grew into the greatest bureaucratic system in the world. Many of the best brains in Britain are chosen annually by competitive examination for this work, and they go out to India to devote their lives to the service of that country. As an alternative to misrule by irresponsible chieftains or rapacious officials, government by skilled administrators responsible to an official superior was a great advance, but bureaucracy has its drawbacks, and the problem of obtaining intelligent and effective criticism of the administration became increasingly difficult after the Mutiny. The results of the disappearance of the Company in 1858 are, therefore, not entirely satisfactory, and after sixty years of great administrative development means are being sought to revive some of the better parts of the old regime, and to modify the grip of the bureaucratic system.

When the duties of the Company were transferred to the Crown, India consisted, as it does to-day, of two great divisions. First there is British India, made up of the three old presidencies enlarged by later conquests, and of a number of other provinces—such as the Punjab and Assam—which had been acquired by the Company. In each of these a separate government had been organised with a governor or commissioner at its head, who was helped by the usual executive council, and assisted in the details of administration by the Civil Service. Above all these separate governments was the Government of India, represented by the Viceroy with his Council, who had his headquarters at Calcutta, or in the summer at the hill-station of Simla. These provinces were the only part of India

British India.

ruled directly by the British, and here only were the great works of irrigation and development carried out by the direct effort of the Government.

The Native States.

The rest of India is composed of native states varying in size from petty principalities consisting of a few backward villages to countries as big as European states, with as many as twelve million inhabitants. The native states play an important part in India, for they comprise about a third of its area and contain nearly a quarter of the total population. Dalhousie's policy had been to absorb these states whenever possible within the direct administration of British India, but that policy was repudiated by Canning in 1859, and since then Britain has worked to preserve the native states, restoring both Baroda and Mysore to native rulers after they had been administered for a time by the Government of India owing to the bad government of their rajahs. This new policy has met with great success, for the native states have formed a useful half-way house where the problems of East and West can be worked out under joint supervision. The native princes have proved very loyal to their engagements, and when in 1877 Disraeli arranged that the Queen should be proclaimed Empress of India, he gave a personal tinge to the rather abstract idea of the Government of India. At home Disraeli's proposal was derided as a piece of useless bombast, but he appreciated truly the importance of pageantry and colour in dealing with the East. The native states are bound to the British Raj by a variety of treaties, which guarantee their external security and the independence of the prince in internal affairs. The British Resident at the native court has a task requiring great tact and common-sense : he must not appear to infringe the independence of the prince, and yet he must endeavour to persuade him to good government and honest treatment of his subjects. In many states the chiefs are so progressive that the principal reforms of British India have been introduced, while others are still in a primitive state of patriarchal life. This strange medley of semi-independent states, some large, some small, but all owning the suzerainty of the British power, is an integral part of the British system in India.

The British Resident at the native court.

Thus the main lines of British power were already laid down by 1858, and have remained practically the same until to-day. Externally, too, there has been but little alteration, for with the annexation of the Punjab the natural frontiers of India had been reached. But the

Frontier policy.

NDIA IN 1920.

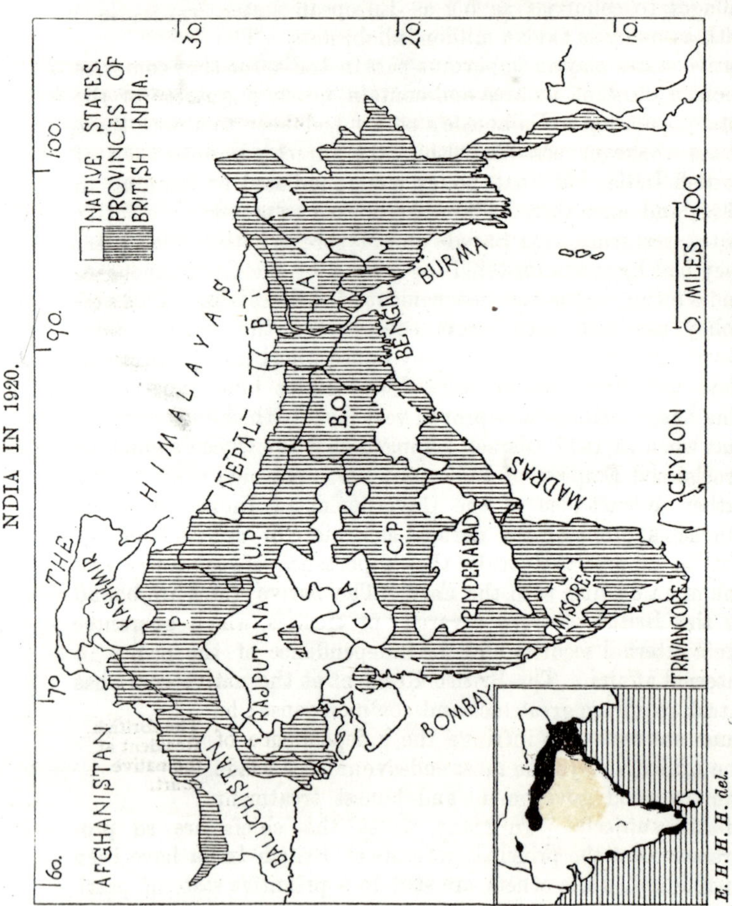

E. H. H. *del.*
P. = *Punjab.* U.P. = *United Provinces.* C.I.A. = *Central India Agency.* C.P. = *Central Provinces.* B.O. = *Bihar and Orissa.* B. = *Bhutan.* A. = *Assam.*

The black on the little map shows areas where the average density of population is above 512 per square mile. [A similar density to that of the industrial districts of Lancashire and Yorkshire.]

trouble on the north-west frontier was still a source of alarm. Fear of Russia was still uppermost in men's minds, and soldiers discussed whether it were best to meet the enemy on the line of the Indus, in the foothills of the Himalayas, or beyond the mountains on the further side of Afghanistan. This latter suggestion had many champions, but it needed one thing that was impossible to obtain, and this was the permission of the Amir of Afghanistan. Successive chiefs were firm in wishing to exclude both British and Russian influence, and when in 1876 the Viceroy, anxious to defeat the Russian schemes, urged the Amir to receive a British Resident, he was met with a polite refusal. Meanwhile in Europe, Russia and Britain were at loggerheads. After a successful war against Turkey, Russia had made that country sign the Treaty of San Stefano, but this agreement seemed too favourable to Russia, and at the Berlin Congress Beaconsfield forced her to amend it (July, 1878). As part of the diplomatic duel Russia sent an embassy into Afghanistan, and rather unnecessarily this was made a pretext for war with the Amir.

Afghan War, 1878–1881.

At first success crowned British schemes; the Amir fled and died in exile, and his son Yakub Khan made an alliance with the British. But soon the troubles of 1841 were repeated, the British Resident at Kabul was murdered and a period of bitter fighting set in, during which Roberts made his famous march from Kabul to Kandahar—318 miles in 23 days. In England Gladstone had returned to power in 1880, and the Liberal Government wished to withdraw from Afghanistan as soon as possible. Ripon, the new Viceroy, realised the impossibility of trying to force a weak ruler on a discontented nation: a bold step was taken, and Abdurrahman, who had for several years been an exile with the Russians, was recognised as Amir. The policy was entirely successful; the new ruler was supplied with arms and money, and all through his life remained loyal to his engagements. A few years later the British and Russians by mutual agreement defined the borders of Afghanistan, and it was recognised that no violation of that frontier by the Russians would be allowed.

Despite the friendship between the Amir and the British, there has been frequent trouble on the border with the wild tribes of the hills. Peshawar, the frontier station, has had to send small expeditions to punish their aggressions; while the great pass is watched by the Khyber Rifles. The importance of this protective work, and the necessity of guarding the frontier, was recognised by Lord Curzon in 1901, when he organised this border-land as a special frontier province, but the fear of Russian aggression has steadily decreased, and the Anglo-Russian agreement of 1907 did much to smooth away misunderstandings.

In one place only has British power in India been widely extended since the Mutiny, and that is in Burma. Once again the bad behaviour of the Burmese Government, its ill-treatment of merchants, and its deliberate refusal of compensation or improvement led to war, and the matter was brought to a head by the knowledge that the King of Burma was negotiating a treaty with France. Mandalay was occupied within ten days after the troops left Rangoon, and the Government of India determined to do away with the source of trouble. The whole of Upper Burma, all that was now left of the Burmese Kingdom, was annexed, and became a part of British India.

(2) Burmese War. 1885-1886.

"With respect to the frontier raids," wrote Dalhousie in 1856, "they are and must for the present be viewed as events inseparable from the state of society which for centuries past has existed among the mountain tribes. They are no more to be regarded as interruptions of the general peace in India than the street brawls which appear among the everyday proceedings of a police-court in London are to be regarded as indications of the existence of civil war in England." This is equally true of the smaller frontier wars which have occurred since the Mutiny, for though in some cases they have proved both difficult and expensive, they are really only police operations on a large scale.

(3) Frontier Wars.

India is almost entirely an agricultural country: in England ninety per cent. of the population live in large towns, while in India the number is only ten per cent., and there are only some nine cities with more than 200,000 inhabitants. Most of the people earn their living as agriculturalists, often farming a few acres with the greatest care and patience. The old village community was a self-sufficing

Economic development.

unit, but the introduction of roads and railways is working a change in India, and by opening distant markets is altering the life of the country. India produces large quantities of cotton, while the tea which was introduced by Dalhousie into Assam has become a most important staple crop. Jute for the mills of Dundee, and rice from the paddy-fields of Burma, are other staple products of India.

When the Company first traded with India it brought back cotton goods woven on hand-looms by native workers, which competed with the woollen manufactures of England. Gradually the cotton industry grew in England and began to find a market for its goods in India, and with the introduction of machinery the English cotton goods quickly beat the Indian hand-made cloths. Lately, however, machinery has been set up in India, and a growing number of cotton-mills around Bombay are weaving the coarser cloths, in competition with the looms of Lancashire. Jute mills, too, have been built, and thus the raw material is manufactured on the spot.

The decay of the native industries is a constant text of the Indian Nationalist, who sees in the whole process a deliberate attempt to destroy local manufactures for the benefit of English mills. From the same point of view he condemns the adoption of a Free Trade policy, which was undertaken in 1878. The Lancashire millowners were most anxious to have the Indian import duty on cotton goods abolished, and their agitation was successful, though the Viceroy, Lord Lytton, declared that he only supported the proposal because he was convinced that a policy of Free Trade would be of great value for India as a whole. A small import duty was imposed in 1898, but it was balanced by a corresponding excise. Recently, however, India has commenced a policy of protection by removing the excise.

Administrative work.

Since 1858 the whole administrative system of British India has become increasingly efficient. Great attention is given to the peasant cultivator, for the largest part of the Indian revenue comes from the land tax, and the peasant is the backbone of India. The whole question of land tenures has been carefully examined; the rules as to borrowing money, and as to the acquiring of land by purchase, have been regulated so that the peasant shall not fall into the hands of the money-lender or the speculator. Irrigation schemes are in operation in many places, while the canals in the Punjab have turned a desert into a fruitful countryside, and a million farmers are settled along their banks.

But the Government has had to face a terrible problem in dealing with the famines which occur in India at intervals, owing to the failure of the rains. India is so great a country that drought does not afflict the whole land at one time. Thus there is food if it can be brought to the sufferers. This is now undertaken by Government, and by means of roads and railways the famine districts are relieved, and public works opened for the employment of the able-bodied men who are out of work for the time being. The regulations for dealing with a drought are drawn up in the famine code, and any part of India can be given relief at a short notice. Though the more accurate statistics which are now compiled bring home the horrors of a drought, the new administration has altered the real meaning of famine, for in the old days the inhabitants of vast districts were swept away by literal starvation. In another matter there has been less success, and the plague which first appeared in India in 1896 has not yet been stamped out of existence.

The wor the district officer.

All this special work, as well as the whole of the ordinary administrative work of British India, is carried out and supervised by the members of the Civil Service. The district officer, who is responsible for a tract of country often larger than an English county, is primarily responsible for collecting the revenue and maintaining the peace, the two essential functions of the old government. But his activities are never ended; he supervises the change in holdings, he arranges for loans to agriculturists who need them, he is a magistrate and responsible for the control of the inferior courts, and when necessary he arranges for famine relief. To the people of India he is the living embodiment of the mysterious power of government, and on his energy and honesty their welfare generally depends.

As a natural reaction against this very efficient system of

bureaucratic government there has grown up in India since the Mutiny the Nationalist movement. The result of the clash of East and West, and of the introduction of Western education, was at first a tendency among educated Indians to despise their own civilisation, and to study and adopt Western ideas and Western ways. Now, however, although the high-caste Hindus are crowding into the Indian universities so fast that it is quite impossible to deal with them properly, there is a revival of Hindu religion and "national" ideals. A new generation has grown up which does not remember India before the days of British control, and this generation has become very critical of the good results of British rule. Often in their eagerness to prove the greatness of their own people, the Nationalist writers draw a rosy picture of the past which would surprise their ancestors could they see it. This growth of criticism is the natural result of the development of education which has been fostered by the British for over a century, and its very existence is good, so long as it is reasonable and honest. The system of education in India has helped the Nationalist movement in two very distinct ways. The great decision that English should form the basis of instruction has given educated Indians a common language, a thing they never possessed before: while the very books which they read in their study of English—Burke, Macaulay, and such writers—have introduced their minds to new ideas, and moulded their political demands. The young Indian graduate has been brought up on British ideas of freedom and responsible government, and when he criticises the government of India he does so with the unmeasured vehemence and even the phrases of Burke. This development has only been possible since Britain has maintained peace and the rule of law in India, for as yet there is no such thing as an Indian nation. But the long period of peace has given a chance for educated people to think, and thus there is growing up, chiefly among the students of the universities, a feeling of unity, and a vague groping after methods of expression. Part of the discontent with the present system is due to the great numbers of students turned out yearly by

Nationalist movement.

Effect of Western education—

—and period of peace.

the universities, often with only a superficial training, who are unable to find posts of a kind to which they feel themselves entitled.

The Nationalists generally claim three main reforms. They wish for the grant of responsible government on the same lines as it exists in the Dominions of the Empire. They claim a very much larger share in the actual administration of their country; and while the thoughtful Nationalist does not wish to expel the British element from the Civil Service altogether, he wishes to restrict it as far as possible. Lastly, the Nationalist wishes to place a protective tariff on imported manufactures in the hope of encouraging the development of Indian industries.

Nationalist claims.

These demands have been gradually developed, but a great impetus was given to the growth of native claims by the rule of Lord Ripon, who was Viceroy from 1880 to 1884. The Viceroy was a confirmed Liberal who had previously held office as Secretary of State for India, and he came to his new post determined to infuse a liberal element into the machinery of government. It was Ripon who made peace with Afghanistan and who handed back Mysore to a native dynasty, but his social and political activities were still more important. He was anxious to encourage the development of local self-government, and so arranged for the election of district boards whose duties were to consist of the organisation of local administration; but here Ripon's faith was only partly justified, for the local boards were often quite incompetent, and were alarmed at his attempt to limit the power of the district officer. Ripon also proposed to extend the jurisdiction of native judges so that they could try Europeans, and this proposal raised a storm of protest from the Anglo-Indians which was hotly re-echoed at home. But what was perhaps the most far-reaching of Ripon's reforms was his repeal of the Press restrictions. By this means the native press was freed from harassing limitations, and at once enabled to develop freely. Unfortunately the vernacular press quickly became an instrument of violent and scurrilous abuse and exercised a thoroughly pernicious influence.

Ripon's policy. 1880-1884.

Ripon's policy, and the opposition which it had created among the Anglo-Indians, awoke the feelings of educated Indians, and they began to organise themselves to express their opinions. In 1885 there was founded the Indian National Congress which has since played a large part in Indian politics. From the first the Mohammedans regarded the Congress with suspicion, and it was composed almost entirely of high-caste Hindus, self-elected and representing the small but vociferous class of people educated in Western ideas. The Viceroy, Lord Dufferin, had encouraged the Congress, hoping that it would act as a safety-valve and assist the Government by turning its attention to questions of social reform. But the members of Congress soon found themselves at differences over such vital questions, though they all agreed on the need for political reform, and so they clamoured at once for a larger share in the administration and for the development of Parliamentary government. Meanwhile the improvement of communications had made such meetings much more easy; the congress habit grew, and meetings of every sort were frequently held. They were attended often by the same individuals, the professional classes, and the lawyers found a special delight in framing high-sounding resolutions, though they generally refrained from proposing practical reforms.

The National Congress, 1885.

Although India was an autocracy, there were not wanting the germs of a constitutional system: besides the District Boards of Ripon's time, and the municipalities of the larger towns, there had also been formed a series of legislative councils. In the old days, the Governor had possessed power to legislate by ordinance, but in Dalhousie's time a special Legislative Council for India was inaugurated, which consisted of the Governor-General's executive council strengthened by members from the other Presidencies. After the Mutiny this system was found to be clumsy, and by the Act of 1861 separate legislative councils were set up for the Provinces, as well as for the Government of India, and some Indians were appointed as members. These Councils, however, were not to be little parliaments; they had no right to ask questions or to deal with any matters except such laws as might be laid before them. The growth of liberal ideas in England, and the demands of the Indians themselves, soon led to yet another change. The Indian Councils Act of 1892 arranged for the election by municipalities and by district boards of certain members for the Legislative Councils, though the right of election was thinly veiled by the use of the term "nomination." The powers of the Councils too were enlarged; they were allowed to discuss and to ask questions, but the Government retained an official majority by its appointed members, and could thus always control the business if it was considered necessary.

Act of 1892.

The Congress movement and the vague demands put forward by the Indian progressives met with but little help or encouragement from the great Civil Service in India. Some of the officials who had worked for so many years for the good government of the country had lost their sense of proportion; they thought of an efficient bureaucratic government as an end in itself. This lack of imagination, and the half measures of the Act of 1892, encouraged a violent movement among the extremists of the Nationalist party. They began to agitate against the methods and even the aims of British rule, they condemned the constitutional action of the Congress party, and they preached the necessity of crime to bring about their political ends. Affairs were now in such a state that it needed but a spark to set the straw alight, and there came not one spark, but a whole shower. Lord Curzon as Viceroy had wished to improve the administration of Bengal, and for this purpose had divided that province into two. In this striving after efficiency he ignored the loudly expressed sentiments of the Bengalis, and his action quickly led to trouble. The great victory of the Japanese over the Russians (1904–1905) showed that Europeans were not always invincible when fighting Orientals, while the Russian demand for an elected Parliament seemed to mark the triumph of liberal ideas. All these events had a great effect on India. An immense flood of enthusiasm poured through the towns of Northern India; students crowded to Japan to learn from this new Eastern country the secrets of regeneration, while in India numerous small factories

Growth of unrest.

Swadeshi movement.

were set up in the hope of doing without British manufactures, which were subjected to a widespread boycott. A sinister side to the movement was the wave of criminal agitation which swept across the country. Officials were assassinated, even Indians, if in Government employ. Bands of schoolboys were organised to commit outrages, and their associations were placed under the protection of Shiva or Kali, while the memory of the old Mahratta chieftain Shivaji was revived, and his veneration organised as a cult throughout the Mahratta country. Against this storm of anarchy the Government stood firm, but while it endeavoured to repress the evils of the movement, it had nothing to offer in answer to the more reasonable of the Indian demands.

Such was the situation which confronted the Liberal Government which came into power in England in 1906. True to their oft-asseverated principles they were bound to look with sympathy on liberal movements wherever they occurred, but anarchy and crime had to be suppressed. John Morley, the new Secretary for India, grasped the situation with a firm hand; side by side with measures of repression he carried out a scheme for the reform of the Legislative Councils, by which their size was enlarged, and in the Provincial Councils the official majority was abolished. Other alterations were made, an Indian was appointed to the Viceroy's executive Council and two Indians to the Secretary's Council in London. These reforms, however, proved of little real value. The elected members were really chosen by extremely few constituents, and in the councils they were cursed with the possession of power without responsibility; power to criticise every action of the Government, without the responsibility of formulating or carrying out any definite policy. The provincial governments, too, were closely controlled by the Government of India, which in turn was increasingly directed from Whitehall. In 1911 the Partition of Bengal was rescinded by the King-Emperor in person at a great Durbar at Delhi, and at the same time the Government of India was removed from Calcutta to the ancient capital of Delhi.

Morley-Minto Reforms. 1909.

Delhi Durbar. 1911.

It was the influence of the Great War of 1914 which raised

again the question of the future of India, and raised it in a form which called for a definite declaration of policy. The claim of the Allies that they were fighting on behalf of liberty was echoed in India, and the part played by India in the war led to her recognition in the War Cabinet: it was obvious that in any readjustment of Imperial relations the claims of India would have to be seriously considered. In the early days of the war India had been vaguely promised large reforms, but as time went on and the promises took no practical form people began to be impatient. At last, in 1916, at Lucknow, the National Congress drew up a definite scheme of political reform which practically amounted to Dominion Home Rule. At the same time the Moslem League, a body which had been formed in the agitation of 1906, agreed to the same scheme. This alliance between Hindu and Moslem extremists was important, for usually the two religions are bitterly hostile.

Effect of War in India. 1914.

In England the Secretary of State for India made a statement in the House of Commons on August 20th, 1916. "The policy of His Majesty's Government, with which the Government of India are in complete accord, is that of the increasing association of Indians in every branch of the administration, and the gradual development of self-governing institutions with a view to the progressive realisation of responsible government in India as an integral part of the British Empire." This definite statement of policy laid down the principles which were in future to guide the relations between Britain and India, and thus it marks a turning-point in Indian constitutional development. The Secretary for India and the Viceroy carried out an inquiry to see what "substantial steps" towards self-government could be taken at once. They recommended a system of modified responsible government in the provinces, by which a number of "transferred" subjects, such as agriculture, education, local self-government, etc., should be dealt with by native ministers, helped by an enlarged council. "Reserved" subjects should still be left to the bureaucratic heads of departments. By this means they hoped to train Indians through responsibility

Montagu-Chelmsford Report, 1918.

to fit themselves for further power. The Government of India itself still remains a bureaucracy, though the Legislative Council is to be reorganised on parliamentary lines. A much greater number of Indians are to be admitted to the services. Finally, Parliament is to undertake a periodical inquiry into the working of the scheme, and to make the necessary adjustments, and place further subjects under popular control as it may see fit.

On paper the scheme may appear clumsy and difficult to work, but it is an attempt to train people in the art of self-government by giving them the great burden of responsibility. It is hoped that those who are so anxious to urge reform will realise, by holding office, the difficulties of sweeping changes, and so become practical statesmen. In any case, the working of any scheme of responsible government really depends on the co-operation between the present governors of the country and the educated Indians. Another problem arises from the small number of the educated classes ; even a most liberal estimate shows them as a mere fraction of the vast population of India. If the coming changes in government mean only a transfer of power from an efficient bureaucracy to a self-seeking oligarchy of Brahmins or Moslems, who will exploit the peasant, the new developments cannot be for the good of India. But the great task in India will be the creation of an intelligent electorate : at first the most generous estimate can only find a total electorate of five millions out of a population of three hundred and fifteen millions. How far this task is possible the future alone can show, but with the Act of 1919 embodying these reforms India is now entering on a great experiment, the result of which no one can forecast.

Government of India Act, 1919.

Books.—Most of the books on this period are controversial, or else official Government reports and blue-books. T. W. Holderness, *Peoples and Problems of India* [Home University Library], is an interesting sketch. J. D. Anderson, *Peoples of India* [Cambridge Manuals], gives a brief account of the chief races of India. The Montagu-Chelmsford Report contains a useful historical introduction. Easily accessible accounts of some of the frontier wars are published by Nelson, *e.g.* E. Candler, *The Unveiling of Lhasa;* M. Durand, *The Making of a*

Frontier; Winston Churchill, *The Story of the Malakand Field Force.* There is an interesting historical article on India in the *Round Table* No. 29 [Dec. 1917].

1858. East India Company abolished.
1878–1881. Afghan War.
1880–1884. Lord Ripon Viceroy: political reforms.
1904–1905. Russo-Japanese War. Swadeshi movement.
1919. Government of India Act.

CHAPTER XV

The New Egypt

BRITAIN's interest in Egypt is largely due to her position in India: any country holding Egypt could attack India by way of the Red Sea, and quite cut off all communications with England, except by the long sea route round the Cape. Thus during the nineteenth century it has been Britain's policy to prevent other countries from obtaining control of Egypt. This has not always been easy, for Egypt was part of the Turkish Empire, and during the last century the "sick man of Europe" was rapidly breaking up, and the various European powers were either annexing portions of Turkish territory for themselves or helping to carve out new states such as Greece or Serbia. Britain herself did not at first wish to possess Egypt, and refused the suggestion that she should occupy it, but at last she found herself forced to do this and to supervise the organisation and administration of the country.

Napoleon in Egypt. 1798.

The great Napoleon dreamt of Eastern conquest, and invaded Egypt with a large army, but he soon found that he had to reckon with Britain. Sir Sidney Smith spoilt Napoleon's destiny by holding the little town of Acre in Palestine and so preventing a great Eastern campaign, while Nelson's victory of the Nile destroyed the French fleet. Napoleon realised that his plans had failed, and slipped back to France leaving his army to its fate.

The next great problem which Britain had to face was the growing power of Mehemet Ali. This Albanian adventurer had won his way by skill and the unscrupulous use of military power to the position of Pasha, or Governor of Egypt, and had forced the Sultan to recognise him. He organised an army and a fleet, and began a series of successful campaigns; he conquered the Sudan, he seized Palestine, and even threatened the Sultan himself. "We would have conquered Constantinople if you hadn't stopped us," said a dragoman to a British officer in Egypt recently, and this is probably true. Britain stepped in to bolster up the power of Turkey, and Mehemet Ali was forced to stop his victorious conquests; later, when he seemed once more to be determined on an aggressive policy, Britain forced him to withdraw to Egypt and to give back Syria to the Sultan (1841). Although Mehemet's attempts to encourage education, and to increase the trade of his country, show an enlightened policy, yet his love of military expansion cost vast sums of money, and the consequent taxation and government monopolies were ruinous to his people.

Mehemet Ali. 1806-1849.

The disadvantages of the long voyage to India round the Cape were very great, and a quicker route was needed, especially for mails and important passengers. This was found by means of Egypt, and an "overland" route had been established by which the mails were carried from the Mediterranean across the Isthmus of Suez to the Red Sea. Still only a little traffic could go by this route, and men began to revive an ancient scheme for cutting a canal through the isthmus. As early as 1830 the British Government had surveyed the course for a canal, but the plan was not taken up, and it needed the energy and imagination of a Frenchman, Ferdinand de Lesseps, to push the scheme to success. So doubtful were the British of the proposal, that the Government took no shares in the company which was floated, and it was even feared that a canal would divert the world's traffic so greatly that London would become a mere backwater. In 1869 the Canal was opened, and the sea route from England to India was thus shortened by some four thousand miles, though at first sailing ships made little use of the new route.

Suez Canal. 1869.

With the great development of steamships the Canal soon became a huge success, for coal was so dear that it was well worth while to save the money by paying Canal dues. The British Government soon changed its ideas about the canal. In 1875, only six years after it was opened, Disraeli seized the opportunity to buy all the Canal shares held by Ismail, the extravagant Pasha of Egypt. By this bold move the British obtained a large interest in the canal itself and a say in its administration. The Canal is still administered by a company, but for practical purposes it is run on an international basis: it has been declared neutral in case of war, and no distinction is made between any nation in the levy of Canal tolls. These rules for the status of the Suez Canal were taken as the basis for the rules for the new Panama Canal.

The development of trade with India and the East by way of the Canal, and the growth of Australia and New Zealand, gave Britain an entirely new interest in Egypt, but it was a very different series of events that made Britain the controlling power in Egypt. Mehemet Ali's grandson Ismail became Pasha in 1863, and soon after received the title of Khedive, or Viceroy, from the Sultan. Ismail was a man of most extravagant tastes and wasteful habits; he borrowed money wherever he was able, and spent it with reckless abandon. In the thirteen years from 1863 to 1876, he had increased the public debt of Egypt from three million to eighty-nine million pounds. The whole of Egypt was groaning under a system of oppressive taxation, and those who had subscribed to the various loans feared that they would never see their money again. Under these circumstances, the two powers most interested, Britain and France, conducted an inquiry into the finances of the country. Ismail was deposed in 1879, and succeeded by his son Tewfik, while the Dual Control of Britain and France was established to secure that a rigid economy was carried out in the finances of the country. This arrangement was brought to an end in Egypt by an outbreak of violence which was due to various causes. The necessary financial reforms were distasteful to many, while the army was full of discontented officers; feeling was aroused against Western interference, and a move-

The Dual Control. 1879-1882.

ment broke out under Arabi Bey, an Egyptian officer, which led to riot and bloodshed. Arabi adopted the catchwords of Western progress: he claimed Egypt for the Egyptians, and demanded that the Khedive should accept "responsible" ministers, of which number he was of course to be one, and thus he gained the ear of many Western liberals. The British Government under Gladstone was loth to interfere: it negotiated with the other powers, it called an international conference, and finally the British and French fleets sailed to Alexandria. Here matters came to a head: riots had broken out, and a demand was made that Arabi should stop making fortifications. When this was refused the forts were bombarded, and a little later sailors were landed to restore order in the town, which Arabi had given up to blood and pillage. Thus England found herself committed to restoring order in Egypt, but she had to do the work single-handed, for before the bombardment the French fleet had withdrawn. With much reluctance Gladstone sent troops to Port Saïd, whence Sir Garnet Wolseley led his men first to the lines of Tel-el-Kebir, which were successfully carried, and thence to the capital, where Arabi surrendered.

Arabi's rebellion. 1882.

Thus British power was established in Egypt; but it had been officially declared that the only object of this expedition was to re-establish the power of the Khedive. This was true, for Gladstone was most reluctant to increase Britain's Imperial responsibilities, but the logic of facts forced Britain to take over the control of the country. The Dual Control was gone: the country was disorganised by Arabi's rebellion, while the state of affairs in the Sudan was very threatening. Thus Britain was forced to stay in Egypt, at least until a new organisation was built up, and as time went on her responsibilities for Egyptian progress became increasingly great. Early in 1883, Lord Granville, the British Minister for Foreign Affairs, declared that it was the duty of the British Government to give the Khedive "advice with the object of securing that the order of things to be established shall be of a satisfactory character, and possess the elements of stability and progress." A year later, he explained it was

British occupation.

indispensable that such "advice" should be followed by the Khedive on all important matters.

Lord Cromer (1883-1907): his difficulties.

The man through whom Britain gave this compulsory advice was Lord Cromer, who first went to Egypt under the auspices of the Dual Control to reorganise the finances of the country. From 1883 to 1907 Cromer was British Agent and Consul-General in Egypt, and to his wisdom and courage the development and prosperity of modern Egypt are very largely due. When he first went to Egypt he found a country over-burdened with debt, with a down-trodden and exhausted population: he left Egypt a new country, with a sound financial system, an elaborate system of irrigation, and the promise of increasing wealth from the development of the staple crop of cotton.

Cromer's work in Egypt was hampered in many ways by the ill-defined position of Britain and the doubt about the future relations between Britain and Egypt. France particularly was very sore at recent developments. Up till 1882 she had very large interests in Egypt. After Napoleon's defeat French influence was still supreme in Egypt, French officers trained Mehemet Ali's troops, Frenchmen were to be found in every office of his administration, while French archæologists explored the wonders of ancient Egypt. French energy and skill had completed the Suez Canal, and thus opened a new highway between East and West; French money had been largely invested in Egyptian loans, and thus France had been Britain's partner in the Dual Control. But at every turn it seemed that Britain had reaped where France had sown: it was Britain who had foiled Napoleon's schemes, Britain had forced Mehemet back to Egypt, Britain had gained a large interest in the Canal, and now the Dual Control was gone and Britain the established power in Egypt in its place. It was natural for France to feel annoyed, and to forget that the developments of 1882 were due to her own refusal to co-operate with Britain. And French annoyance found expression in a constant attempt to frustrate British policy in Egypt, and in frequent inquiries as to when Britain would fulfil her promise and withdraw from Egypt.

Another difficulty was found in the system set up by the

Dual Control for dealing with Egypt's debt. By the Law of Liquidation of 1880, about half the revenue of Egypt was set aside to reduce the debt and pay the necessary interest, and to manage this affair various international bodies were set up in Egypt. These continued to exist after the establishment of British control, when their usefulness had quite disappeared. Thus Cromer had his hands tied, and it was not till the Anglo-French Entente of 1904 that any alteration could be made.

Another difficulty arose from the old arrangements made between the European powers and Turkey. Fearing the doubtful course of justice in the dominion of the Turk, the various European powers had early made a series of treaties with the Sultan, known as the Capitulations, by which their citizens were exempt from Turkish jurisdiction or taxation. These Capitulations extended to Egypt as part of the Turkish Empire; and thus there were a confusing series of consular courts, which tried cases in which Europeans were concerned, while the Government of Egypt found itself unable to make the Europeans living in Egypt pay their share towards the administration of the country.

Loss of the Sudan.

But the worst trouble which Cromer had to face was the problem of Egyptian defence against the growing peril of Dervish raids from the Sudan. That country had been conquered by Mehemet Ali, but it was the haunt of slave-traders, who were often in league with the Egyptian rulers. Englishmen such as Gordon, acting under the Egyptian Government, had tried to stamp out the slave trade, but this policy had led to discontent. In 1881 the Mahdi appeared, claiming to be an inspired prophet sent to lead the Sudanese to the oonquest of Egypt, and preaching a holy war against Christian and Turk alike. The Egyptian Government found itself powerless to deal with the Mahdi's fanatical supporters; the Egyptian army was in a deplorable state, and more ready to throw down its arms and flee than to face an enemy. The British Government feared to find itself entangled yet more deeply in Africa, and attempted to separate the Sudanese problem from the question of the occupation of Egypt. The defeat of Egyptian troops soon showed them that this was impossible, and they determined to order an evacuation of the Sudan. This policy was unpopular in Egypt, but the British Government sent out General Gordon to carry through this measure (January, 1884). It appears, however, that there was some misunderstanding in the matter, and Gordon, on arriving at Khartum, found himself shut up by the Mahdists. In England the Government was immersed in domestic affairs, and delayed action for month after month in the vain hope that something would turn up. Finally, in August, Lord Wolseley was despatched to Gordon's relief, but the advance was slow in the face of the enemy and the natural difficulties of the Nile and desert. When on January 28, 1885, a light column came in sight of Khartum, they saw the Mahdist flag flying over the town. Gordon had been killed just two days before. Thus the Sudan was evacuated, but hardly in a statesmanlike way: the blow to the Egyptian Government was such that the future reconquest of the Sudan became almost a necessity. In England, too, there was a great outburst of feeling, for Gordon's personality had caught the popular imagination; rightly or wrongly, the country felt that

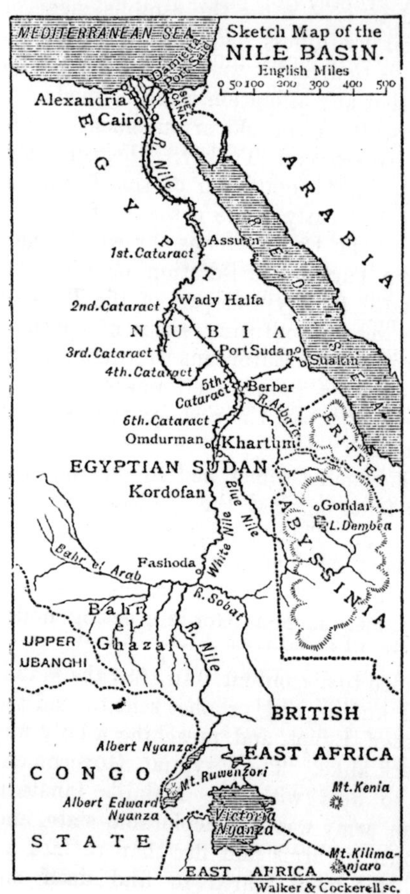

Walker & Cockerell sc.

Death of Gordon. January, 1885.

Gladstone was to blame, and his ministry narrowly escaped defeat.

Despite these various difficulties, Cromer was able to carry out a number of reforms in Egypt, which have raised that country from a state of bankruptcy to a position of increasing prosperity and wealth. The system of finance was carefully controlled: the rate of interest reduced, and in time the actual amount of the debt itself was also reduced. Meanwhile, the growing prosperity of Egypt is shown by the fact that although the revenue doubled between 1883 and 1912, the actual amount of taxation per head has fallen steadily.

Cromer's work: (1) Financial reorganisation.

But Cromer early realised that an extensive policy of irrigation and public works was needed to secure the prosperity of Egypt; and so successful had been his handling of the debt that he was able to raise a new loan for necessary public works. The new loan was amply justified, for the whole prosperity of Egypt depends on the great engineering schemes that were inaugurated. An ordinary map gives a very wrong idea of Egypt, for it shows a wide stretch of country with a river running through it. But Egypt is the Nile valley and its delta: on either side are barren deserts, with here and there an oasis of palm trees with a small spring or pool. The valley is a few miles in width, and the old Greek writer Herodotus spoke the truth when he said that Egypt is the gift of the Nile; no rain falls in Egypt, and so the fertility of land depends on the annual flooding of the Nile, when the great river overflows its banks and spreads a layer of fertilising mud over the countryside. A dry year may mean a poor flood and the loss of a vast proportion of the crops, while violent floods may sweep away the villagers' cattle and destroy their houses. Cromer's scheme was to harness the Nile by a great dam, and thus to regulate the floods: by this means some land could be irrigated all the year, and so made to bear two crops, while much land that was seldom reached by the floods would be assured of a yearly supply of water. The first work was to repair and develop earlier irrigation works, and the barrage at Cairo was restored. In 1898, however, larger plans were adopted, and

(2) The Nile irrigation schemes.

a vast dam was built across the Nile at Assuan in Upper Egypt, and so was formed a huge reservoir which made it certain that there should be plenty of water even in the driest years of all.

To Britain, Egypt was important as a cotton-growing country, and these great irrigation schemes increased the cotton crop immensely, while sugar-cane was introduced and soon became an important crop. These various developments went hand in hand; the improvement in the finances made it possible to raise money for the irrigation schemes, these schemes brought more land under cultivation, and the increase in the cotton crop made Egypt wealthier and so better able to bear the burden of its debt.

(3) Development of cotton.

Meanwhile, the other services were being reorganised: the police were reformed, and the use of the lash as an aid to collection of taxes abolished; English advisers were attached to the chief government offices. The army, too, was built up upon new lines; the men were well treated, well paid, and gradually began to take a pride in their regiments. Instead of the cowardly Egyptian levies, who threw down their arms and fled in panic from the Mahdists, the army now consisted of well-drilled, well-disciplined troops, officered by Englishmen, who were soon to prove their value in a lengthy campaign.

(4) Re-organisation of the army.

The reconquest of the Sudan had long been in men's minds, and though Gladstone's Government decided on the policy of withdrawal after the tragedy of Gordon's death, many people both in Egypt and in England recognised that the struggle would have to come. Besides the sentimental desire to avenge the death of Gordon, and to win back what had till recently been an important province of Egypt, there were other practical considerations. It was felt that the Nile valley was an economic unit; the control of the Sudan was necessary for any satisfactory treatment of the irrigation problem as a whole. In 1896 it was decided to begin the attempt, with a force of British and Egyptian troops under the command of General Kitchener. The Mahdi's successor, the Khalifa, opposed the advance inch

Reconquest of Sudan. 1896-1898.

by inch, but Kitchener was a man of great administrative ability, and, building a railway as he went, he carefully organised his lines of communications, and thus made sure of his supplies. After several battles, Kitchener at last reached the ruins of Khartum, and there, outside the new city of Omdurman, he fought a great battle and inflicted a crushing defeat upon the enemy. The Khalifa was soon after killed, his followers fled in confusion, and thus, after twelve years, Gordon was avenged and the Sudan reconquered. Just after this great victory Kitchener heard that a French explorer, Major Marchand, had reached Fashoda, a village on the Nile still further south of Omdurman, and had there raised the flag of France. This seemed a threatening incident, for France had been continually exploring the north of Africa and pushing her power westward from her colonies of Tunis and Algiers; and now she might claim, through Marchand, the possession of the Upper Nile. Kitchener did not hesitate a moment; he left all the war correspondents behind, and went himself to meet the French explorer and to deny his right to be there. Although the matter caused some ill-feeling at the time, France withdrew and the name of Fashoda has been omitted from the maps of the Sudan.

The reconquest of the Sudan had been carried out jointly by Great Britain and by Egypt: it was therefore agreed that it should be ruled jointly by the two countries. This altered the position of Britain in Egypt, for she now possessed jointly with Egypt a huge southern country. Since the establishment of the Anglo-Egyptian Sudan, that land has progressed very greatly: during the twelve years of Dervish supremacy the population was considerably reduced by slave-raids and fighting, but since the reconquest it has practically doubled. The aim of the Sudanese Government is to introduce the cultivation of cotton on a large scale, for the growing demand of the cotton-spinners of Lancashire promises an excellent market. To do this irrigation is needed, and so a vast scheme for the control of the Nile has been worked out: a large part of the upper waters of the river is lost by evaporation from the wide marshes through which the White Nile wanders. It is now hoped to attack these marshes, and to confine the stream within its proper banks, thus saving a large amount of water for irrigation purposes: as a first step to this the sudd or water-weed, which had choked the Upper Nile during the Mahdist period, has been cut through, and thus navigation of the river is opened up once more.

The ill-feeling between France and Britain came to a head in the Fashoda affair, and during the negotiations which followed several points at issue were settled. Soon after, however, a more general arrangement was effected, and under the influence of King Edward VII an agreement was reached in 1904 between France and England, which included a friendly settlement of all the disputes between the two countries—some of them dating from the earliest days of colonisation. For Egypt this arrangement was of great importance. France undertook "not (to) obstruct the action of Great Britain . . . by asking that a limit of time be fixed for the British occupation, or in any other manner." In practice this meant that Cromer was able to do away with a large part of the arrangements of the Law of Liquidation and so to put the finances of Egypt on a still better footing. Although the Capitulations still remained, the removal of friction between France and England was a great gain for the Egyptian Government.

Anglo-French agreement, 1904.

Lord Cromer laid down the reins of government in Egypt in 1907, after many years of unremitting labour for the good of the country, and was succeeded by Sir Eldon Gorst, who had formerly acted as his subordinate. The new Consul-General was called upon to face a serious domestic crisis, in the outburst of crime and violence connected with the Nationalist movement. To understand this development, it is necessary to glance at the different classes of the population in Egypt. In 1907 the population numbered a little over eleven millions, and the Nile Valley was nearly twice as thickly populated as the most densely populated European country, Belgium. Of this population by far the largest number is made up of the Fellaheen, the blue-shirted tiller of the soil. For many centuries he has been little better than a slave, ground down under the heel of the Turk and burdened with taxes till he could scarce call his soul his own.

Sir Eldon Gorst. 1907-1911.

In many cases the Fellah owns the land he tills, and Egypt is largely a land of small proprietors, but long oppression has left him with little initiative and little interest in anything beyond the question of the annual floods. The Turco-Egyptian, on the other hand, is the class which monopolised power under the old régime, and frequently got rich at the expense of the Fellaheen. It still provides a large number of members of the Civil Service, and from it the Khedive's ministers are usually chosen. It is among this class, too, that the chief opposition to British rule has developed, for British rule has limited their powers, and the teaching which they have received in the Government schools while training for the Civil Service has introduced them to the idea of liberty, and so recruited the ranks of the Nationalists. Besides these two groups of Mohammedans there is a class of native Christians, the Copts, who represent some of the most ancient inhabitants of Egypt. Although numbering less than a million, the Copts are an energetic and businesslike community, and many of them are artisans and skilled workmen of various types. Lastly, there are the Europeans: Greeks and Italians who form the shopkeepers of the larger towns, and British and French merchants and business-men. The number of Europeans in Egypt has been increasing rapidly of recent years, and it was Cromer's wish to sweep away the barrier of the Capitulations, which made the Europeans a privileged class within the state, and thus to build up an Egyptian nation consisting of all these different classes.

Population of Egypt.

When Britain first found herself established in Egypt Lord Dufferin, the Ambassador at Constantinople, was sent to report on the situation. He suggested a constitution which should train the Egyptians in the work of government, and see how far they were capable of such responsibility. A series of elective Provincial Councils was set up; while the central government was assisted by a council and an assembly composed partly of elective and partly of nominated members. These bodies had but little power, and the system was merely an experiment. "I should have been wanting in my duty if I had attempted to conceal the inherent difficulty of endowing an Oriental people that has been ground down for centuries by the most oppressive despotism with anything approaching to representative government: but I have no hesitation in declaring that if only it is given fair play, the reorganisation of Egypt upon the lines now approved by Her Majesty's Government has every chance of success." Such was Lord Dufferin's appreciation of the situation in 1883.

The Nationalist movement.

The Nationalist movement in Egypt is not unlike the similar movement in India, and it springs from somewhat similar causes. In both countries Britain has provided an efficient system of administration, honest justice, and a successful bureaucracy whose skill has aided in the development of the country. In both countries, too, Britain has taught the story of liberty, and some of the younger generation, fired by that story, are now claiming an immediate enjoyment of that liberty to its very fullest extent. To such a claim Britain with her frequently avowed principles is forced to turn a sympathetic ear, but two great questions at once arise. How far are Western institutions suitable for an Oriental people, and how far are the vast, inarticulate masses, the Fellaheen in Egypt, and the lower castes in India, to be entrusted to the care of their vociferous fellow-countrymen?

Unfortunately, the Nationalist movement in Egypt took on an evil form: outrages occurred, murders were committed, while the native press flooded the country with virulent articles of a most provoking type. Cromer had steadily ignored newspaper agitation, but a serious affray just before he left Egypt called for stern punishment, while Sir Eldon Gorst, despite his liberal feelings, found himself bound to suppress the more outrageous of the native papers. Although more power was given to the Provincial Councils, and they obtained control of local education and certain public works, the agitation continued, for the leaders thought that the quickest way to attain their end was by clamouring for the withdrawal of the British from Egypt. When Gorst died in 1911, Lord Kitchener was appointed to succeed him, a visible sign that the British Government would not give way to a campaign of force, and matters very speedily improved.

During the three years that Kitchener controlled affairs in Egypt a new policy was begun. A scheme of political reform was drafted, which substituted a single Chamber composed mainly of elected members for the old double Chamber system, and the new Chamber was given very much larger power in controlling the action of the ministers, who had to explain most carefully their reasons for any action against its wishes. But Kitchener's great work was devoted to an attempt at emancipating the Fellaheen from his bondage to the usurer, and to stimulating his interest in political affairs. Thus it was hoped to create a body of public opinion which would help to balance the fervid schemes of the Nationalists. Though the Fellah was often the owner of his little holding, he was usually in the hands of an unscrupulous moneylender, who would advance him money on the security of the crops. In this way he often lost his land. To prevent this practice, the Government made a law that no holdings of five acres or less could be forcibly sold for debts. Government savings banks were established in each district; seed, too, was supplied direct by the Government, while public cotton-markets were set up, so that the Fellah could weigh his cotton and see the latest current prices, and thus avoid being swindled by a rascally middleman. Such were Kitchener's plans, and for their results we must look to the future.

Lord Kitchener Consul-General, 1911-1914.

Egypt was never actually a part of the British Empire until the outbreak of the Great War, but when Turkey joined Germany in 1914 Egypt was declared a Protectorate, the Khedive was deposed, and a new ruler placed on the throne with the title of Sultan. Thus Egypt's dependence on Turkey ceased, and with it the obligation to pay an annual tribute which had long been a burden on its finances. The British garrison left for France, and was replaced by the East Lancashire Territorial Division, which helped to defend the Canal against Turkish attack in 1915. After the glorious disaster of Gallipoli, a great offensive movement was begun from Egypt, and Allenby swept through Palestine, and was stopped only by the armistice. Since the signing of the Peace, Palestine has been placed under the care of Britain, to whom a mandate has been given for its government, but the immediate future of Egypt was not so easy to decide. The Nationalists objected to Egypt becoming

War in the Near East, 1914-1918.

a Protectorate: they demanded that their country should receive its independence. This demand, however, seemed to ignore the fact that the development of the vast irrigation schemes depended upon British skill and enterprise, and that Britain had a special interest in the safety of the Suez Canal and the control of the Sudan. Meanwhile a Commission was sent out under Lord Milner to examine the problem, and to suggest a solution of the difficulty. The successful establishment of the New Egypt really depends on the extent to which the educated section of the Egyptian population will co-operate with Britain in the development of their country.

The Milner Mission. 1919-1920.

BOOKS.—Lord Cromer tells his own story in *Modern Egypt* and *Abbas II.* Auckland Colvin, *The Making of Modern Egypt* [Nelson], tells a similar story. G. W. Steevens, *With Kitchener to Khartoum* [Nelson], is a brilliant description of the great campaign. W. B. Worsfold, *The Future of Egypt* [Collins' Nation's Library], is a useful little book, based largely on official documents, and brings the story almost up to the war of 1914.

1869. Suez Canal opened.
1879-1882. Dual control. (1880 Law of Liquidation.)
1882-1907. Lord Cromer British Agent. Irrigation and other reforms.
1885. Death of Gordon. Loss of Sudan.
1896-1898. Reconquest of Sudan by Lord Kitchener.
1920. Lord Milner's Report.

CHAPTER XVI

The Tropical Empire

BESIDES the great self-governing Dominions and British India, there lie scattered up and down the world islands and territories which form part of the British Empire. These lands have been acquired or settled at many different times. Some are the remnants of the Old Empire which depended for their prosperity on slave labour and trade protected by a tariff wall, others were captured during the Napoleonic wars, while many have been gained within the last forty years, since the great scramble among the Powers to divide the backward parts of the world. These colonies differ in many ways, but have one common feature : none of them possess responsible government, and so we may call them the Dependent Empire. Most of these colonies lie in or near the tropics and are unsuited to become the homes of white men, but they produce those tropical plants which modern civilisation needs so greatly—rubber, cotton, palm-oil, tea, coffee, sugar, tobacco, and such like. For this reason they are invaluable as sources whence Britain obtains her raw material, and, to a lesser extent, as markets whither she can send her manufactured goods. During the last century, when the great inventions were transforming the means of transport and manufacture, traders and merchants could be found in every land exploring the resources of the world. These pioneers were often more ready than their governments to undertake the work of controlling and organising the backward countries to which they went, and, like their forerunners who adventured to America, they formed themselves into trading corporations. Thus the latter half of the nineteenth century saw the creation of Chartered Trading Companies, and many parts of the Dependent Empire were first developed by companies, and were afterwards taken over by the Crown.

The Dependent Empire.

The more recent expansion of the British Empire was due to the great bid for colonial power made by Germany in the 'eighties. After the success of the Franco-Prussian War and the achievement of German unity, a quickly developing trade and an increasing emigration to America made patriotic Germans feel that they, too, needed colonies whence they might draw their raw materials, and whither they could divert the constant stream of emigrants. At first Bismarck looked with disfavour on this movement, but as it grew he lent it his support, and in 1884 the first German colony was established at Luderitz Bay in South-West Africa. In the same year the Powers met at the Berlin Conference to discuss the whole question of African colonisation,

Berlin Conference. 1884-1885.

and the doctrine was laid down that claims to colonies must be based on effective occupation. From this date the various Powers joined in the scramble for Africa, and by a series of mutual agreements the whole of Africa was partitioned amongst them; this annexation movement spread also to the Pacific, and even threatened China. As we shall see, Britain obtained a large share in this division.

Divisions of the Dependent Empire.

The Dependent Empire falls broadly into two classes: the Crown Colonies, which are actually British territory, and the Protectorates, where native rulers retain some internal authority under the control and advice of British agents, but have no relations with foreign Powers at all. The Crown Colonies are administered by a governor, who is responsible to the Colonial Office: he is helped by an executive council generally composed of his chief officials. Laws are made by a nominated legislative council, though in some cases there are certain elected members, and care is always taken that special native interests or classes of the population are adequately represented. The native inhabitants of the Dependent Empire are backward races who would inevitably suffer from their contact with European traders unless some strong government were provided. The attempt is made to rule the native justly, to impose peace and prevent his exploitation by the white man: it is now an accepted principle of government to interfere as little as possible with native customs and native organisations, though slave-trading, torture, and human sacrifice are forbidden. Most of the Crown Colonies support their own administration by local taxes, though some have to be helped from the Imperial treasury, but trade to the Dependent Empire is open on equal terms to all nations, and no special treatment is given to the British.

I. The West Indies

The British West Indies consist of some of the oldest settlements of the English in America, together with islands captured from the enemy during the long Napoleonic wars. But the great days when the West Indian merchants had a monopoly of the English market are gone; early in the eighteenth century the sugar-planters began to complain of competition from the French islands, and when their slaves were freed they found it difficult to obtain labour. Free Trade in England forced them to compete with other growers, and when the beet-sugar industry sprang up in Europe, often with the help of government subsidies, the West Indian planter was very heavily hit. Thus the West Indies have undergone a great change: they are now full of small holdings, where negro peasant proprietors grow food for their own use, and sometimes for export, and though there are still large estates, these are often in the hands of blacks. Of recent years attempts have been made to increase the prosperity of the islands by introducing more scientific methods of sugar-making, and by developing fruit-growing as an important industry. A large quantity of tropical fruit is shipped to the United States, and the great popularity of the banana in England is a sign of this development.

Economic changes: decay of cane-sugar industry.

In the West Indies we see at work the opposite process to that which we have studied in the growth of the Dominions. In the lands where white men settled, representative government soon brought in its train responsibility; but, though the West Indies possessed representative assemblies from the very first, yet with the decrease of white men the assemblies withered away and were finally abolished. This process can best be seen at work in Jamaica. Here the emancipation led to serious economic troubles, to financial quarrels between the assembly and the governor, and to various proposals to modify the constitution. At last, in 1865, a small negro rising was suppressed by Governor Eyre with what some people considered unnecessary violence; he was removed, and the local assembly, thoroughly alarmed, voted their own abolition. Jamaica was then made a Crown Colony with a nominated council, but a more liberal element was soon added in a partly representative assembly. Since then the island has prospered, and demands for responsible government are now being heard. The other

Political change: decay of popular assembly.

Jamaica: Crown Colony. 1865.

West Indian settlements also became Crown Colonies, though without the difficulties and disputes which accompanied the change in Jamaica.

The Leeward Islands now include not only the four original islands, but also the Virgin Islands and Dominica, once the home of savage Caribs. As early as 1680 the Leeward Islands had a federal Parliament, which used to meet from time to time to discuss common affairs, but this system fell into disuse until 1871, when it was decided to revive it. Thus at intervals a federal council elected by the councils of the different islands meets under the Governor's direction. But the glory of the old days is gone, as any one must realise who sees the ruined warehouses at Statia, or the dilapidated sugar-mills and overgrown estates of the once well-cultivated Antigua. The old prosperity, however, was founded on the curse of slavery, and no one who sees the negro peasant working peacefully at his little plot can regret the change. Further to the south lies the Windward group, which contains St. Vincent, Grenada, and St. Lucia, from early days claimed alike by French and English, and bandied to and fro during the wars of the eighteenth century until the sea-power of Britain secured them as her spoil. Barbados is still a separate colony, with the proud boast that alone of the British West Indies no alien flag has ever been unfurled upon its shores. To the north of the Antilles lie the Bahamas, a scattered group of coral islands settled by English colonists in the seventeenth century, whose descendants now live by growing fruit for the United States markets. The Bermudas are busy with a similar trade, but their importance is increased by the naval dockyard they possess. But the Bermudas are almost a winter garden for the States, and every year sees a rush of visitors from New York to enjoy the balmy climate of these beautiful islands. At the southern end of the long string of the Lesser Antilles there lie two British islands which recall the chequered story of the West Indies. Tobago, claimed or held in turn by almost every nation which strove for power in these seas, fell at last to Britain by the Peace of 1814. It has been attached to the larger island of Trinidad, which was held continuously by the Spaniards until captured

Island colonies.

by the British in 1797. Trinidad is now a flourishing colony, thanks to its prosperous fruit industry, its oil wells, and its famous asphalt lake.

Besides these different islands there are two colonies on the mainland itself. British Honduras was long the home of English squatters, who felled the precious woods which were needed for making dyes at home. These "Baymen" were regarded by the Spaniards as trespassers on their domain, but various agreements were made which allowed the industry to continue. Finally, in 1798, the settlers repelled a determined Spanish attack, and were definitely recognised as a British colony. The origin of British Guiana is very different: it really represents the early trading settlements of the Dutch around the mouths of the Orinoco. This country was seized by a British expedition during the Napoleonic wars, and its possession was confirmed to Britain by the Peace of 1814. Towards the end of the nineteenth century a boundary dispute arose with the neighbouring Republic of Venezuela, in which the question of the extent of the old Dutch settlements was keenly disputed, and appeal made to ancient documents and even to the Papal Bull of Division, but the matter was settled by arbitration. This colony has now an important sugar trade, but though gold is mined, the mineral wealth is still undeveloped, and the wonders of the South American tropical forest are only partly explored.

Mainland colonies.

II. Africa

The earliest English settlements on the west coast of Africa were connected with the West Indies, for they were the forts and posts established by the company which bought negro slaves from the local traders and shipped them across to the sugar plantations. Some of the West African colonies of to-day are the direct descendants of these early posts, but they are very different in character. Instead of being mere trading forts upon the coast, they are large tracts of land stretching far back into the interior. This change is due to the exploration of the great rivers and to the ensuing scramble for Africa.

The African Company had posts on the Gambia river and along the Gold Coast, but when the slave-trade was abolished these forts seemed but a burden. The new colony of Sierra Leone, with its capital of Free Town, which had been founded in 1795 as a home for rescued slaves, seemed more important in men's eyes. When the last slave-trading company was wound up in 1821, all its settlements were placed under the Governor of Sierra Leone, and a string of British ships worked to suppress the vile traffic which had been one of the most cherished branches of trade in the previous century. The withdrawal from all the forts was contemplated, but a body of London merchants, headed by Maclean, persuaded the Government to allow them to take over the administration of the Gold Coast. Thus from 1831 to 1843 a merchant association controlled the Gold Coast forts, and even extended their influence over some of the inland tribes. But other nations besides Britain were considering the question of abandoning their settlements, and in 1850 Denmark transferred its forts on the Gold Coast to the British. The whole problem was examined by a Parliamentary Committee in 1865, whose report recalls the famous but ineffective words of Pitt's India Act.[1] They declared "that all further extension of territory, or assumption of government, or new treaties offering any protection to native tribes would be inexpedient ; and that the objects of our policy should be to encourage in the natives the exercise of those qualities which may render it possible for us more and more to transfer to them the administration of all the governments, with a view to the ultimate withdrawal from all, except, probably, Sierra Leone."[2] Thus a policy of abandonment was advocated, and as a step in this direction all the settlements were again placed under the Governor of Sierra Leone. But economic pressure was too strong for such desires : the steady growth of a West African trade changed men's idea of the value of the settlements, and the sudden appearance of Germany as a rival led to an outburst of annexation which gave shape to the four British colonies we must now examine.

Sierra Leone. 1795.

[1] See page 116.
[2] Quoted in C. P. Lucas's *Historical Geography*, vol. iv.

The settlement on the Gambia was the first British post in West Africa, and it now consists of a small Crown Colony at the mouth of the river, and a Protectorate proclaimed in 1894 by agreement with the French, which stretches some two hundred miles up the river. This narrow strip is bounded on either side by French territory, and much of their trade comes down the vast waterway. Further south lies Sierra Leone, and here too the Crown Colony was extended in 1896 by the proclamation of a Protectorate over a portion of the hinterland. The Gold Coast was still a scattered group of British posts sandwiched in between the forts of other nations until the Dutch sold their stations in 1871–1872: this gave Britain a continuous coast-line, but led almost at once to a war with the Ashantee kingdom of the interior, whose hordes had invaded the British protected zone. The Ashantee proved an impossible neighbour, and after further fighting the country was declared a Protectorate in 1901, and the British sphere pushed still further afield over the northern territories. One of the most difficult questions in this Protectorate is the problem of domestic slavery: it has existed from time immemorial, and any sudden attempt to wipe it out would probably end in disaster. The slave traffic has, therefore, been prohibited, and the law courts will not recognise the existence of slavery. Thus it is hoped that in time the evil will disappear. The colony of Nigeria was founded in a different way. All through the nineteenth century British merchants were trading to the Oil Rivers, as the many mouths of the Niger Delta were called. The appearance of rival companies, French and German, made the British merchants combine and form the United African Company in 1879. Their energy won for Britain at the Berlin Conference the recognition of her interest on the lower Niger. Two years later, in 1886, the Royal Niger Company was formed to administer and develop the inland territory; while the coast-line became a Protectorate. The Company gained for Britain trading rights and influence right up to the borders of Lake Chad, but it was involved in several petty wars with local chiefs in its endeavour to put

British West African colonies: (1) Gambia.

(2) Sierra Leone.

(3) Gold Coast.

(4) Nigeria.

down the slave-hunts. In 1900 the Company's administrative duties were taken over by the Crown, and the country organised as two Protectorates, which were amalgamated in 1914.

The West Coast of Africa has always had an evil name because of the pestilential fevers bred in the river swamps: in old days it was a regular death-trap for Europeans, and

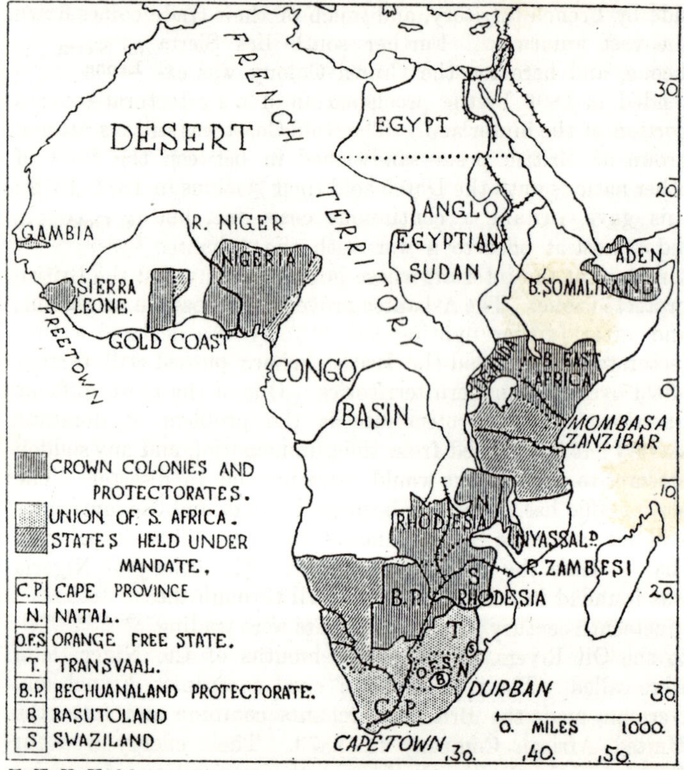

E. H. H. H. del.

even now with improved sanitation and quinine as a medicine it is a most unhealthy place. The hope of making money in trade, or of gaining experience and adventure in administrative work, still takes men to the West Coast, and the Liverpool School of Tropical Medicine is working to minimise the dangers of the life. From Liverpool the

West African trade.

Elder Dempster ships sail regularly to the West Coast, and return with wealthy cargoes of hides and palm nuts, ground nuts and cacao, thus bringing the raw material for leather, soap, margarine, and cocoa making, and for many another important industry which draws its very life from this great trade.

Central and East Africa.

Thus the first settlements on the West Coast were due to the slave trade, but the Central and East African colonies owe their origin to a different series of events—to the great explorations of the nineteenth century, to the old East Indian trade, and to the British advance from the Cape into Rhodesia and from Egypt into the Sudan. At the beginning of the nineteenth century hardly anything was known about the interior of Africa; men had regarded the great continent merely as an obstacle which they must circumnavigate before they could reach the Golden East. This self-satisfied outlook disappeared before the French Revolution, and the British were the pioneers of exploration, though they were quickly followed by great travellers of other nations, both French and German. One of the most famous explorers was David Livingstone, a Scotch missionary in Bechuanaland, who became an explorer in the course of his work. He crossed Africa from west to east, following the Zambesi to its mouth. Seized by the zest for discovery, he set out again, and in 1859 reached Lake Nyassa in Central Africa. His picturesque reports stirred people at home: the Universities' Mission to Central Africa began work in the new country, and in 1875–1876, after Livingstone's death, Scotch missionaries came to work in memory of their hero, while a small trading company also appeared upon the scene. But all was not plain sailing: the white men stoutly opposed the slave raiders, while Rhodes' schemes of expansion from the south affected this little settlement. So between 1889 and 1891 the great explorer, Sir Harry Johnston, was sent to Nyassaland; a Protectorate was established and friendly agreements made with the local chiefs, and also with the Portuguese who held the coastal territory. Just at this time Rhodesia was founded, but Nyassaland remains a separate Protectorate, growing both cotton and tobacco.[1]

(1) Nyassaland Protectorate.
(2) Rhodesia.

[1] For Rhodesia, see page 165.

Further north the discovery of the Great Lakes, and the romantic way in which a letter from Livingstone, asking for missionaries, at length reached England, led to the dispatch of a party by the Church Missionary Society to Uganda in 1876. Some time after, a French Roman Catholic mission arrived in the country, and there followed a series of quarrels in which religious and political motives were hopelessly confused, while the cruelties of the slave trade still further entangled the problem. The British East Africa Company now extended its power over Uganda, but soon found itself in financial difficulties and in 1894 the British Government took the country over as a Protectorate. Even then its troubles were not at an end, for some of the Sudanese troops mutinied; but the reconquest of the Sudan from Egypt, and the extension of the Uganda boundary to meet that of the Sudan, soon removed the cause of trouble. Uganda is now in touch with the sea, either by steam-boat down the Nile, which has been opened by the cutting of the sudd, or by means of the Uganda railway to Mombasa. Since the re-establishment of peace, and the destruction of the slave trade, the missionaries have done a great work of civilisation, and there is developing in Uganda what promises to be a native Christian state in the centre of pagan and Mohammedan Africa. The coast-line of what is now British East Africa was early subject to the Arabs, who expelled the Portuguese traders and re-established themselves on the coast. When the British set themselves to stamp out the slave trade, this coast-land was important to them, for the Arabs were great slave merchants. The Sultan of Zanzibar was recognised as an independent sovereign, but he was forced to denounce the evil trade, and a British squadron was based on Zanzibar to patrol the coast. The French, however, became suspicious, and so in 1863 an Anglo-French "self-denial" treaty was made, by which each country promised to refrain both from Arabia and from the Arab coast of Africa. But the appearance of a new rival in Germany altered the state of affairs. The British consul at Zanzibar, David Kirke, had already urged his Government to proclaim a Protectorate over the mainland, and had made arrangements with the

(3) Uganda.

(4) The Sudan.

(5) British East Africa.

Sultan for this purpose. But this had not been done, and in 1886 by agreement with Germany the mainland territory was divided. Two years later the British East Africa Company was formed to administer the country, but in 1894 it was taken over by the Imperial Government. The great work was at once undertaken of driving a railway through to the shores of Victoria Nyanza, and the construction of this Uganda railway secured the destruction of the slave trade and linked the Lake Settlement to the coast. In East Africa there are high plateau lands fit for white men to dwell on, and empty of natives, and there is already a strong nucleus of a resident white population there. Along the coast lands Indians are settling in large numbers, and the future of East Africa is an interesting problem. "Greatly changed is the land that Livingstone knew, wherein—at Chitambo—his heart lies buried. For more than twelve years there have been no slave-raids by Arab, Yao, Bemba or Angoni-Zulu—raids which often turned a natural paradise into an uncultivated wilderness, making burnt-out villages, stinking corpses, starving people, man-eating lions and hyænas common sights and incidents in the experience of all travellers during the nineteenth century. Mission schools exist in almost every centre of population ; the young men frequently go away in numbers to earn money in South Africa, and return to spend it on the purchase and cultivation of land around their own homes. Perhaps there is no part of tropical Africa in which the advent of the white ruler has created more good and done less harm than in British East Africa." [1]

When the spoils of Africa were divided, Germany was displeased with her share. She hoped that, if she aided the Boers, South Africa might fall into her net, but the South African War, and still more the Union, prevented that plan from succeeding. Her other wish was to extend her sway right across tropical Africa, while Britain wished to construct the Cape-to-Cairo railway as far as possible under British control. The mandate for the government of German East Africa has now fallen to Britain, and the Cape-to-Cairo railway may yet be built and operated under British control.

[1] Sir Harry Johnston, in *Britain across the Seas: Africa*, p. 212.

III. The Sea Route to the East

Besides these mainland colonies, Britain possesses a number of naval posts which have enabled her to retain the command of the sea. These lie along the great trade routes, and though the change from sail to steam has made some of less importance, they are still useful as cable stations. The old route to the East Indies is studded with such places. Gibraltar is the

Gibraltar. 1704.

key of the whole system. It was captured by Rooke in 1704, and ceded to Britain by the Treaty of Utrecht. Since then it has remained in British hands despite a lengthy siege at the close of the American War of Independence. Its value lies in its use as a base for the Mediterranean fleet, and in old days it played an important part by separating the French Mediterranean and Atlantic fleets. Since the opening of the Suez Canal, Gibraltar's importance has increased. It is well armed and provided with large docks and coaling stations, and it is governed in military fashion. The island of St. Helena in mid-Atlantic was

St. Helena. 1651.

occupied by the East India Company in 1651, and became the regular port of call for all their fleets, playing the same part as did the Cape for the Dutch Company. Its greatness is now a thing of the past, for few ships call there except whalers, but it is a cable station, as is the little island of Ascension further north. The next station on this route was the Cape, for its capture from the Dutch made it a regular British depôt, and the usual place where officers from India spent their short leave. North-west of Madagascar the islands of Mauritius and Seychelles were used by the French as the naval base from which their fleets could raid the British factories in India, or prey upon the regular fleets which passed to and fro upon the ocean highway.

Mauritius. 1810.

Mauritius fell to Britain in 1810, and though organised as a Crown colony, care was taken to preserve French laws and customs. It has now some 370,000 inhabitants, of whom a large proportion are Indians, either temporary labourers or settlers engaged in sugar growing. Seychelles was separated from Mauritius in 1903.

On the newer route to the East, through the Mediterranean, Gibraltar is still the first great port. The next is the tiny island of Malta, seized from Napoleon's invading Malta.
troops in 1800, and retained at the Peace of 1800.
Vienna. Its docks and harbour have been greatly developed, and it is now a port of call and coaling station for the Navy. Cyprus was leased to Britain by Turkey in 1878 in return for a promise of aid against Russia, if that Cyprus.
country proved aggressive. It was annexed at 1878.
the outbreak of war with Turkey in 1914. The people depended almost entirely on agriculture, and the lack of a regular rainfall often led to great distress; a scheme of irrigation has altered this, but aid has been necessary from Imperial funds.

The Suez Canal is the most vulnerable point on this route, and despite its international character, its defence is a great problem. The mandate for Palestine has been entrusted to Britain, and thus the Eastern approach is now covered. At the southern entrance of the Red Sea lies the port of Aden, in Arabia. The port was a flourishing market for Eastern goods in the old days of Eastern trade before the discovery of the Cape. With the revival of an overland route across Suez, it again became important, and was seized by the East Aden.
India Company in 1839. It was used as a naval 1839.
base for the protection of trade and the suppression of piracy, and is now an important coaling station, subject to the Governor of Bombay. The African coast of Somaliland opposite was declared a British Protectorate in 1884, after Egypt had withdrawn her claims as a result of the evacuation of the Sudan. It was annexed to secure the control of the straits, and is of little value in other respects. Between Aden and Bombay there stretches away to the northward the great inlet known as the Persian Gulf. From early times this coast was policed by the East India Company, for the local sheiks were famous as daring pirates or as energetic slave-traders. The Navy carried on the good work, and the Gulf was thoroughly surveyed and its waters charted. Trade, too, developed with Southern Persia and with Mesopotamia, and so when in 1907 a convention was signed with Russia, it was

definitely recognised that the Persian Gulf was a British "sphere of influence." The German plan to carry the Berlin-Bagdad railway to a port on the Persian Gulf alarmed British statesmen who feared an attack on India. They wished to control such a port, and to emphasise their demand annexed in 1914 a small piece of territory at the head of the Gulf. The government of Mesopotamia has now been entrusted to Britain by a mandate.

IV. The East Indies

In the East there are some British colonies which do not form part of the Indian Empire, although their story is interwoven with that of the East India Company. Of these the most famous is Ceylon. The Dutch trading settlements along its coasts were captured in 1795, and were attached to Madras until 1801, when Ceylon was made a separate colony. The European settlements were still confined to the coast, but in 1815 war broke out with the natives, and the whole island came under British control. There are still only 9000 Europeans in its population of four millions, but Colombo does a vast trade in tropical products. Coffee was at one time the principal crop, but it was attacked by a strange disease, and tea now flourishes in its place, along with cocoanuts, rice, and rubber.

Ceylon. 1795.

Further east in the Malay Straits there are a group of British possessions, which recall the old days of the struggles between English and Dutch for the trade of the Spice Islands. Although the English were driven from the spice trade, the Dutch paid little attention to the Malay Peninsula, and preferred to hurry through the straits on their way to richer lands. Through this passage, too, sailed ships of the East India Company on their way to China, and towards the end of the eighteenth century servants of the Company began to take interest in the Malay Peninsula, and so there came into being the Straits Settlements. These now consist of Malacca, acquired from the Dutch in 1824, Penang, settled by the Company in 1786, and Singapore, annexed by Sir Stamford Raffles in 1819, by agreement with the local rajah.

Straits Settlements.

Of these, Penang is now a flourishing port busy in exporting the tin and rubber of the interior, while Singapore is one of the greatest ports of the world. It is the very hub of all the trade between East and West: no less than nine cables radiate from Singapore, while fifty steamship lines make it a port of call. In 1913 the immense number of 27 million tons of shipping entered and cleared from the Straits Settlements.

On the Peninsula itself there are a number of small Malay states, which for long were in a condition of anarchy. In 1874 a Protectorate was established, and in 1895 the four most important states agreed to form a federation. Since 1909 a federal council has met annually for common business, while a British resident in each state assists with the organisation and administration of the government. Railways and bridges have been built, an efficient police force set up, and good government established in place of the previous misrule. The whole system is supervised by the Governor of Singapore, who is High Commissioner for the Peninsula. Besides these four federated states, there are other Malay states on the Peninsula which do not form part of the federation. The climate is extremely hot, but the Peninsula has great possibilities; tin is mined very abundantly, and rubber is grown.

Federated Malay States.

The large island of Borneo was for long almost a stranger to European trade. The Dutch had vague claims over the country, and the East India Company tried in vain to establish trading stations. Now, however, the north of the island contains three British Protectorates, whose wide variations show how loose a term the word "Protectorate" is. Sarawak was built up by the energy of Rajah Brooke, a retired officer of the East India Company, who helped the local rajah to put down a rebellion and was in return granted the province (1841). In 1888 Sarawak was recognised as a Protectorate, and there is the strange sight of a private English gentleman ruling as an Eastern rajah, and recognised as such by the British Government. The north-west of the island is ruled by a chartered company formed in 1881 to secure the good government of the country: the company does not trade itself, but is content

Protectorates in Borneo.

with the work of administration, and its country is recognised as a Protectorate. Between the two lies the native state of Brunei, which became a Protectorate in 1888, while the island of Labuan is a Crown colony controlled by the Governor of Singapore. Borneo grows rubber and tobacco, but much work has still to be done in exploring the tropical forest.

The East India Company's monopoly of the trade to China was abolished in 1834, and it was hoped that competition would reduce the price of tea in England. But the sudden arrival at the port of Canton of traders unaccustomed to the ways and methods of the Chinese only led to trouble, and soon to the outbreak of war. When peace was made in 1842, the sparsely populated island of Hong Kong at the mouth of the Canton river was ceded to Britain, and this unpromising-looking place soon developed into a great port, for its various waterways provided good shelter for shipping, while it was excellently placed for trade. It quickly became the port from which Chinese labourers went abroad to seek their fortunes, first to Australia in the gold rush of 1851, and since then to various parts of the world. In 1913 over 300,000 Chinamen passed through the port. Further north along the coast Britain holds the port of Wei-hei-wei, which was leased from China in 1898. It was acquired chiefly for use as a naval base, and has had to receive help from Imperial funds.

Hong Kong. 1842.

V. The Pacific

The Western Pacific is studded with groups of picturesque islands, some large volcanic outcrops covered with tropical foliage, others mere low-lying coral atolls crowned with cocoanut palms and surrounded by a barrier reef, on which the ceaseless thunder of the surf beats eternally. The romance of the Pacific has seized the modern world: R. L. Stevenson himself spent the remainder of his life in a charmed existence at Vailima in Samoa, while modern writers can hardly tear themselves away from the beauty of the South Sea Islands. Many of these islands were first discovered by the Spaniards sailing westward from South America to the Philippines; but they were practically

The South Sea Islands.

rediscovered by French and English explorers in the eighteenth and early nineteenth centuries, as their names well show.

As these islands became better known in England and Australia, three types of people began to visit them. The missionaries were early in the field. The London Missionary Society led the way in 1796, and was soon followed by Presbyterians and Roman Catholics. Paton, the great Scotch missionary, made a name for himself in the New Hebrides, while Selwyn, the first Bishop of New Zealand, founded the Melanesian Mission with its policy of "a black net with white floats"—a self-supporting native church. Sometimes religious differences were made the excuse for native feuds, as happened more than once at Fiji, but the missionaries found their chief enemies in men of their own race, for some of the traders hated the missionary because he tried to protect the native. The trader began to visit the Pacific seeking for sandalwood and bêche-de-mer, and also for copra (or cocoanut kernel). From Fiji they early traded to China for tea, and to avoid the East India Company's monopoly Sydney merchants formed partnerships with Americans. But these traders often did evil to the natives, for they introduced such harmful things as raw spirits and cheap firearms. Still more harm was done by the growth of the labour traffic. The first attempt to get native labour for New South Wales from the New Hebrides was made in 1847, and as sugar plantations sprang up in Queensland so this trade developed. The islanders were supposed to enter freely into an engagement to serve as indentured labourers for a term of years, but the actual traffic frequently degenerated into little better than a man hunt. Unscrupulous skippers, looking only to their profits, cared little whether the natives understood the terms of their contract, and often kidnapped them without going through the form of asking their consent. This, of course, led to reprisals, and in 1871 the saintly Bishop Patteson was murdered in the Santa Cruz group by some outraged natives, who took vengeance on the first white man they could catch. Attention was thus called to the villainy that was going on, and in 1872 an Act was passed extending jurisdiction over this trade. Three years later another Act created the

High Commissioner for the Western Pacific. 1875.

office of High Commissioner of the Western Pacific, and this new official was to enforce the earlier Act, and to protect the natives from illtreatment by Europeans.

Meanwhile, events in Fiji had led to the annexation of that island; the drama of the early days of New Zealand was being re-enacted. A crowd of disreputable settlers, who helped the natives in their blood feuds, had been succeeded by more respectable traders from the States and from Australia; they appealed in turn to Britain and America for annexation, and when this was refused they attempted to organise a government of their own. At last the growth of internal disorder, and the appeals of the native king, backed by the demands of Australia and New Zealand, who wished to secure a port on the way to the western shores of America, forced the British Government to give way. In 1874 Fiji became a Protectorate, and has since then become important, both as a station on the Imperial cable between Australia and British Columbia, and as a tropical farm for growing sugar, cocoanut, rubber, and bananas.

With the appointment of the High Commissioner, who was also the Governor of Fiji, things quickly began to improve. The labour traffic was regulated, and has by now been practically abolished, while the dealings of traders with natives were strictly supervised. Meanwhile, the attention of other nations had been drawn to the Pacific. France, who had sent some early exploring voyages in the eighteenth century, occupied New Caledonia in 1853, and eleven years later had turned it into a penal station, much to the disgust of New South Wales. The growing claims of Germany alarmed the Australian colonies, who regarded the Pacific as their preserve. At last, by a number of different agreements, the islands of the Pacific were assigned as Protectorates to the different Powers, and many came under the control of the High Commissioner, though some were transferred to the Dominion of New Zealand. Since the end of the Great War, the German islands south of the line have been entrusted by mandate to the British Empire.[1]

The carving up of the Pacific.

[1] New Guinea is entrusted to Australia, Western Samoa to New Zealand, and the question of mandates raises great constitutional problems within the Empire, see p. 204.

Thus, in the Pacific, as in Africa, the advent of the European trader has brought in its wake the national flag, for however reluctant a government might be, it ultimately found itself forced to assert its power in order to control its subjects, and to prevent their harmful exploitation of the backward races.

BOOKS.—There are few handy books other than the volumes of Lucas' *Historical Geography of the British Empire.* Sir H. H. Johnston, *Britain across the Seas: Africa,* is a vivid summary well illustrated. *The Opening-Up of Africa,* by the same author, in the Home University Library, is useful. H. H. Montgomery, *The Light of Melanesia,* gives a description of mission work in the Pacific. E. Jenks, *The Government of the British Empire,* gives a clear account of the system of government throughout the Empire.

1795. Sierra Leone established.
1815–1880 (circ.). Reaction against further expansion.
1865. Parliamentary Committee advises withdrawal from West Coast of Africa.
1884–1885. Berlin Conference.
1888. British East Africa Company.
1889. British South Africa Company (Rhodesia).

INDEX

PRINTED IN GREAT BRITAIN BY WILLIAM CLOWES AND SONS, LIMITED, BECCLES.